The Cultural Dimensions of Peacebuilding

The Cultural Dimensions of Peacebuilding

Marty Branagan

ANTHEM PRESS

Anthem Press
An imprint of Wimbledon Publishing Company
www.anthempress.com

This edition first published in UK and USA 2026
by ANTHEM PRESS
75–76 Blackfriars Road, London SE1 8HA, UK
or PO Box 9779, London SW19 7ZG, UK
and
244 Madison Ave #116, New York, NY 10016, USA

First published in the UK and USA by Anthem Press in 2025

British Library Cataloguing-in-Publication Data
A catalogue record for this book is available from the British Library.

Library of Congress Control Number: 2026942638

ISBN-13: 978-1-80136-050-0 (Pbk)
ISBN-10: 1-80136-050-2 (Pbk)

This title is also available as an eBook.

CONTENTS

FIGURES

ACKNOWLEDGEMENTS

This book was primarily written on the unceded lands of the Anaiwan Aboriginal Nation, shared now with Gumbaynggirr, Dhungutti, Kamilaroi and other Aboriginal people.

With many thanks to:

Peace Studies students and staff at the University of New England, Australia.

The incredibly patient, pleasant and professional Jebaslin Hephzibah, Mario Rosair, Phiriya Durairaj, Courtney Young, Jessica Mack, Pradhiba and everyone at Anthem Press. Also, Deanta's Nandhini Ravi and Gomathy Ilammathe.

The staff at Lieu de Mémoire, Le Chambon-sur-Lignon, France.

Professor Kazuyo Yamane, Ritsumeikan University, Kyoto, Japan.

Woody, Francesca and Ronan. Gillian Branagan and the extended family.

My friends and colleagues in the Australian peace movement, especially Wendy, Nina, Eva, Ariel, Frank, Lindsay and Jacques.

Peace-builders, activists and advocates everywhere.

In memory of Elise Boulding and Johan Galtung.

Chapter 1

INTRODUCTION

Most of us – maybe even arms dealers – want to live in peace and safety. Yet wars[i] continue to rage across the planet. Massacres by military forces or terrorists, school shootings, women raped and murdered by men, knife attacks – every day a new atrocity blares from the radio or across huge screens in gyms, railways stations and homes, causing widespread anxiety, despair and feelings of powerlessness. Is this violence just human nature and inevitable? Should we rely on governments and the United Nations to provide solutions? Or are the causes – and solutions – closer to home, in our cultures, thoughts, words, actions and everyday life?

As a lecturer in Peace Studies[ii] at Australia's University of New England, these questions were first brought home to me starkly in 2014 as I was flying to Istanbul, Türkiye, for the International Peace Research Association's 25th global conference.[iii] Below, in Palestine/Israel, Iraq, Afghanistan and Syria, there were horrendous, ongoing armed conflicts, while all around me on the plane residents of the region were engrossed in films filled with violence. Was there a connection?

In this chapter, we'll start to examine these questions by looking at what is meant by 'culture' and discussing different forms of violence, including 'cultural violence', before getting some background to the book and an overview of the topics it will examine. We'll conclude with an introduction to militarism, peace and cultural peace.

---

i War is a state of intense armed conflict between different countries or different groups within a country, usually of considerable duration and magnitude.

ii UNE's Peace Studies celebrated 40 years in 2022. It's discussed further below and in the chapter on Peace Education.

iii I was hoping that the benefits of attending the conference would outweigh the enormous carbon footprint of flying there.

Culture

We often think of culture as something only the wealthy enjoy – expensive objects and performances we find in art galleries and opera houses, things created by talented artistes for a small number of wealthy, 'high-brow' people to enjoy. But culture is much broader than that, being the 'network or totality of attitudes, values and practices of a particular group of human beings'.[1] Everyone has some relationship to culture and some interaction with it. We all consume culture whenever we watch a movie or listen to music. We also *contribute* to the culture (or sub-cultures) of a society by the clothes and hairstyles we wear, the language we use, how we engage with social media, the things we eat and the interactions between generations, to name but a few areas. Sometimes this is denigrated as 'popular culture', but it is culture nonetheless.[2]

Why look at culture if we want to cultivate peace? Surely most wars are ended by high-level negotiations involving governments and powerful institutions, while reducing levels of interpersonal violence (such as male violence towards women) requires stronger laws and punishments. That may be the case, but in both examples, the violence will continue or re-erupt *if the underlying causes are not addressed.* Those underlying causes may be economic (such as extreme poverty living next to extreme wealth) or environmental (severe drought causing migration), but they also include cultural factors, such as inundation with violent films and video games, or language and narratives that encourage violence or ignorance of peaceful alternatives. Also important are the quality of a society's education, journalism and arts sectors; how history is portrayed; our public spaces; and how children are parented and educated. Is there gender equality and tolerance of diversity? Do the society's religions or spiritual practices encourage division and hatred or tolerance and inner peace?

Culture affects every aspect of our lives. On a 2022 BBC Arts Hour programme,[3] a diverse panel grappled with the question of how society can be improved after the COVID-19 pandemic, especially in light of the climate and biodiversity crises (or catastrophes, as one put it). All agreed that culture is an essential element of our lives, giving them meaning, and connecting us with each other and with nature. It is through culture, they argued, that some of the most profound and sustainable transformations can be embedded.

Different Forms of Violence

Direct violence is easy to see in the form of wars and physical attacks, and this includes *ecological violence*, which is destruction and degradation of the environment (which is greatly increased by war). *Domestic* and *psychological violence* are less obvious, as is *structural* (or *slow*) *violence*, which is where people die from a lack of food or water or housing, even within wealthy countries.[iv] It is not for lack of these resources but because of systemic failures of governance and inequitable economic systems. Equally hidden are the attitudes and values (the *cultural violence*) that create or justify *direct violence* and *structural violence*.[v] These different types of violence interlock and reinforce each other, with *cultural violence* at the foundation of the behaviours and beliefs which lead to the more visible forms of violence.[4] There is increasing recognition of this from politicians concerned about community violence levels, with statements such as 'We need to change the culture', but little indication of how this should occur.

In this book we will examine how our cultural interactions can contribute to a peaceful society or a militaristic one. We'll see how language; movies; history, museums, parks and gardens; journalism; education; families and parenting styles; gender issues; the arts; and religion can contribute either to cultural violence or to cultures of peace. Delving into these diverse areas means that the analysis is multidisciplinary while being centred in Peace Studies theory.

Cultural Violence

Culture is rarely neutral. As Johan Galtung[5] observed, sometimes cultural factors can support violence. For example, in Northern Ireland, Protestant Unionists (i.e. those favouring remaining in a union with Great Britain) believe they have a right to march through Catholic Nationalist suburbs while singing songs that celebrate their past military victories over the latter. Both sides have long used murals to affirm their identity and glorify armed violence against each other – while Irish jokes have been used by English people to put down the Irish and intimate that this whole nation is stupid, even though it had kept alive a great deal of Western learning and culture during the Dark Ages. This culture is now beginning to change as there is pressure from below and above for peace, and people are actively working

iv Although structural violence is less obvious than direct violence, far more people die from it.

v Alternative terms for structural and cultural violence include exploitation, oppression and harm, but these don't capture the notion that they are both forms of violence which psychologically and physically impact negatively on people and ecosystems. In this book, the term 'violence' will stand for all three of direct, structural and cultural violence, unless stated otherwise.

on cultural ways to create peace, such as by involving diverse groups in painting murals with peace themes. Songs such as *Zombie* by the Cranberries, *Sunday Bloody Sunday* by U2 and Sinéad O'Connor's *Famine* have criticised the violence, both historical and recent, and contributed to a society that is much less violent than it was a few decades ago.

In a less obvious example, TV ads are a major part of Western cultures, yet they can often contribute to structural or ecological violence. Advertisements for four-wheel drives (SUVs) glorify vehicles driving through remote environments, yet this behaviour adds to global warming, erodes creek beds and makes moves to exclude vehicles from sensitive environments (such as beaches in National Parks) harder to achieve. Encouragingly, in a 2023 landmark ruling (no pun intended), one such ad has now been banned in the UK by the Advertising Standards Authority for breaching social responsibility in an environmental context, after a complaint by Adfree Cities, a network of groups trying to get advertising out of public spaces.[6]

Advertising in general may encourage more consumption of products which are unnecessary or produced in unethical, degrading and/or polluting circumstances, such as sweatshops in the global south, while television may bias our perceptions of conflicts:

> By selecting what we read and what television we watch, we are forming images of the world situation and the way it works that differ from the way others see it. These images become very deeply-rooted in our psyches, making learning new things much harder and less likely. Where we choose to live, with whom we associate, how we spend our time, what we buy, and how we vote all contribute to the system that drives many intractable conflicts.[7]

So, cultures can have violent aspects, inasmuch as they can legitimise, support or contribute to direct, ecological and structural violence. For example,

- Militaristic or xenophobic songs may contribute to fighting between ethnicities or religious groups.
- Sexist or homophobic music videos can create or maintain stereotypes and contribute to sexual and domestic violence.
- Saturation of car industry advertisements can contribute to ecological violence.
- Product placement in movies of smoking or junk foods can exacerbate structural violence and lead to poor health outcomes.

Cultural violence is:

> any aspect of a culture that can be used to legitimize violence in its direct or structural form. Symbolic violence built into a culture does not kill or maim like direct violence or the violence built into the structure. However, it is used to legitimize either or both, as for instance in the theory of a Herrenvolk, or a superior race.[8]

It may be exemplified by religion and ideology, language and art, empirical science and formal science. Cultural violence makes direct and structural violence look or feel 'right', or at least not wrong. The study of cultural violence highlights the way in which the act of direct violence and the fact of structural violence are legitimised and thus made acceptable in society.

Samuel Huntington's influential book on the 'clash of civilizations' claimed that:

> The fundamental source of conflict in this new world will not be primarily ideological or primarily economic. The great divisions among humankind and the dominating source of conflict will be cultural. Nation states will remain the most powerful actors in world affairs, but the principal conflicts of global politics will occur between nations and groups of different civilizations. The clash of civilizations will dominate global politics. The fault lines between civilizations will be the battle lines of the future.[9]

Right-wing populists in the United States and Europe have had widespread electoral gains by drawing, often implicitly, on Huntington's argument 'particularly as it related to hostility, competition, and conflict between the West and Muslims'.[10] While many scholars have been critical of Huntington's argument, and there are now corporations more powerful than many nation-states, it does illuminate how culture is not an incidental or trivial phenomenon, but an influential force in the contemporary world.

From Cultural Violence to Cultural Peace

Culture can thus be a powerful promoter of consumerism, militarism, nationalism, totalitarianism or other ideologies. Art-forms such as racist literature or music can contribute to *cultural violence,* wherein they inspire direct violence, or they can be psychologically violent.

Is it possible to transform these cultures and make them more peaceful? A pioneer of cultural peacebuilding was Quaker and peace sociologist Elise Boulding, who espoused the need to understand the world deeply so we can change it effectively. Therefore, to cultivate peaceful cultures, we need to understand the cultural violence that pervades many societies. If we can become aware of it and how it permeates so many aspects of our daily lives, we can begin to make the small changes (in how we speak, parent, educate and so on) which are the necessary first steps in creating broader cultural change. If we can understand where cultural peace already exists, we can amplify it in a more sophisticated and effective way.

Therefore, the first part of each chapter focuses on the current state of play, critiquing cultural violence, while the second part examines some of the positive currents towards cultures of peace. Some chapters will contain more critique than solutions, such as the one on violent films (Chapter 3), which at the moment far outweigh pro-peace films. Others, such as Chapter 4, on 'Existing Peaceful Cultures', are more positive, aiming to inspire reflection about existing real-world alternatives.

There is some cross-over of subject matter, for example with educating for peace through theatrical means being relevant for both the education and artistic activism chapters, and gender being relevant for many issues. Space does not allow for an in-depth examination of some major topics of relevance, such as social media and information and communication technologies, which I have covered elsewhere.[11]

Background to the Book

The book's approach is informed by my background as a long-term activist and artist, which has been woven into my academic theorisation and writing in the field of Peace Studies. The book, and the university unit it is based upon, sprang from the realisation that, while both activism and academia are valuable in building peace, the arts, humour and creativity are essential elements in any successful nonviolent campaign.

Exploring this vein further led to an understanding of the enduring quality of cultural icons, such as the social critiques of authors Charles Dickens, Arundhati Roy, Toni Morrison and Marcel Pagnol; the peace dove of Picasso; and the poetry of Australian Aboriginal rights activist Oodgeroo Noonuccal. These many forms of cultural advocacy or resistance flow in a constant current in one direction, while deeply-embedded militaristic narratives that support war, violence and powerful weapons companies flow the opposite way. While we can 'appeal to elites' such as governments to reduce violence from the top down, we can also act at grassroots levels in our everyday lives to shift our cultures away from violence (in all its forms) and towards peace. This is often slow and subtle work, but it underlies sustainable change and can sometimes result in unexpected shifts.

The book is designed to stimulate both thought and action, and is down-to-earth and practical rather than highly theoretical. It is solutions-oriented, aimed primarily at the grassroots level of ordinary citizens' daily lives, in the belief that this will translate upwards into larger cultural change, and support top-down change. It is about thinking globally and acting locally.

As such, some of the analysis inevitably arises from my Australian context, where I have been embedded in participant-observation of 'artistic activism'[vi] since the 1982–3 campaign to preserve Tasmania's Franklin River from damming. With a range of fellow activists, we have engaged in writing and performing songs; journalism; poetry; street-theatre at blockades, rallies and festivals; radio plays; graffiti; making banners and life-sized puppets; exhibiting artworks with activist and protest themes; and organising joint exhibitions. I have also taught art, nonviolence and artistic activism and produced two illustrated novels, including *Locked On! The Seventh and Most Illegal in the Hitchhiker's Guide Trilogy*.[12] This participant-observation research informed my 2013 monograph *Global Warming, Militarism and Nonviolence: The Art of Active Resistance*, part of which explored the role of the arts, creativity and humour in aiding peace, environmental and social justice campaigns, including civil disobedience and nonviolent direct action. I found that artistic activism has educative, communicative and community development qualities; builds solidarity; fortifies, emboldens and enlivens activism; impacts diverse audiences in manifold ways at multiple levels; has tactical benefits; and lessens violence and burnout.[13]

This emic (insider) research inevitably has biases and limitations, but it also has many advantages over research by movement outsiders. With many movements infiltrated by police or corporate security, and at times heavily repressed by the state and opponents, outsiders asking questions will struggle to gain similar access and understanding.

This participant-observation research includes stints in Borneo,[vii] Northern Ireland, and recently France and Japan, and peace conferences in Türkiye, Japan, India and Austria, but has primarily been situated across the Australian continent, including in activist, counter-cultural and permacultural intentional communities.[viii] Australia is a westernised, colonised,

---

vi Artistic activism is defined at the start of Chapter 10.

vii My 1994 novel *Horizontal Lightning*, by [pseudonym] 'Simon Ellis', was inspired by working with Borneo's semi-nomadic Peran people to save their rainforest homelands from logging.

viii Intentional communities are conscious attempts to create a cooperative, alternative way of life outside mainstream society. They are often designed around a social ideal or collective values and interests and usually involve shared resources and responsibilities. Permaculture is described in Chapter 5.

wealthy nation but with pockets of extreme poverty. It is situated in the global south and home to the oldest continuous human cultures on Earth. (These are struggling with the ongoing impacts of dispossession, genocides and intergenerational trauma but still hold much wisdom.[ix]) It's hoped, therefore, that the book has broadly applicable insights for readers in the global south and north.

Diverse Voices

The book tackles some confronting topics and challenges our own beliefs and practices, but it is also meant to be accessible to a wide range of readers. One way it does this is by including many diverse voices, such as proactively seeking those of women. It also includes the voices of graduate and undergraduate students who have studied the unit *Creating Cultures of Peace*, which I created within Peace Studies at the University of New England in Armidale, Australia, as I felt that examining the cultural roots of violence and positing peaceful cultural alternatives were essential for sustainable peace and to complement our other academic offerings.[x]

Informed by the egalitarian praxis initiated by Paulo Freire[14] and Augusto Boal,[15] Peace Studies units are taught collegially, and the lecturers don't presume that we have all the knowledge or that students are empty vessels to be filled. Instead, we recognise that everyone in the classes brings wisdom, unique perspectives and valuable insights gained through lived experience in different environments and professions.

---

ix While Australian Aboriginal people have long been denigrated as 'primitive' by the settler-colonial state, they produced some of the world's first scientists, astronomers, ecologists, philosophers, bakers, chemists and doctors, and they holistically and sustainably managed Country (the environment) for at least 60,000 years. With over 250 Aboriginal nations found across the land now called Australia, and many more language groups, Aboriginal people often spoke numerous languages (and some continue to do so, despite attempted cultural annihilation) and worked actively for peace between the nations and with the environment.

x Our other units cover post-conflict peacebuilding; nonviolent action; environmental peace and security; conflict resolution, mediation and negotiation; refugee issues; and globalisation as if people and ecosystems matter. Unfortunately, ever-decreasing funding for Australian universities, and particularly the humanities, arts and social sciences, allied with corporatisation and top-heavy management, led to our reconciliation and cultural peace units being cut in a euphemistic 'curriculum development framework' project.

In accordance with the inclusive nature of many social movements, the author has tried to minimise jargon where possible and write in a straightforward manner accessible to a general readership as well as peace scholars and students. It contains a broad-brush, non-linear overview of many topics rather than claiming to be exhaustive, but there are in-depth examinations of the most interesting or pertinent issues and developments.

Chapter Summaries

1. Introduction

Defines culture not just as elite and stratified but as something in which everyone is involved, both consuming and contributing to it through the language we use, the movies we choose to watch, how we raise and educate our children, the newspapers we read, the music we make and listen to and so on. Such culture may appear innocuous or neutral but is rarely so, contributing in myriad ways to whether our societies are warlike or peaceful. I've introduced concepts such as cultural, structural, direct and ecological violence and will shortly define militarism, the military-industrial complex, peace and cultural peacebuilding.

2. Language, Narratives and Discourses

Language affects not just how we communicate but how we think and behave (e.g. sexist language contributes to and maintains patriarchal systems of thought and behaviour). This chapter describes the many violent, militaristic or derogatory terms used in everyday speech and argues that this is both a reflection of and contributor to more violent societies. The chapter also looks at other forms of expression such as tone and body language, conversation dynamics and dialogic processes, and describes applied peace linguistics processes which can counter violent communication and transform it into communication which cultivates peaceful relationships and communities. The chapter describes dominant narratives and discourses, seeking to expose invisible assumptions, embedded in our communication, which underlie our societies' beliefs and processes.

3. Screen Violence and Peace

Explores through numerous examples the increasing prevalence of violent actions, imagery and themes in contemporary English-language films. It describes how this may be depicted as 'comedy violence' or callous, careless 'psycho violence'. This violence has increasingly occurred in children's films, often having undergone a process of 'violentisation'[xi] – turning gentle children's stories into more violent movies. Looking at the effects of this violence, the chapter shows how it may contribute to more aggression, bullying and violence, as well as a fearful society more likely to accept militarism and violent solutions. It also often supports other forms of structural, cultural and ecological violence, such as promoting unhealthy products, harmful body images and discriminatory or demeaning stereotypes. The chapter examines the reasons for this filmic violence, such as the financial imperatives of the film industry and the powerful military-industrial complex, and examines how violent films are often deceptively advertised and poorly reviewed and classified. Finally, the chapter explores ways of reducing movie violence, such as through censorship, classification or action by parents and community campaigners, and provides examples of films which aim to minimise or oppose violence in its various forms.

4. Peaceful Societies Already Exist

Peace is a relative state and may occur on small or large scales and for short or long periods. This chapter describes the many societies currently living in a state of relative peace, some of them having done so for long periods, with peacemaking and peace cultivation embedded in their cultural, social, political and economic fabric. Such societies range from small communities in Africa, Asia and South America to relatively undeveloped nations such as Bhutan to wealthy, developed Nordic nations such as Norway. They include countries such as Costa Rica, which have survived – indeed thrived – without military defence. The existence of these nations helps challenge the common assumptions that humans are naturally aggressive and warlike, that war is an inevitable aspect of human nature and societies, and that military defence is essential. The chapter focuses on the cultural elements of those societies which contribute to their peaceful nature, and asks whether and how these elements can be utilised more widely in other societies to build towards a more peaceful world.

5. Peace History: Museums, Memorials, Parks and Gardens

This chapter argues that much of conventional history is the history of violence and that our history curricula and institutions are being militarised by powerful vested interests. At the same time, a great many nonviolent

xi Violentisation is the process of making something more violent.

movements – which have effectively created social change and altered the course of history – are under-recognised. Additionally, there are other biases in conventional histories which ignore feminist, indigenous and other perspectives. Peace movements have been a dissenting voice in this militarisation of history, challenging it and providing alternative narratives, 'landscapes of remembrance' and 'sites of conscience' such as subaltern peace histories, museums, memorials and parks which are acting for positive peace. Their uncovering of untold stories is an important way of countering museums and historical practices that privilege militarism by focusing entirely or mainly on great battles and leaders (usually men). They can facilitate remembering (such as of white-washed genocides) while aiming to be constructive, future-oriented and peace-promoting, and to use their power to educate and shape society to prevent historical traumas or conflicts caused by war from taking place in societies today. The chapter also interrogates the role of war memorials, name and event changes, and controversies such as the removal of colonialist statues, occasioned by movements such as 'Black Lives Matter'.

6. Peace Journalism and Writing

Mainstream media often demonstrates a pro-war bias or at least supports the maintenance of military spending and the supposed necessity of violence in international and intra-national problem-solving. The poor investigation of militarism may occur because of an enculturated respect for militarism, fear of upsetting powerful interests, ignorance, unconscious bias, poor teaching of journalism or simply laziness – it is easier to parrot official statements by the 'masters of war' than to seek out alternative views or views from its victims. The involvement of corporate vested interests in the decision-making processes of defence spending occurs at a covert level through the selective presentation of information to the public by the mass media. This allows the military-industrial complex to promote military operations as necessary and even desirable and to promote continued military spending for national and even global security reasons. This chapter describes how much of conventional media can (consciously or unconsciously) contribute to conflicts and militarism, whereas peace journalism specifically aims to reduce conflict and promote peace.

7. Domestic Peace

Chapter 7 explores the realm of parenting and the home in their role of either creating damaged people prone to violence (such as Stalin and Hitler) or people who act for peace. Childhood experiences shape emotional makeup and beliefs, and scars from repetitive hurts can affect behaviour much later, with many 'normal' social behaviours being in fact defensive vestiges from intergenerational mistreatment as humanity acts out its collective trauma in manifold ways. More positively, peace and democracy start at home, and parenting can change the world. Making children's emotional well-being our top social priority brings benefits for all of humanity, so our child-rearing choices can be the most powerful agents for positive social change and planetary healing. Moving from authoritarian to authoritative parenting and promoting children's emotional intelligence enable them to grow to have the healthiest and most rewarding relationships with others and fulfil their potential. There are no perfect parents or family arrangements, however, and child-rearing is best approached as a communal enterprise which takes into account the role of gender, games and sport in detracting from or promoting peace.

8. Peace Education

Following the previous chapter on domestic peace, this chapter describes systems of education which aim to create well-rounded youth capable of living and acting peacefully in the world. It explores the role of education in determining whether citizens are violent or peaceful; docile and apathetic or empowered and assertive; ignorant and easily led or well-informed and independent; passive consumers who acquiesce with violent systems or active citizens who use nonviolent methods of conflict transformation. In short, how can our education systems ensure more peaceful, engaged societies? The chapter describes some innovative programmes designed to bring children from warring communities together so they can learn to understand each other better, and discusses education systems (such as in alternative schools, Peace Studies departments at universities and arts-based projects) which make a conscious effort to promote harmonious co-existence and counter the pro-military aspects of much of the history that is taught in schools, as discussed in Chapter 5.

9. Gender, Sexuality and Peace

This chapter discusses the role that gender plays in whether a society is militaristic or peaceful. It gives a summary of women's contributions to peacebuilding, citing some of the many examples of women at pivotal points of nonviolent campaigns and at the forefront of peace activism, partly because they suffer the most from war, along with children. It describes the overwhelming evidence that, where women's inclusion is prioritised in peacebuilding missions, peace is more likely, particularly when women are in positions to influence decision-making. On the other hand, the increasing entry of women into military forces is better understood not as liberation but as the newest stage of militarising global capitalism. Men are both socialised in terms of violence generally and towards women, as well as suffering under militarism. They are often constrained by societal notions of masculinity, or adversely affected by 'toxic hyper-masculinities' promoted in the violent movies discussed in Chapter 3. Social movements continue to advocate for the liberation of both women and men from harmful cultural and social conditioning.

10. Artistic Activism

Explores the many examples of creative people all over the world using the arts, humour and creativity to create a more peaceful, equitable, just and sustainable planet. This occurs in every medium imaginable, from puppetry, prose and punk to classical, liberation and resistance music. The chapter explores exuberant protests in South Korea, postering in Russia and Hong Kong, and assertive, confronting critiques clothed in beauty. Artistic activism can provide oases of freedom of expression, move people from fear to engagement, make issues personal and cause deep changes in people's worldviews. It can increase empathy, find common ground, heal divisions, unite and get people laughing.

It can expose direct, structural and cultural violence. It can strengthen nonviolent movements for change and aid the dynamics of those movements as well as prevent violence. We also explore the question of whether disquieting, challenging art promotes peace or adds to cultural violence. The chapter describes outbursts of counter-cultural activity, such as in the anti-war and civil rights movements of the 1960s and 1970s, and discusses the social criticism role of popular music, including rock, reggae, rap, hip hop and Australian Aboriginal and African protest music.

11. Peace Within

Beginning with the premise that finding a measure of *peace within* is essential for creating peaceful cultures and societies, the chapter describes a range of practices – spiritual, religious and secular – which can still the mind and contribute to inner peace. These include developing mindfulness and the ability to listen deeply through meditation, yoga, tai chi, jogging, walking in nature and trying to establish a deep connection with nature and communities. For others, it involves the calming effects of listening to music or viewing art, engaging in creative or expressive practices, or spending focused time with loved ones. The chapter also explores the pro-peace aspects of religious or spiritual traditions such as Buddhism, Taoism, Hinduism, Islam, Judaism, earth-based spirituality and Christianity, and how action for a better world – such as nonviolent activism, setting up alternative or parallel systems and engaging in prefigurative politics – can lead to a reduction in cognitive dissonance and a growth in internal peace. The chapter describes how this inner peace can lead to peace more widely – in homes, workplaces, institutions, communities, societies and nations.

*

I hope you'll find the book illuminating, and you will consider ways of applying your learning and reflections to your lives. Before looking at various aspects of culture and whether they contribute to militarism or peace, it's important to understand what is meant by militarism.

Militarism

The term militarism refers to a political, social, cultural and discursive orientation of a people or government to maintain a strong military force and be prepared to use it aggressively to gain power; defend, promote or expand national interests and values; and win economic or political advantages. It may include the predominance of a professional military class in the administration or policy-making of the state and the exaltation of military virtues and ideals.

Although conflict is a normal and even healthy feature of societies which embrace diversity, and some levels of violence are inevitable, militarism tends towards a 'hawkish' political orientation, favouring aggressive foreign policies, and armed violence as the 'fall-back' or ultimate option for conflict resolution. This requires the maintenance of large, permanent armed forces trained to use extreme violence against people, places and objects when ordered to do so. High levels of military spending are common, usually to the detriment of other areas of government spending, such as health, education, welfare and environmental care. Although such spending is characterised as for defence, it is just as often used for neo-colonialism, territorial and market expansion, and attempting to secure resources such as oil.

Although militarism is often associated with terms like 'dictatorship' and presumed to happen in countries other than our own, this book will show how it is embedded in most countries and in the daily practices of peacetime. Militarism is a complex phenomenon which influences people and institutions towards violent paradigms and practices, often using subtle mechanisms such as language, discourses and narratives. As we will see in the next chapter, pervasive but subtle discourses and hidden power structure play an important role in leading people towards accepting militarism. These discourses help to create our personal and cultural selves and underpin numerous cultural notions such as patriotism, morality and perceptions of 'the other'. We'll see in later chapters how things like entertainment violence, toy guns, war journalism and co-opted education are forms of cultural violence which support militarism. To give an example, one junk email you may have received promotes a 'Military Grade Tactical Waist Backpack', the implication being that 'military grade' means high quality. How a backpack is 'tactical' is hard to fathom.

The Military-Industrial Complex

Militarism also relies on and is encouraged by a variety of industries, such as arms manufacturers. This is often termed the military-industrial complex, a physical manifestation of militarism involving a complicated and secretive conglomeration of entities that supply armies, navies and air forces with fighter and surveillance planes, battleships, nuclear and 'conventional' weapons, drones, armoured vehicles, munitions, fuel, housing, infrastructure, food, information and communication technologies, and a range of other goods and services. (Security personnel, police, prison corporations and gun owners are also customers.) Corporations such as Halliburton are also involved in rebuilding states after their military subsidiaries have contributed to their destruction.[16]

The title of this complex has been expanded to include media, entertainment, finance and academia, while terms such as 'military-entertainment complex'[17] are used to describe particular manifestations. (For simplicity's sake, I will generally just use the term 'military-industrial complex'.) Militarism and war are big business, worth trillions of dollars,[18] and this complex has a vested interest in ensuring that they continue so that 'defence' spending and its enormous profits are maintained. It achieves economic and political war-dependence through its phenomenal lobbying power and 'revolving door' connections with governmental elites.[19]

What Do We Mean by Peace and Cultural Peacebuilding?

Just as there are different forms of violence, peace can have many definitions and forms.[xii] A simple form is a ceasefire or peace treaty, which Galtung

---

xii Anders Reagan argues that '[d]espite significant disagreement between peace researchers on a standardized definition of peace, there seems to be overwhelming consensus that "peace" – in all its varied academic conceptualizations – always

described as merely *negative peace*, as this form of peace may be highly unstable unless the root causes of the conflict are addressed, and the warring parties make concerted moves towards more deep-seated and sustainable *positive peace*. UNE Peace Studies' Helen Ware prefers describing war as *Peace Zero* and ceasefires as *Peace One*, since achieving ceasefires is often difficult and a positive, necessary step towards more substantial peace. After achieving *Peace One*, post-conflict societies should attempt to progress towards ever greater levels of peace (*Peace Two, Peace Three* and so on). For the sake of simplicity, however, I'll continue to use Galtung's more widely recognised terms.

For Rebecca Oxford, peace is holistic and comprised of six interconnected elements. *Intercultural peace* is one of the key elements of her peace model, which also includes *inner, interpersonal, intergroup, international* and *ecological peace*: 'The future of the whole planet rides on decisions about these aspects of peace.'[20] These elements can be further categorised as a peace triangle, the base of which is *inner peace*. The other two sides are *social peace* and *ecological peace*.

> *Inner peace* is placed at the bottom as the foundation of social and ecological peace. Interpersonal, intergroup, intercultural, and international peace – all forms of *social peace* – are linked with *inner peace*, because building and maintaining social bonds require some degree of peace within the heart. *Inner peace* [...] also influences *ecological peace* by offering insightful motivation to cherish the environment in which we live, move, and have our being.[21]

Elise Boulding's book *Cultures of Peace: The Hidden Side of History*, based on her study of civil society during the second half of the twentieth century, attempted to integrate the human needs for both autonomy and connectedness; emphasised connection among family, community and government; and encouraged networking, relationship and listening: 'Put in the simplest terms, a peace culture is a culture that promotes peaceable diversity'.[22] For Boulding, a peace culture includes

> lifeways, patterns of belief, values, behaviour, and accompanying institutional arrangements that promote mutual caring and well-being as well as an equality that includes appreciation of difference, stewardship, and equitable sharing of the earth's resources among its members and with all living beings.[23]

---

relates to the social welfare of interacting sentiences' (2023 'Reframing the ontology of peace studies', *Peace and Conflict Studies*, vol. 29, no. 2).

Empowerment and Action

Just as we inadvertently (and sometimes intentionally) contribute to militarism, we all – not just powerful entities and rich people – can play a constructive role in reducing it and the dynamics that lead to destructive and intractable conflicts.[24] This requires empowerment and understanding what we are doing to make our cultures more militaristic or peaceful:

> [P]eople need to be empowered with knowledge, self-esteem, skills, and resources, as well as by directly engaging in peacebuilding efforts. Empowerment has a direct relationship with human security, which consists of physical safety, economic well-being, social inclusion, and the full exercise of human rights.[25]

It also requires taking action individually and collaboratively to cultivate positive peace. Thousands and even millions of people acting independently, or preferably in organised movements, can change the 'tipping point' of a system, transforming it into something much more peaceful, just and sustainable. Building momentum through myriad cultural ways at all levels of societies can shift the tides of public opinion and behaviour so that governments and corporations are forced to follow where the people have led.

As we will see, a commitment to creating cultures of peace has many aspects, most of which, such as viewing movies and consuming mass media, we already have a connection with. It can involve 'everyday nonviolence' – deliberate actions taken by a person or group to improve themselves and society, through language; screen choices; investigating peaceful cultures; understanding nonviolent history; parenting and educating for peace; gender and sexuality awareness; artistic activism; and seeking spiritual balance.

In the next chapter, we'll commence this journey by looking at the language, communication styles, discourses and narratives we use, and how they can constitute cultural violence or create small but significant ripples of peace around us.

Notes

1 Marwick, Arthur 1998 *The Sixties*, Oxford University Press, Oxford, p. 11.
2 Ibid.
3 ABC Radio National 19 January 2022.
4 Galtung, Johan 1990 'Cultural violence', *Journal of Peace Research*, vol. 27, no. 3, pp. 291–305; Galtung, Johan 1969 'Violence, peace and peace research', *Journal of Peace Research*, vol. 6, pp. 167–191.
5 Galtung 1990.

6 Skopeliti, Clea 2023 'Toyota SUV adverts banned in UK on environmental grounds', *Guardian*, 22 November, www.theguardian.com/media/2023/nov/22/toyota-suv-adverts-banned-in-uk-on-environmental-grounds?CMP=share_btn_link

7 Burgess, Heidi and Burgess, Guy 2022 'About the things you can do to help limit destructive conflict blog', *Beyond Intractability*, www.beyondintractability.org/about-things-you-can-do

8 Galtung 1990, p. 291.

9 Huntington, Samuel P. 1993 *The Clash of Civilizations and the Remaking of World Order*, Simon and Schuster, New York, p. 22.

10 Haynes, Jeffrey 2019 'Introduction: The "Clash of Civilizations" and relations between the West and the Muslim world', *The Review of Faith & International Affairs*, vol. 17, no. 1, pp. 1–10.

11 Branagan, Marty 2013 *Global Warming, Militarism and Nonviolence: The Art of Active Resistance*, Palgrave Macmillan, pp. 143–175.

12 Branagan, Marty 2018 *Locked On! The Seventh and Most Illegal in the Hitchhiker's Guide Trilogy*, Irene Publishing, Sparsnäs.

13 Branagan 2013, pp. 176–216.

14 Freire, Paulo 1972 *Pedagogy of the Oppressed*, Penguin, Harmondsworth; Freire, Paulo 1985 *The Politics of Education*, Macmillan, London.

15 Boal Augusto 1979 *Theatre of the Oppressed*, Pluto Press, London.

16 Boyle, Peter 2005 'Halliburton in Australia: The publicly funded war profiteer', *Green Left*, 16 March, www.greenleft.org.au/content/halliburton-australia-publicly-funded-war-profiteer

17 Kang, Inkoo 2013 'Tales of the military-entertainment complex: Why the U.S. navy produced "Battleship"', *Movieline*, 6 February, http://movieline.com/2013/02/06/military-entertainment-complex-hollywood-pentagon-relationship-battleship-zero-dark-thirty/

18 Bandow, Doug 2021 'War is big business', *Cato Institute*, 30 September, www.cato.org/commentary/war-big-business#

19 Turley, Jonathan 2014 'Big money behind war: The military-industrial complex', *Al Jazeera*, 11 January, www.aljazeera.com/opinions/2014/1/11/big-money-behind-war-the-military-industrial-complex/

20 Oxford, Rebecca 2017 'Peace through understanding: Peace activities as innovations in language teacher education', in Tammy Gregersen and Peter MacIntyre (eds.), *Innovative Practices in Language Teacher Education*, Springer, Cham, pp. 125–163.

21 Oxford, Rebecca and Olivero, María Matilde 2023 'Editorial', *Peace Research: The Canadian Journal of Peace and Conflict Studies*, vol. 55, no. 1, pp. 5–14.

22 Cited in Jegen, M. E. 2001 'Cultures of peace: The hidden side of history by Elise Boulding', *Fellowship*, vol. 67, no. 9–10, p. 24.

23 Ibid.

24 Burgess and Burgess 2022.

25 Askerov, Ali 2020 'An interdisciplinary academic field- Peace and conflict studies', *Researchgate*, February, www.researchgate.net/publication/339416022_An_Interdisciplinary_Academic_Field-_Peace_and_Conflict_Studies, p. 28.

Chapter 2

LANGUAGE, NARRATIVES AND DISCOURSES

Language affects not just how we communicate but how we think and behave. Our language doesn't only reflect our view of the world – it *shapes* it. For example, sexist language contributes to and maintains patriarchal systems of thought and behaviour, as does 'mansplaining', a term recently coined to describe the phenomenon of a man explaining something to a woman 'in a condescending, overconfident, and often inaccurate or oversimplified manner, typically to a woman already knowledgeable about the topic'.[1]

In another example, the widespread adoption of the innocuous and vague term 'climate change', rather than the more accurate 'global warming', was pushed by states with oil interests, such as Saudi Arabia and the United States.[2] By diluting the urgency and obscuring the cause, this has delayed action.

Linguist Edward Sapir argued in 1921 that the 'real world' is to a large extent unconsciously built up on the language habits of society. That is, language has a measurable influence on the formation of thought, which is a precursor to action leading to behaviours, policies and institutional practices.[3] So, language is a powerful tool, and how we use it can make a significant difference to society and to how we think.

It can provide subtle or unconscious support for dominant paradigms on a widespread, everyday basis, or it can undermine them. For example, language can be used to exclude certain people or groups through the use of derogatory terms such as 'wog', 'poof', 'nigger' or 'slut'. As a result of concerns about how this language can translate into bullying or encourage physical violence, there has been a strong push to outlaw such terms or at least make them socially unacceptable. This in turn has been denigrated, often from more conservative quarters of society, as 'politically correct' – supposedly because it limits people's freedom or dictates how they should speak. Others counter this by saying that such language is simply offensive and 'politically wrong'. According to the Mental Health Commission in the Australian state of New South Wales (NSW):

> Language is how we express the ideas in our minds, and is therefore a most powerful agent that can reinforce separation, stigma and discrimination or, instead, work to overcome our differences and emphasise the things we have in common.[4]

Feminist attempts to counter sexist language, such as using Ms instead of Miss or Mrs, are one example of a group recognising that language has power and that sexist language has contributed to the oppression of women. As a lecturer, I still get many essays – some written by women – which talk about 'the origins of man' or otherwise use 'man' to stand for all people (e.g. chair*man*, spokes*man*, *man*power, *man*ning) – even though this automatically skews one towards an acceptance that men are primary and women are secondary or just associates of men.[5]

Universities are now making conscious attempts to counter sexist language and encourage gender-neutral language. There are still many terms, however, such as black market, black looks and black magic (as opposed to white magic) which reinforce racist stereotypes that black is bad or illegal while white is good and legitimate.[i] An early film example was the villain in Charlie Chaplin's *The Gold Rush* (1925) being called 'Black Larson'.

Violent Language

There has been less realisation that our language can contribute to violence or peace. In the appendix is a list of common phrases which stem from war, militarism, guns or violence. You can see from this list that our language is filled with such terms. By themselves, they may seem quite tame, especially if you've grown up with them and never given them a second thought. But they can have a cumulative impact.

For example, constant use of 'war words' in workplaces, such as 'execute', 'blunt instrument' and 'war room', or the advice to 'keep your head down' (relating to trench warfare and avoiding being shot), creates the impression that employees are in a war zone, competing with each other or a hostile world.[6] This can impact on workplace morale and interrupt workers' intellectual capacity, communication, sleep patterns and digestion. Substituting those terms for more positive, engaging words can make a difference in how workers interact.

---

i There are exceptions, of course, such as 'in the black' (profitable, financially solvent) and 'to white-ant' (to undermine from within).

You might come across other phrases or find yourself saying these ones without thinking, as I have. My son's 'Pause Game' (stopping a game for a short period) became, by the age of 12, 'Ceasefire', while 'I bags [claim] the front seat' became 'Shotgun front seat'. Soccer parents say to forwards: 'Get into position and then pull the trigger' or 'Fire a corner in', while TV commentators say things like 'She's a trooper'.

At school barbecues, parents emerging with large BBQ tools claim to be 'bringing out the heavy artillery' or 'the big guns'. At weekend tennis, people talk about a serve 'like a bullet' or how someone 'killed it'. There's even a lolly called a 'Warhead'. The avocado we serve is no longer mashed but 'smashed'. A UN conference talks about 'diving into the trenches of sustainable development.' A sci-fi book by Monty Python's Eric Idle talks about how comedians 'die', 'kill an audience', 'slay them' or 'knock them dead' with a 'punchline' or a 'knockout gag'.[7] In the United States, you can buy a can of water called 'Liquid Death' with a melting skull on it, which lets you 'murder your thirst'. In Australia, you can buy 'Slap Ya Mama' seasoning, which could be viewed as a harmless joke or one more aspect of our culture which legitimises domestic violence. Joe Biden, when US vice president, led a task force exploring the issue of gun violence and said, apparently without irony, that there was no 'silver bullet' to solve it.[8]

Even nonviolent activists fall into this trap, talking about 'the weapons of nonviolence', 'a death of a thousand cuts' or how an author 'punches home a message'. A campaign against the US military presence in Darwin, Australia, is called 'Give 'em the Boot'. Activists use terms such as the 'fight for social change', 'the fight against Adani coal mine' and 'the battle against Santos CSG in the Pilliga'. In the case of the Sea Shepherd group, the narrative is reinforced by their skull and crossbones symbols and controversial tactics.

The 2018 movie *A Wrinkle in Time* has a message of opposing violence but then urges people to 'fight' evil and become 'warriors'. A classic example is the term 'fighting for peace' which is something the so-called 'realists' believe is necessary and effective, whereas critics say that it's a contradiction in terms and that fighting simply contributes to cycles of violence and pushes peace further away. (In Australia's foreign military excursions, we have been 'fighting for peace' for more than 100 years with only limited success.) Such critics advocate nonviolent strategies, arguing that the means must be compatible with the ends (prefigurative action). They prefer phrases such as 'to work for peace'.

Even seemingly-innocuous phrases such as 'toast soldiers' (slices of toast that young children dip into boiled eggs) may normalise at an early age the concept of soldiers as something harmless, accepted by the family and home, something fun and tasty like 'ANZAC biscuits'. The bikini was named after the site of atomic tests that deeply affected both human and environmental health. There are also numerous sports metaphors which encourage aggression and competitiveness.

When these terms occur in tandem with all the others described in the list, we can see that there is a pattern of a language which has been filled by warlike or militaristic paradigms. This militarism-influenced language is just one of many factors which might predispose us to accept militarism and continue to allow our taxes to be poured into 'defence' and the wealthy, pervasive military-industrial complex which supplies it. In other words, the casual use of military terminology in everyday speech acts to integrate militarism into the cultural subconscious and to normalise militarism:

> More than just a linguistic quirk [...] the militarisation of language reflects the militarisation of society; it normalises the military as a part of everyday life.[9]

Language and Religion

The final chapter examines the role of religion and spirituality in cultivating peaceful cultures. It's worth briefly noting here, however, that religious language is not necessarily peaceful. As one student noted on a *Creating Cultures of Peace* online discussion forum:

> As I thought about the way language can be violent and the example given about how activists might say something like 'keep fighting the good fight', I started thinking about my upbringing in the Christian church and how often violent language is used in hymns and so forth. 'Onward Christian Soldier, marching as to war' springs to mind, and phrases like 'the army of God', 'spiritual warfare', and so forth. It surprises me that such violent language is used really, if the belief is that Jesus came to bring peace and that God is a God of peace, and Christianity a peaceful religion it doesn't seem a good fit! (Although of course the Old Testament, being largely a history text, is very violent.) I would feel very uncomfortable if I were to attend a church service where such songs or language were used now, especially the idea of Christians being soldiers. To me, that is the opposite of what should be happening.

Peaceful Language

Are there expressions which could replace these terms without losing their dramatic impact? Can we retrain ourselves to use more peaceful language, such as 'use a hose instead of a watering can' rather than 'use the scatter gun approach'? Or we could try 'feed two birds from one bowl' rather than 'kill two birds with one stone', as advocated by the People for the Ethical Treatment of Animals. Such a change might have a surprising impact. As Michael Fox notes, 'language and dialogic processes are a common feature in [...] peaceful societies; effective conflict resolution processes are employed in their daily lives'.[10] He argues that the values that are central to extant peaceful societies provide a vocabulary that promotes and sustains peace-building processes. The Xingu tribes of Brazil, for example, value tranquil, self-contained behaviour over aggression; being a warrior has no value in this society.[11] Likewise, Souillac and Fry[12] contend that indigenous peaceable societies maintain a values vocabulary that promotes 'relationship, responsibility, reciprocity and redistribution', with an Australian Aboriginal example being their frequent use of the terms 'sister', 'bruz' (brother) and 'cuz' (cousin) with a wide range of people. The peaceful language and dialogic processes that are used to support and maintain trade, ceremonial connections, governance and negotiation are fundamental to these peace systems.[13] Cooperative, communal and collaborative values and language that promote the whole society rather than the individual are emphasised. This peaceful values vocabulary sees the enculturation of peacefulness into each successive generation. Peacebuilding language and dialogue are essential components of the ongoing maintenance of peace systems. Brian Martin's *Verbal Defence*[14] and Marshall Rosenberg's *Nonviolent Communication: A Language of Life*[15] are useful resources for those interested in this area.

Reviving Aboriginal Place Names

An important shift in Australia, which was accelerated by the Black Lives Matter movement's emergence, is the increasing use of Aboriginal place names. This can be seen in a wide variety of settings, from the Awabakal and Wonnarua signage in the NSW Kurri Kurri rest area to the callers and texters on national radio broadcasters ABC Classic and youth station Triple Jay, to letter writers to the Sydney Morning Herald. This shift has created a source of pride for indigenous traditional owners, has educated indigenous youth and the wider community, and has become a long-overdue acknowledgement of ongoing ownership and connection, despite the predations of colonialism. It helps reverse cultural violence and erasure, moving the country towards sustainable peace.

Most linguists agree that language can be defined as a systematic way of conveying our aspirations, ideas and feelings, and also a way to share opinions and facts (although not all agree with 'linguistic determinism', the notion that linguistics is the prime determinant of behaviour). There is now an emerging field of peace linguistics, described by Gomes de Matos as 'the study of the interaction of language and peace for improving human communicative life'.[16] Labelling peace linguistics as a distinct field of linguistics highlights the importance of the teaching and use of peacebuilding language. Structured conflict resolution methods, also known as 'applied peace linguistics', provide educational pathways that support people to become peaceful language users, further fostering cultures of peace.

Other Forms of Expression

Language is just one aspect of communication. It is complemented by other forms of expression, such as:

- Tone of voice,
- Engagement styles: passive, assertive, aggressive or passive-aggressive,
- Body language, for example, conversing with children at eye level or standing over them,
- Maintaining eye contact or being distracted (such as by mobile phones),
- Interrupting constantly and dominating the conversation space versus listening well and allowing equal time.

As one *Creating Cultures of Peace* student commented:

> I am a town planning contractor working in a different office every day, so I'd like to think that I have seen quite a bit of different environments and how this affects the employees in these shires. Language I think is less important in these scenarios than behaviour towards employees, staff meetings and breaks. The language used in country shires tends to be fairly informal and a lot of these 'military' terms are used, but I have found that the tone is a lot more casual and less demanding. Offices located in urban areas tend to want things done now, like right now, ASAP, etc., and I have found that this is more likely to add stress to terms than the words themselves. Informal tones and the feeling of endless amounts of time to do things (even if there isn't) create a lovely environment to work in and significantly reduce the worry created by terms such as 'deadlines'. Office culture also helps with creating a friendly environment to talk about worries and ask others for help. When staff meetings are held over morning tea, cake and coffee, it creates an open space to not only discuss workloads but, if you are busy, it also creates opportunities for others to step up and offer help (a frequent occurrence). I think that although words have a huge impact on how

we react to things, a person's tone, font in email, and other surrounding language are more important.

Gerard Vanderhaar's article 'A Manner of Speaking'[17] was an early exploration of this area, giving a practical introduction to the gentle art of communication (or the art of gentle communication), based on what he calls *active listening*. He begins by pointing out that: '[m]ost people with whom we converse won't be skilled in a non-violent dialect. Some will be aggressive, asserting their own egos and putting others down. Others will talk much more than they listen.'

His approach is simple but not necessarily easy, and it can be liberating. He emphasises the idea of *space* in conversation, that is, giving others space to express themselves, their thoughts and, perhaps most importantly, their needs. Vandehaar advocates developing nonviolent dialects, giving pointers on how to be assertive and the value of maintaining a 'gentle and soothing, rather than a sharp or demanding' vocal tone.[ii] These practices are calming for both the speaker and the listener. Finally, he mentions the need for *ahimsa*, a term from Jain and other Eastern traditions which means 'without violence' or, more broadly, respect for all living things.

Respect for women's voices, however, is often missing in mixed conversations, according to the pioneering work of Dale Spender on sexism in conversation dynamics, which investigated the subtle and not-so-subtle ways by which women endure an unequal share of conversation time and have their ideas dismissed or taken over by men.[18] Looking to indigenous cultures can often provide solutions to problems ranging from biodiversity loss and global warming to how conversation dynamics occur. One indigenous practice is the 'talking stick', which is passed from person to person so it is obvious who is speaking and should be respected as such, and to prevent frequent interrupting, talking over people and dominance of loud, talkative people over quieter ones, who may have important things to say but do not get the chance to say them.

For Peace Studies pioneer, Elise Boulding, creating peace cultures involves not just language and how we deal with difference creatively, but how we listen: 'The other key word in peace culture is "listening." Any group of people that is really listening with their hearts to each other is practicing peace culture'.[19]

---

ii If done carelessly, it can also be damaging to chastise others over their use of unintentionally offensive language.

Narratives and Discourses

Power operates in a number of ways, including through knowledge and language, suggesting that power is not just possessed by those in official or elite positions of authority.

Theorists such as Pierre Bourdieu, Antonio Gramsci, Hannah Arendt, Jacques Derrida and Noam Chomsky have provided profound insights into the diverse ways by which language can influence, shape and shift dominant power structures. Their collective work portrays language as a complex and paradoxical tool in the context of power. Language may validate, preserve, justify and perpetuate prevailing power structures. Simultaneously, it may weaken, undermine, expose vulnerabilities in, and challenge them, often embodying acts of resistance.

Narratives and discourses are made up of the language we use as well as other factors, including who controls them, what is discussed and what is omitted in any topic. According to Michel Foucault, discourse can be described as a meta-narrative through which we construct our social reality.

> Discourse is not simply that which translates struggles or systems of domination, but is the thing for which and by which there is struggle, discourse is the power which is to be seized.[20]

Discourse plays a significant role in shaping specific worldviews that Foucault terms 'regimes of truth' that subsequently influence societal actions. These discursive regimes become deeply ingrained in our everyday beliefs, guiding the behaviours we embrace to conform with these convictions. Through this prism, existing power structures are reinforced and perpetuated by prevailing discourses, and this intersection of discourse and power dynamics is where resistance often emerges.

Discourse is a strategic resource, a fundamental arena of struggle over societal power dynamics, and a crucial medium through which we construct our social reality, negotiate our relationships and reinforce – or challenge – existing power relationships and dominant ideologies.[21] It can influence the formation, internal cohesion and success of nonviolent civil resistance and peace movements by shaping public opinion, developing a rationale for participation, creating mobilising emotions to persuade people to act, and organising social movements.[22]

Narrative is a form of discourse that encompasses a sequential arrangement of events presented in a particular order and recounted through the process of narration. Narrative allows us to construct and convey meaning and beliefs; understand cultural values; explain human behaviour and mental processes; develop perception of the self; explore existential questions and ethical dilemmas; comprehend and interpret political ideologies and power dynamics; and analyse social structures, interactions and changes. Narrative underlies everything from literature and movies to legal instruments.

Militaristic Narratives

A common term or narrative phrase used by politicians who wish to portray themselves as strong or effective is 'war on.' We have a 'war on drugs' which has been fairly unsuccessful as it mainly impacts on and criminalises individual consumers, keeps drug use unregulated and dangerous, keeps prices high, and finances criminal and violent groups.

We have a 'war on weeds' which was part of the 'green revolution' and the rise of agri-business – large-scale monocultures dependent on multinational corporations to supply pesticides, synthetic fertilisers and heavy fossil fuel use.

The 'war on disease' has been perhaps the most successful of these 'wars', although it has relied on scientific research (often cooperative and international) rather than warlike methods (usually secretive and competitive), and could be more successful if the trillions poured annually into arms, battleships and warplanes were to be spent on more research, hospitals, water, mosquito nets, health education and poverty reduction such as through land redistribution.

Other examples include the 'war on crime' and the 'war on cancer'. Least successful has been the 'war on terror', formulated as 'a potentially endless struggle against an infinitely extended enemy, that permeates all borders, and may inhabit any sphere'.[23] Although vast amounts of resources have been poured into it, many argue that it is unwinnable and contradictory, like 'fighting for peace', and has been pushed by the arms industry which profits from a continual state of war.

Combative Political Cultures

In Australian politics, as elsewhere, we have an *opposition*, a group of politicians whose *job* is to *oppose* the government's position or actions rather than work *with* them for the good of all citizens. This likely contributes to the combative culture and adversarial nature of our political system.

Countless management books quote military language, strategists such as Sun Tzu and war heroes like Winston Churchill and George S. Patton, despite the impacts this can have on workplace morale, as noted above. Similarly, Bill Shorten, the former Federal Opposition Leader, cites military rather than political thinkers as his main influences. He admires the meticulous preparations that John Monash made during World War I, but Napoleon is his hero for his maxim of finding the enemy's weakest point and concentrating the attack there. This seems to exemplify a great deal of Australian politics (where both the major parties pour billions annually into new military equipment and war museums) as well as politics elsewhere. It is combative and emotionally puerile, filled with petty point scoring, constant mudslinging and personal attacks (particularly towards any women, such as former Australian prime minister Julia Gillard, who struggle to gain and remain in the higher offices). A conciliatory, cooperative approach to leadership would lead to considered policymaking and visionary leadership and be far more effective. The latter is certainly more appreciated in other institutions, such as universities and businesses.

This might seem utopian, but it does occur in some cultures, as we will see in Chapter 4. To get there more widely, cultural changes through peace education, improved parenting, peace journalism, gender equity and inner work are all useful, as we'll see in other chapters. Changing the language communication styles, discourses and narratives is also important. Can we resist warlike narratives by developing new narratives and discourses that emphasise cooperation and collaboration?

Narrative Power Analysis

Narrative power analysis (NPA) is something developed by the social change organisation SmartMeme. Stories or narratives, they argue, are fundamentally important to human existence and a crucial site for activism because they 'shape and inform how we see the world'.[24] By conducting an NPA – an analysis of the prominence of certain narratives and the power structures supporting them – activists are better able to identify the dominant myths, cosmologies and assumptions surrounding a given issue, and are thus better placed to develop alternative narratives that effectively counteract these prevailing orthodoxies.

An NPA asks certain questions, such as 'Which stories define cultural norms? Where did these stories come from? Whose stories were ignored or erased to create these norms?' NPA is designed to uncover what Reinsborough and Canning label as the 'dominant culture', described as 'stories that validate [...] political agendas' and which have 'become invisible as they are passed from generation to generation – carrying assumptions that become "conventional wisdom"'.[25] In Chapter 3, we'll examine a few of these conventional assumptions.

Discursive and Narrative Resistance

Narratives are vitally important aspects of conflicts and social change movements. Peace scholar and director of the Tokyo-based Toda Peace

Institute, Kevin P. Clements, writes of the Palestine–Israel conflict, which flared up again in October 2023, that the violence is only part of the conflict:

> The second battle is for control of the narrative. Israel immediately moved into a victim narrative, comparing the Hamas assault to 9/11, Pearl Harbour and the Holocaust. President Biden called the Hamas attacks 'pure evil'. All of these comparisons are intended to evoke memories of swift and 'legitimate' military action and 'vengeance'. Hamas, on the other hand claims that its actions are justified by years of blockade, oppression and humiliation. Gaza, for example, is often referred to as the largest open-air prison in the world. The world's media (led by the United States) promotes the first narrative while pro-Palestinian states and free Arab media the second. Neither narrative, however, can be used to demonise, and justify unrestrained bloodshed against the other.[26]

One common narrative is that most revolutionary changes to societies and their cultures have occurred through violence. Jonathan Schell challenges this narrative, arguing that the United States, French and Russian Revolutions were primarily achieved through shifts in the attitudes, behaviours and institutions of the masses.[27] Even at the time, this was understood by some, such as John Adams, second president of the United States, who wrote to journalist Hezekiah Niles in February 1818:

> But what do we mean by the American Revolution? Do we mean the American war? The Revolution was effected before the war commenced. The Revolution was in the minds and hearts of the people [...] This radical change in the principles, opinions, sentiments, and affections of the people was the real American Revolution.[28]

Yet the narrative that violence is useful or necessary persists widely, in governments, armed forces and the military-industrial complex, in those who demand the right to bear arms, and in groups who argue for 'revolutionary violence'.[iii] Reducing war, militarism and gun violence, and channelling activist groups towards nonviolent means, requires subverting this narrative and replacing it with one cognisant of the power of concerted, disciplined, well-organised and strategic nonviolent action.

A related narrative is that armed forces are a normal and essential part of any nation, although this is in fact only a recent construct. They are

iii Violence is never revolutionary. It's the status quo of elites.

thought to be essential for defence and that there are no alternative methods of defence. However, a 'heretical' article in *New Internationalist*, 'What If [...] Armed Forces Were Abolished?' questions this narrative:

> The justifications given for retaining armed forces don't stand up. There's a common belief that soldiers are needed to defend a country, in case of invasion. Yet many of the world's most militarily active countries prepare their forces for fighting abroad – not at home. Equipment belonging to British armed forces, for example, is often designed for fighting in desert conditions. It would be of far less use if Russian troops landed in Cornwall. In the unlikely event that Russian troops *did* land in Cornwall, there can be little doubt that British troops would be deployed to guard government buildings, military installations and sites of commercial importance. But defending people and towns would be some way down the list of priorities. Acts of mass non-co-operation with invaders by civilians might well be a more effective form of resistance.[29]

Despite the punitive power of weapons such as nuclear bombs and the concentration of power among wealthy elites, it is often small actions and shifts by the masses which build up the pressure for major changes. Any attempts to create a more peaceful society come up against powerful, influential opponents, but the thoughts, conversations and activities of ordinary people can still make a difference. The desire of youth in Eastern Europe to listen to Beatles' music in the 1960s and 1970s, for example, was one of many cultural factors that undermined the pillars of the totalitarian USSR Empire. Such discursive shifts in societies, seemingly random, undirected and insignificant, have been responsible for the nonviolent and occasionally unexpectedly swift demise of many oppressive, heavily armed regimes that seemed impregnable. Successful nonviolent resistance is not just

> mass uprisings and other heroic acts of defiance [...] [but is] located in countless non-heroic practices that make up the realm of the everyday and its multiple connections with contemporary global life.[30]

Counter-narratives

Let's look at an example of a counter-narrative created by a novelist. To do something with 'military precision' implies that doing something in a military way is to do it well. This can be contrasted with anarcha-feminist novelist Ursula Le Guin's description of a military campaign, which promotes a diametrically opposite view: that the hierarchical methods of militaries are extremely inefficient:

> Atro had once explained to him how this [the army] was managed, how the sergeants could give the privates orders, how the lieutenants could give the privates and sergeants orders, how the captains [...] and so on and so on up to the generals, who could give everyone else orders and need take them from none, except the commander in chief. Shevek had listened with incredulous disgust. 'You call that organization?' he had inquired. 'You even call it discipline? But it is neither. It is a coercive mechanism of extraordinary inefficiency – a kind of seventh millennium steam engine! With such a rigid and fragile structure what could be done that was worth doing?' This had given Atro a chance to argue the worth of warfare as the breeder of courage and manliness and the weeder-out of the unfit, but the very line of his argument had forced him to concede the effectiveness of guerrillas, organized from below, self-disciplined. [...] Later Shevek explained to Atro that he now understood why the army was organized as it was. It was indeed quite necessary. No rational form of organisation would serve the purpose. He simply had not understood that the purpose was to enable men with machine guns to kill unarmed men and women easily and in great quantities when told to do so.[31]

This is an example of someone using the arts to encourage people to think differently, to challenge and resist common narratives in order to build a more peaceful culture. Even simple phrases can shift a narrative, such as 'Black is beautiful' which came to express a growing sense of pride and self-affirmation among African Americans.

Linguistic violence often relies on authoritarian, monological, aggressive and calculative methods. For Cay, avoidance of linguistic violence is necessary but not sufficient:

> [O]ften silence is violence; frequently, unless we break the silence, we are being complicitous to the violence of the situation. However, in breaking the silence, our aim should be to avoid counter-violence, in its physical forms and in its verbal forms. Efforts to advance peace and justice should occupy the space between silence and violence.[32]

Pacific discourse that underpins positive peace means moving from avoiding violence to assertively negating it. More peaceful (or 'politically correct') discourse can be achieved through legal methods (which are often backed by physical coercion), but this compromises any commitment to nonviolent methods. Instead, it can be achieved by widespread adoption of inclusive language, affirmation of diversity and a positively nonviolent discourse that is democratic, dialogical, receptive and mediative.[33]

Economic Narratives

Our economic cultures can be part of militarism or of cultivating peace. In 'Why We (Continue to) Fight', a chapter of her book *War and Delusion,* Laurie Calhoun argues that '[e]conomically speaking, nearly all of modern society is in complicity, whether directly or indirectly, with the military'.[34] This is a big claim, as many of us presume we don't support the military, and we may even oppose it through our statements, attendance at peace marches and so on. However, militaries are supported through our taxes, and it's not easy to withdraw our taxes, especially now that we pay taxes (such as the UK's VAT and Australia's GST) on so many products. How then can we withdraw our financial support for militarism? How can we use what Tim Gee[35] calls our 'economic counterpower' to reduce militarism?

One way is through creating a new narrative around ethical investment and its flipside: boycotts, divestment and sanctions. We may be unwittingly investing in militarism through the banks we use. A report, 'Don't Bank on the Bomb',[36] for example, claims that the Commonwealth Bank, ANZ, AMP, Westpac and Macquarie Bank all finance nuclear weapons companies. Deciding to boycott these banks and reinvest our money elsewhere, and alerting the banks and our networks as to why, is a way of countering their persuasive PR campaigns and contributing to an economic cultural narrative which values peace and does not profit from war or the preparation for it.

Further Exploring Pro-Peace Narratives

To explore this area more deeply, specifically pro-peace narratives are described in David Swanson's book *War Is a Lie*[37] and Michael Karlsberg's article 'The Power of Discourse and the Discourse of Power: Pursuing Peace through Discourse Intervention',[38] while anarchist scholarship by Rusche[39] provides an intriguing alternative perspective. Like Karlsberg, Rusche is critical of Western liberal peacebuilding narratives which have led to less effective and even counter-productive outcomes in fostering peace after violent conflicts. He asks what an alternative to the reliance on state-building could look like, and proposes emancipatory peace practices based on anarchism (egalitarian, non-hierarchical organising) that build on direct action and prefigurative politics – enacting now at grassroots levels what people would like to see in the future at wider scales. This would also involve strengthening autonomy, decentralisation, horizontality rather than hierarchies, and consensus decision-making rather than voting (which can alienate up to 49 per cent of a group), as well as challenging all structural forms of domination through radical forms of self-determination. As with suggestions that nations can defend themselves nonviolently, all this challenges the dominant narrative that hierarchical, armed states are an inevitable part of civilised societies.

Another useful resource is Reinsborough and Canning's *Re:Imagining Change – How to Use Story-Based Strategy to Win Campaigns, Build Movements and Change the World*, a call to innovate our strategies for collectively addressing the escalating social and ecological crises of the twenty-first century. Knocking on doors, writing letters, organising petitions and community meetings, and planning occasional street protests are no longer enough. Contemporary activists need to know how to generate eye-catching symbols, tell captivating stories, tap into popular dreams and hone their effectiveness through real-world experiments. Moving beyond smart 'issue framing', this envisages

> a movement of movements with the power, creativity, and vision to change the world by changing the stories that shape our collective destiny. [It's about] holistic social change practices – shifting from issues to values, supplementing organisation building with movement building, and exploring creative new strategies to be more effective and strategic in confronting systemic problems.[40]

As with this book, their approach is about thinking big, challenging the powers-that-be and creating deep change from the ground up, because 'people-powered grassroots movements, led by those who are most directly affected, are the engines of true social progress'.[41] For them, innovation is much more than just improving what is already happening in social movements. Rather, it requires rethinking underlying assumptions and finding the courage to re-imagine what could happen. This is partly the work of this book – not just critiquing current problems (as with many academic books) but describing the importance of imagining better futures and giving examples of people doing so.

*

In this chapter, we've discussed the role of language and communication in maintaining cultural violence or building positive peace, before introducing the notion of discourses and narratives as vital for constructing social reality, propping up militaristic paradigms or facilitating nonviolent social change. Together, these have a cumulative effect, added to by cultural violence (or peace) in the many other spheres we examine in this book. In the next chapter, we look at the power of film to desensitise, create fear, disempower and maintain acceptance of war and militarism or, alternatively, inspire people to act for peace.

Notes

1 'Mansplain', Dictionary.com, https://www.dictionary.com/browse/mansplain
2 Poole, Stephen 2006 *Unspeak,* Grove Press, New York, pp. 42–49.
3 Sapir, Edward 1921 *Language, an Introduction to the Study of Speech*, Harcourt, Brace and Company, New York.
4 NSW Mental Health Commission 2014 Living well: Putting people at the centre of mental health reform in NSW, NSW Mental Health Commission, Sydney, p. 4.
5 See Sczesny, Sabine, Moser, Franziska and Wood, Wendy 2015 'Beyond sexist beliefs: How do people decide to use gender-inclusive language?' *Personality and Social Psychology Bulletin,* vol. 41, no. 7, pp. 943–954.
6 May, Andrew 2015 'Why war words in the workplace massacre morale', *Sydney Morning Herald,* 29 January, www.smh.com.au/lifestyle/why-war-words-in-the-workplace-massacre-morale-20150128-12zvla.html
7 Idle, Eric 1990 *The Road to Mars: A Post-Modem Novel,* Vintage, New York.
8 Rucker, Philip 2013 'Biden says "no silver bullet" exists to solve the problem with gun violence', *Washington Post,* 11 January, www.washingtonpost.com/politics/white-house-insists-obama-will-push-for-assault-weapons-ban/2013/01/11/55b6e032-5c05-11e2-88d0-c4cf65c3ad15_story.html
9 Hawking, Tom 2016 'Our casual use of military jargon is normalizing the militarization of society', *Quartz,* 30 November, https://qz.com/847577/our-casual-use-of-military-jargon-is-normalizing-the-militarization-of-society
10 Fox, Michael 2014 *Understanding Peace A Comprehensive Introduction*, Routledge, New York.
11 Fry, D. P., Bonta, B. D. and Baszarkiewicz, K. 2009 'Learning from extant cultures of peace', in J. D. Rivera (ed.), *Handbook on Building Cultures of Peace*, Springer, New York, p. 13.
12 Souillac, G. and Fry, D. P. 2014 'Indigenous lessons for conflict resolution', in P. Coleman, M. Deutsch and E. Marcus (eds.), *The Handbook of Conflict Resolution: Theory and Practice*, 3rd edition, Jossey-Bass, California, p. 607.
13 Fry, Bonta and Baszarkiewicz 2009, pp. 14–20.
14 Martin, Brian 2015 'Verbal defence', in *Nonviolence Unbound*, Irene Publishing, Sparsnas, pp. 104–147.
15 Rosenberg, Marshall B. 2015 *Nonviolent Communication: A Language of Life*, 3rd edition, Puddle Dancer Press, California.
16 Gomes de Matos, Francisco 2014 'Language, peace and conflict resolution',in P. T. Coleman, M. Deutsch and E. C. Marcus (eds.), *The Handbook of Conflict Resolution: Theory and Practice*, 3rd edition, Jossey-Bass, California, p. 183.
17 Vanderhaar, Gerard A. 1990 'A manner of speaking', in *Active Nonviolence: A Way of Personal Peace*, Twenty-Third Publications, Mystic, CT, pp. 30–35.
18 Spender, Dale 1980 *Man Made Language*, Routledge & Kegan Paul, London. See also Dudding, Adam 2017 'Are men really talking too much? We've done the maths', *Stuff,* 12 March, www.stuff.co.nz/life-style/life/89851118/are-men-really-talking-too-much-weve-done-the-maths
19 Boulding, Elise 1999 'Elise Boulding on peace cultures and living with difference', *Ikeda Center,* 5 February, www.ikedacenter.org/resources/elise-boulding-peace-cultures-and-living-difference
20 Foucault, Michel 1981 'Order of discourse', in R. Young (ed.), *Untying the Text: A Post-Structuralist Reader,* Routledge and Kegan Paul, Boston, pp. 52–53.

21 Fairclough, Norman 2001 *Language and Power,* 2nd edition, Routledge, London.
22 Davis, Joseph E. 2002 *Stories of Change: Narrative and Social Movements,* SUNY Press, Albany.
23 Ross, Daniel 2004 *Violent Democracy,* Cambridge University Press, Cambridge, p. 2.
24 Reinsborough, Patrick and Canning, Doyle 2010 *Re:Imagining Change – How To Use Story-Based Strategy To Win Campaigns, Build Movements and Change The World,* PM Press, New York.
25 Ibid.
26 Clements, Kevin P. 2023 *Director's Statement: The Hamas-Israel Conflict,* Toda Peace Institute, 13 October, https://toda.org/global-outlook/2023/directors-statement-the-hamas-israel-conflict.html
27 Schell, Jonathan 2003 *The Unconquerable World: Nonviolence and the Will of the People,* Metropolitan Books, New York.
28 Tenth Amendment Center 2014 'John Adams: The meaning of the American revolution', 24 April, https://tenthamendmentcenter.com/2014/04/24/john-adams-the-meaning-of-the-american-revolution/
29 Hill, Symon 2021 'What If… Armed forces were abolished?', *New Internationalist,* 7 October, https://newint.org/features/2021/08/09/what-if-armed-forces-abolished
30 Bleiker, Roland 2000 *Popular Dissent, Human Agency and Global Politics,* Cambridge University Press, New York, p. 278.
31 Le Guin, Ursula K. 1974 *The Dispossessed,* HarperCollins, New York, pp. 305–306.
32 Cay, William C. 1998 'The practice of linguistic nonviolence', *Peace Review,* vol. 10, no. 4, p. 547.
33 Ibid.
34 Calhoun, Laurie 2013 *War and Delusion: A Critical Examination,* Palgrave MacMillan, New York, p. 194.
35 Gee, Tim 2011 *Counterpower: Making Change Happen,* New Internationalist Publications, Oxford.
36 Beenes, Maaike and Snyder, Susi 2018 *Don't Bank on the Bomb,* PAX and ICAN, Utrecht, the Netherlands.
37 Swanson, David 2016 *War is a Lie,* 2nd edition, Just World Books, Charlottesville.
38 Karlberg, Michael 2005 'The power of discourse and the discourse of power: Pursuing peace through discourse intervention', *International Journal of Peace Studies,* vol. 10, no. 1, Spring/Summer, pp. 1–23.
39 Rusche, Jonas 2022 'Imagining peace outside of liberal statebuilding: Anarchist theory as pathway to emancipatory peace facilitation', *Alternatives,* vol. 47, no. 1, pp. 18–44.
40 Reinsborough and Canning 2010, p. 11.
41 Ibid., p. 12.

Chapter 3

SCREEN VIOLENCE AND PEACE

About 90 per cent of movies, 68 per cent of video games, 60 per cent of television shows and 15 per cent of music videos have some form of violence, according to psychologist Caroline Fitzpatrick.[1] In this chapter, we will examine the increasing violence of films (mainly English language) through a number of examples, including children's movies. We'll also discuss how they are often deceptively advertised and poorly reviewed and classified, and how they may support structural, cultural and ecological violence. We'll look at the reasons for and effects of this filmic violence, and explore ways of reducing it.

*

In the first movies made, violence was often merely alluded to, or occurred off-screen, or was handled subtly compared to what we are now used to. This caused the on-screen death rate to be very low – even though deaths still occurred as part of storylines. In the 1920s, it was distasteful to show someone being killed on screen, although it did happen occasionally. By the 1940s, violence in films was more prevalent, although it was used mainly to portray the evilness of characters and was often hidden.

In the years after World War II, several UK murders of women by men resulted in extremely light sentencing and even complete acquittals. Numerous popular books and films centred sympathetically on 'war heroes emasculated by a post-war world and striking back at the women around them'.[2] Examples include the movies *They Made Me a Fugitive* (1947) and *The Flamingo Affair* (1948), and the books *The Pursuit of Purpose* by Raymond English (1947) and *A Wreath of Roses* by Elizabeth Taylor (1949).

With the introduction of Western movies, a movement towards more violent movies began, as thousands of 'Indians' and the odd bad cowboy were killed, with the killers showing little emotion or reflection on what they were doing. Western movies were also some of the first to show deaths openly, with blood and flesh-tearing gunshot noises often followed by slow and painful deaths.

Sometimes the line between fictional and real violence dissolves, as shown by accidental but lethal shootings on the sets of *The Crow* (1994) and *Rust* (not yet released).

Movie violence does not just involve guns. The editor of the *Sydney Morning Herald's* 'Good Weekend' magazine professes to be a fan of American crime shows as a way to relax after work, noting however that 'this seems strange when you stop to think about it'.[3] She continues that 'anyone who is there with me on the *CSI/NCIS/Law and Order* ride knows how often people get stabbed on the small screen. And how regularly they miraculously survive such incidents', before citing a trauma surgeon's observation that in real life even the smallest knife wound can be life-threatening. She concludes: 'In short, knives are way more dangerous than popular culture would have us believe'.[i] [4] The same could be said for guns. In movie after movie, the 'good guys' (generally white males) unerringly shoot the 'bad guys' (generally non-white males) while usually managing to avoid being shot, even by machine-gun fire.

Modern movies rarely show the physical consequences of violence. In one study of major films, researchers found a median number of 16 violent actions per film (not including implied violence) in which '[a]lmost 90% of violent actions showed no consequences to the recipient's body, although more than 80% of the violent actions were executed with lethal or moderate force. Fewer than 1% of violent actions were accompanied by injuries that were then medically attended'.[5]

A common and predictable theme is the resolution of problems through violence, seen, for example, in the *Secret Life of Pets* (2016), *The Lion King* (2019) and 2009's 'blockbuster' *Avatar* movie. The latter is all the more disappointing because *Avatar* starts with some superb ecological concepts and social critiques that challenge anthropocentrism and racism.

Often, killing the bad guy is portrayed as the only possible solution, such as in *Sleeping with the Enemy* (1991).

'Psycho' Violence

Movie violence also has themes of comedy, humanising weapons and callous, uncaring violence. For example, the leads in *Valerian* (2017) show no empathy for all their newly dead comrades – they stroll casually away from them,

---

i The UK's National Monument against Violence and Aggression is a sculpture formed of 100,000 knives seized by police or surrendered during weapons amnesties (Robson, Frank 2021 'Razor's edge', *Good Weekend*, 18 September, p. 11).

chatting jokingly as if their comrade's lives were of no consequence whatsoever. And as Elena Lazic writes, few of the films involving sexual violence explore the impact and trauma, specifically the psychological consequences and lived reality of such violations; there is a lack of engagement beyond shock value.[6]

In recent years, there has been an upsurge in what could be termed 'psycho violence' in movies – brutal violence casually executed by someone enjoying themselves – with no compunctions about hurting fellow humans (or animals – but to a lesser extent). This was obvious in the 1995 film *Dead Man*, starring Johnny Depp, where a dead man's head is graphically crushed beneath the boot of another. In *Cody Banks: Secret Agent*, the hero sets someone on fire in this prime-time show described as 'comedy/drama', while his girlfriend watches with glee as the bad guy dies. This normalisation of the acceptability of violence towards the 'bad guys' seems one reason why there was so much rejoicing in the United States at the death of Osama bin Laden, even though he was illegally and summarily executed without even the pretence of a trial.[7] For some people, rejoicing at any person's death is regarded as callous. As poet John Donne wrote in 1624, 'Any man's death diminishes me, because I am involved in Mankind [*sic*]; and therefore never send to know for whom the bell tolls; it tolls for thee'.

The *Walking Dead* series (2010–22) also portrays brutal violence – a person shot point-blank through the head, a pick slammed into a skull – but this is supposedly okay if the 'humans' are zombies – subhumans we can't reason with. But throughout history, military and political leaders have similarly demonised their enemies, portraying them as subhuman to encourage easy, conscience-free killing, where people are narrowed down from a multitude of diverse individuals to one undifferentiated mass.

For example, Jewish people were characterised in Nazi state propaganda broadcasts, films and newspapers as *untermensch* or 'subhumans', while in Rwanda, radio stations incited the Hutus to genocidal violence by calling the Tutsi people 'cockroaches'. So cultural violence has very real impacts. In Australia, the One Nation party claims that all Muslims are ordered to overthrow all nations and governments,[8] and there is no place for them in 'our' country, by which they mean white and Christian (conveniently ignoring 60,000 years of Aboriginal history).

Australian environmentalist Bob Brown recalls that when he was in jail for three weeks during the 1980s Franklin River civil disobedience campaign, he was forced to attend a film chosen by prisoner vote.[9] The film was *Caligula* (1979), which he regarded as extremely violent, perverted, sadistic and incest-filled. He asks, is this really appropriate viewing for prisoners convicted of rape and murder?

'Comedy Violence'

About 37 per cent of media aimed at children have scenes of physical or verbal violence.[10] According to psychologist Peggy Drexler, research has revealed that 'the most violent films are actually the ones aimed right at kids'.[11] Even in children's cartoons, there are characters frequently punching others or expressing a desire to do so, and this behaviour is often sanctioned by the narrative voice. Yet boys and girls younger than seven can struggle to distinguish between fantasy and reality, may interpret a violent act as 'real' and are highly likely to imitate what they see.[12]

In *Nanny McPhee* (2005), which is in other respects a wise and enjoyable tale, a pair of diabolical nurses are 'hit women' (the name doesn't sound right) trying to extract a man's kidneys. This plot device is often portrayed as 'comedy violence' – violence we sometimes can't help laughing at but which adds to the big picture of widespread and normalised entertainment violence.

There is also a lot of unprovoked and casual violence, such as in the 2015 *Pan* movie, where the heroine punches someone just to stop them from talking. Movie violence is now so normalised that it's widely acceptable for J.M. Barrie's fairly innocuous *Peter Pan* story to now involve people being hit in the face with a metal bucket or hit over the head with a shovel.

'Violentisation' in Children's Movies

Pan is one example of Hollywood taking a children's story and making it much more violent, in a process that can be called 'violentisation'. Another example is the screen version of *Cat in the Hat* threatening someone with a kitchen chopper and having a car crash, and there are military references to periscope sights. None of these scenes were in the original book by Dr Seuss, who was emphatically pro-peace, as shown in his 1984 book *The Butter Battle Book,* which reflected Cold War concerns about nuclear war.

Other examples of violentisation are the quaint and gentle *Peter Rabbit* story, violentised in the 2018 movie, and the lightweight Archie comic strip for children, which was turned into *Riverdale,* a murder mystery series.

The popular 2011 movie *Adventures of Tintin* has more use of guns than originally, including machine guns, which are largely absent from the original comic strips and later books. There is attempted use of torture, while a crew member is said to be 'handy with a razor'. There are new and longer fight scenes; these involve bottles, cranes and even a grenade launcher. The Thom[p]son 'twins', for some reason, are obese, unlike in the comic strips, and this seems part of a tendency towards exaggerated body types in films, discussed below. The violentisation of *Tintin* is directly counter to the evolution of the comic strip, which began as a crude, violent, racist polemic but ended as decidedly pro-peace and multiculturally tolerant, and critical of arms dealers and dictatorships of all political persuasions.[13]

A 2008 movie remake of the humorous TV series *Get Smart* involves more violence and less humour. Its supposed 'comedic violence' involves a man shot point-blank for asking a question, another man being stapled on the head and the 'Control' boss smashed in the face with a fire extinguisher.

Today's generation of children and adolescents has been the most immersed in these fictional realities that film violence creates; consequently, their experiences in comparison to their parents are overwhelming. Forty years ago, children did not start watching television regularly until at least the age of four, whereas it is now common for infants of just four months old to be regularly interacting with digital media.[14]

Effects of Film Violence

Most people who watch violent media don't engage in direct violence. However, evidence strongly suggests that violent films encourage aggression and violence, at least in some people, with other risk factors being 'bias toward hostility, low parental involvement, participant sex, physical victimization, and prior physical fights'.[15] Immersion in such films may also desensitise us, so that violent solutions (e.g. wars – and, by extension, our massive levels of military spending) are more acceptable. As Drexler argues:

> Continuous exposure to extreme violence, like the kind exaggeratedly fictionalized in the movies, can begin to desensitize kids to such violence. In *Reducing School Violence Through Conflict Resolution*, authors David W. Johnson and Roger T Johnson cite 'how society has redefined violence as normal and acceptable' as among the reasons violence among teens has steadily increased [16]

How Dangerous Is the World?

Children exposed repeatedly to aggressive content can develop a deformed perception of violence and its actual frequency in real life. This can eventually give rise to 'the impression that the world is an overly dangerous place filled with ill-intentioned people. People that have such a worldview are more likely to interpret an ambiguous or accidental gesture as hostile or as a personal attack'.[17]

Psychiatrist Emanuel Tanay agrees that movie violence instils fear in people, either temporarily or in the long term, causing them to believe that violence is more prevalent in society than it is. This leads them to believe that they need to protect themselves, hence the constant 'need' for guns and to be armed in the United States. By allowing film violence to increase the way it has for the past few decades, 'reality is distorted. If you live in a fictional world, then the fictional world becomes your reality'.[18]

As one student of the Peace Studies unit *Creating Cultures of Peace* observed:

> I vividly remember one of my first jobs as a holiday camp leader, where kids would come and spend a week, sleeping in cabins. It was almost an impossible task to get the kids (generally aged between 8 and 11) to go to bed each night and to sleep through the night because the majority were so frightened by things from horror movies they had watched – convinced that killers like 'Jason' or 'Freddie' would get them, or horrible creatures like 'Chucky' or 'Pennywise'. At least one child would have a nightmare every night, and myself and the other camp leaders would have to spend hours trying to calm them down. If we would try to tell them that they shouldn't watch scary movies like that, they would not hear of it. They would insist that they loved these movies.

I sometimes stay at a beautiful sub-tropical guesthouse in New South Wales which seems to epitomise peace because of its general aura of tranquillity, leafy setting, Buddhist and Hindu images, books about Martin Luther King, Gandhi and Greta Thunberg, and no televisions. There, however, I observed a teenaged girl regard the accommodation not as a place dedicated to peace but as reminding her of the television series *Death in Paradise*, where there is at least one murder per episode. The same girl, on a one-day bushwalk in a spectacular setting, mentioned her concerns, only half-jokingly, about 'dementors', soul-sucking wraiths from the *Harry Potte*r universe. I wondered how her perceptions of those wonderful environments could be so different from mine, and how film violence had made them places of fear rather than relaxed enjoyment.

To feed society's insatiable appetite for violence, Hollywood continues to glorify aggressive outcomes, and this is compounded by technological advances through which society can easily view such content. Leading experts continue to find connections between media consumption and emotional behaviours, affirming the conclusion that film violence does contribute to a fearful and violent society. Furthermore, those most susceptible are children, particularly during cognitive development, and different types of violence may affect children in different ways.[19]

*

In the midst of this violence which saturates our movie culture, it seems strange that we are surprised and outraged at coward punches,[ii] terrorist killings or school massacres. A much-cited 2010 study published in the *Personality and Social Psychology Bulletin* found a 'weapons effect' – consistent in both angry and non-angry people – wherein even the sight or depiction of a gun can make people behave more aggressively.[20] In one experiment, children who watched a movie containing gun footage were more likely to pull the trigger of a real (but unloaded) gun; on average, they pulled it about two to three times and spent four to five times longer holding it in comparison to children who watched the movie with no gun footage.[21]

Filmmaker Robert Altman even blames Hollywood for terror attacks such as 9/11, believing that life was imitating art:

> The movies set the pattern, and these people have copied the movies [...] How dare we continue to show this kind of mass destruction in movies? I just believe we created this atmosphere and taught them how to do it.[22]

Philosopher Michael Fox suggests that a majority of aggression is a result of misplaced fear, perceiving threats that are non-existent, where those suffering from depression, anxiety and other mental health issues are the most at risk of violently acting out.[23] Tim Winton's autobiographical short story 'The Boy Behind the Curtain' is about a boy struggling with a new town and school, who for months surreptitiously aims the family rifle at passers-by. It gives a fascinating insight into how one's cultural milieu can influence children's behaviour:

> We're all steeped in [gun] romance. We've marinated in this cult all our lives; it's inescapable. Even in a country where there is no fetishised right to bear arms, gunplay is a staple of entertainment. Researchers estimate that by the age of eighteen the average American child is likely

ii A coward punch, also known as a cheap shot, one-punch attack, king-hit or, in American English, a sucker punch, is a punch which is often thrown from behind, unprovoked or while the victim is unprepared or distracted. Such a punch is usually considered unfair, unethical or deceptive.

> to have been exposed to as many as twenty-six thousand gun murders on TV.[24]

Tarabay and Warburton[25] suggest that exposure to media violence, such as violence by charismatic characters that is consistently rewarded, may lead to increases in lower-level aggressive behaviours such as bullying. Series like *Wolf Creek*, based on horrific real-life murders, are likely to stop women from hitchhiking and add to the fears of violence they already have. Film violence can also normalise violence, such as in the UK's unlikely *Midsome*r series, where a delightful, bucolic region of rural villages has a serial killer on the rampage each week.

Despite all this, there is little media coverage of high-profile opposition to film violence. Psychologists Kirsh, Mounts and Olczak[26] conclude that there are both short-term and long-term effects, and that:

> Consistently, research has demonstrated that exposure to violent media appears to increase aggressive behavior, thoughts, and feelings in children, adolescents, and young adults [...] This connection has been found using correlational [...] and experimental [...] methodologies. However, in spite of these findings, the impact of media violence continues to be underreported by news services.

Similarly, Kyla Boyse[27] argues that:

- Extensive research evidence indicates that media violence can contribute to aggressive behaviour, desensitisation to violence, nightmares and fear of being harmed.
- Watching violent shows is also linked with having less empathy towards others.
- Most violent acts go unpunished on TV and are often accompanied by humour. The consequences of human suffering and loss are rarely depicted.
- Many shows glamorise violence. TV often promotes violent acts as a fun and effective way to get what you want, without consequences.
- Even in G-rated, animated movies and DVDs, violence is common – often as a way for the good characters to solve their problems. Every single US animated feature film produced between 1937 and 1999 contained violence, and the amount of violence with intent to injure has increased over the years.
- Even 'good guys' beating up 'bad guys' gives a message that violence is normal and acceptable.

Structural and Ecological Violence in Movies

In addition to the effects of increased levels of fear, aggressiveness and direct violence, movies may involve other forms of cultural violence as well as supporting structural and ecological violence. The 2008 *Get Smart* movie features not just gratuitous violence but also 'fat women' jokes, while a strong female character at the start becomes emasculated and turns into a secondary support character. Instead, Maxwell Smart forges ahead, continuing movie stereotypes where men give most of the orders and hold most of the most powerful positions in society. This attitude is embedded in our cultures, from the book and later film *Mayday*[28] where a man takes charge of a pilotless airliner, to signs at pedestrian crossings, usually depicted by males ushering females. There are racial stereotypes too – the baddies are often muscle-bound African Americans and foreigners (often from Eastern Europe), while the heroes are usually white men.

A glaring example is *Geostorm* (2017), where a white American male saves the world from global warming disasters, not through reducing fossil fuel use and deforestation but through the less effective channel of the use of technology. According to David Trend,[29] American film violence legitimises and aids direct, cultural and structural violence by positioning the United States as the centre of the universe, the epitome of goodness, rightness, democracy and power, and white US males as the norm, centre or pinnacle of civilisation, while everyone else is 'other'.

A consequence of this, and the sheer power, wealth and outreach of Hollywood, is the Americanisation of other societies such as Australia's – of the words we use and how we pronounce them[iii] as well as the music, radio, television and movies we consume. While there are many great qualities to American culture, this cultural imperialism may lead to more acceptance of US behaviours and values, and less scrutiny of its inequalities, incarceration rates (one of the world's highest), and its high levels of gun violence, both in the streets and schools, and internationally as the most heavily armed nation in history.

The connection between the fact that the United States exports both real and movie violence first became evident to me when flying over the Middle East to that peace conference in Türkiye, mentioned in Chapter 1. Those terrible conflicts we were flying over – in Palestine/Israel, Iraq, Afghanistan

iii An example is 'new', which in Australia is increasingly being pronounced 'noo' rather than 'nyoo'.

and Syria – mostly involved or were armed by the United States (and other major arms dealers such as Britain and Russia), while all around me the violent films the locals were watching were American (or British). Massive resources are poured into making this film violence slick and alluring, immersing the globe in cultural violence. The implicit message being transmitted is that violence equals power and is glamorous, exciting and acceptable as a method of problem-solving.

Australian journalist Eric Campbell observed the international implications of US film violence on the ground when he encountered mercenaries (called *kontraktniki*) in Chechnya:

> A few of them had shaved their heads and painted green and black on their face. Their Russian uniforms had touches of Rambo action movies – bandanas, tight black singlets, hunting knives strapped to their legs. […] While morale among the conscripts was at rock bottom, this was just the kind of real-life Hollywood fantasy some of the kontraktniki had come for.[30]

Ecological violence is supported in movies through the glamorisation of fast cars and plane travel, with only the occasional exception which favourably depicts bicycle use, such as in *ET* (1982) and *Enemy of the State* (1998). Ubiquitous advertisements that glamorise four-wheel drives (SUVs) complement this, with Australians' penchant for heavier and dirtier vehicles[31] making Australia one of the highest per capita polluters on the planet.[32] There are also advertisements featuring people drinking bottles of alcohol on beaches and rocky river banks, despite the hazards of broken glass for bare feet.

Films may also support structural violence, such as through 'product placement' for wealthy multinational conglomerates such as Coca-Cola, the world's largest 'soft drink' company, long criticised for its human rights, health and environmental record.[33] Although product placement had existed since the start of the movie era, Coca-Cola accelerated it in the 1980s, aided by the company's purchase in 1982 of Columbia Pictures, one of the world's major studios, which had in the previous decade released movies like *Close Encounters of the Third Kind* and *Kramer vs. Kramer*.[iv] Product promotion, such as of BMW vehicles and Heineken beers[v] in the James Bond films, or McDonalds in the

---

iv Product placement of Coca-Cola continues today, such as in King Richard (2022), which also promotes Reebok and Nike in what is otherwise an inspiring film.

v Heineken and Carlsberg are accused by the group Justice for Myanmar (www.justiceformyanmar.org) of supporting the illegal military junta in Myanmar through the tens of millions of dollars in taxes they pay them.

2006 *Pink Panther* movie featuring Steve Martin, soon made its way into the foreground of art, where it has remained ever since.[34]

Ocean's 8 (2018) has been praised for its large female cast, but Zaki Mehchy from the Syrian Centre for Policy Research is highly critical of the series:

> We Arabs need to confront our need for *abawiyya* [paternalism], for the *dhakar* [big man]. These days it seems that you are a hero if you can get money, it doesn't matter how you get it. Even a film like *Ocean's Eleven* glorifies the work of thieves.[35]

Sexism and Systemic Biases

The 2017 *Baywatch* movie portrays extreme body images, with the men being huge, muscle-bound, neckless and engaging in violent or extreme behaviour, while the women are thin but large-breasted. The father in *The Incredibles* franchise (2004, 2018) is ludicrously muscle-bound, while the heroine of the *Lorax* (2012) is impossibly thin, as is the young woman in the *Secret Life of Pets* movies (2016, 2019). Glamorising these body types may push vulnerable women towards insecurity, anorexia and cosmetic surgery, while encouraging men into bodybuilding, steroid use and excessive food consumption (with all its ecological consequences). On the other hand, films that normalise obesity may also be problematic.

Male-on-female violence is promoted through films such as the 2017 *Blade Runner* sequel, where the hero strangles and drowns a woman. Viewing sexual violence frequently – usually depicted as men overpowering women – may lead to acceptance of violence towards women and the idea that women enjoy sexual abuse; women who view a great deal of sexual violence may develop low self-esteem and have poor relationships.[36] According to Radha O'Meara, in Hollywood scripts:

> Male characters are commonly named and described expansively, whereas female characters are often unnamed, highly sexualised, infantilised and meagrely described. Research also shows that male characters dominate time on screen, dialogue on screen, and narrative action.[37]

Other marginalised groups such as non-Caucasians and LGBTQIA+ people also suffer from the lack of diversity in mainstream films. Representation in the fictional world is a signifier of social existence, whereas absence is 'symbolic annihilation' and indicates that you don't count, with the message that many people unconsciously assume being: 'There's something wrong with me'.[38]

Racist stereotypes, such as the idea that white is good and black is bad, can be reinforced through film traditions that put the goodies in white (e.g. Professor Dumbledore in the *Harry Potter* series) while the bad guys wear dark clothes and black hats (e.g. Lord Voldemort). The background music underlines these features and manipulates one's emotions. Violence within films that portray stories of power and heroism creates a clear barrier between the 'good' guys and the 'bad' guys, and this separation can transfer into real life, legitimising certain behaviours and people over others and accepting them into social constructions of right and wrong, thus leading towards more divided and violent societies.

Although we focus on movies in this chapter, it's worth noting that similar observations and criticisms can be made for video entertainment more broadly, such as the *Grand Theft Auto V* video game, the fastest entertainment property to ever gross one billion dollars, which encourages players to have sex with a prostitute, whom they can then beat up or even kill.[39]

Sexism can also be found in game shows, with the usual pattern involving a male compere and more male panellists than female, with examples being the UK's *Mock the Week* and Australia's *Gruen Transfer* and *Celebrity Letters and Numbers.* Adam Hills has hosted *Spicks and Specks* and the UK's *The Last Leg*, but the latter is at least a forum where disability is no barrier to access. Similar sexist patterns can be found on radio, such as Australia's 'Kate, Tim and Joel show' (previously 'Kate, Tim and Marty'), and women usually get to speak less than the men. The lack of diversity in gender, ethnicity, sexual orientation and age can be attributed to the predominantly white, male, middle-class operators of conglomerates who create and disperse our media.

Glamorisation of Smoking

Smoking kills more than 8,000,000 people prematurely every year around the globe, primarily in middle and low-income countries,[40] yet it has long been promoted through tobacco industry sponsorship of movie stars such as John Wayne, Cary Grant and many others.[41] It was also promoted in Australia for many years through film and television advertisements featuring popular figures such as Paul Hogan, and through ubiquitous advertising billboards at the cricket, football, buildings, streets and railway lines. This overt advertising was stopped through an effective twin campaign involving the direct actions of 'Buga-Up' (Billboard-Utilising Graffitists Against Unhealthy Products) who cleverly changed and subverted these ads, and through high-level lobbying and pressure from the Australian Medical Association.[vi]

---

vi Medical doctor, activist and politician Dr Arthur Chesterfield-Evans was a conduit between these two groups. He described the BUGA-UP actions as 'probably the most

While Australia led the way in ending tobacco advertising and making most public places smoke-free, in light of harsher advertising laws and the introduction of plain packaging in countries such as Australia, the World Health Organisation (2015) believes that 'Big Tobacco' is turning to the film industry to infiltrate the minds of vulnerable young people. Tobacco promotion therefore continues subtly through its frequent use in films. For example, in *The Wife* (2018) all the main characters smoke, and there is conspicuous smoking by characters in the background, yet few viewers notice this. Smoking is usually promoted through product placement, in which a film is financed by a corporation such as British American Tobacco in return for some characters (preferably leading ones) smoking (such as the lead in 2018's *First Man*).

Another example is the high-profile World War II film *The Monuments Men,* featuring megastars George Clooney (the director and lead), Bill Murray, John Goodman, Cate Blanchett and Matt Damon, where cigarette smoking features throughout the movie in a prominent way, including as part of the plot. Two non-smokers are shown smoking for the first time, one of them being ordered to do so in a scene where two Americans and a German overtly use cigarettes to defuse a tense situation.

Similarly, cigarettes are a significant narrative element in *Aftermath* (2019), featuring in the romantic moments, and there's obvious product placement of Kool cigarettes in *Respect* (2021). The lead protagonist and narrator in *House of Cards* (2013), played by Kevin Spacey, smokes, as does star Helena Bonham Carter in the 2010 movie *Toast.* The leads in *Atlantic Crossing* (2020) and *Eiffel* (2021) smoke, as does Kate Winslet, made famous in *Titanic,* in *Ammonite* (2020).

In *The Dig* (2021), Ralph Fiennes, famous for playing Voldemort and numerous other high-profile roles, smokes a pipe often and conspicuously, including during a social occasion where three workers share a light. There is also a plot device where his wife lights his pipe for him when he is frustrated and can't light it himself. The other leading character also smokes. In the 2022 French film *Tout Le Monde Aime Jeanne* (Everybody Loves Jean), flouting the indoor smoking rules is portrayed humorously.

The usual pattern is lots of smoking in early sections, with less later, exemplified in *A Call to Spy* (2021). There is strong evidence that glamorising smoking through movies can influence children to take it up and hinder those trying to give it up.[42] Defenders of the practice of depicting smoking might argue that it is historically accurate to have plentiful smoking in dramas set

---

cost-effective health promotion programme ever done' ('Billboard Bandits' 2021 *YouTube*).

when smoking was widespread. That is true, but then the question arises: why are there so many of these historical dramas? How much does Big Tobacco money determine what films and genres filmmakers can afford to produce?

And this excuse falls flat for *Wicked Little Letters* (2023), which is based on a true story with some feminist undertones. The film is pleasantly notable for its inclusive but historically inaccurate colour-blind casting which 'casts people of colour in prominent roles in 1920s England without referencing their race even once'.[43] However, the feisty heroine and her young daughter both smoke, following a long pattern of the tobacco industry associating itself with women's emancipation.[44]

Blasé Reviews and Deceptive Advertising

It's rare that any of this film violence features in the trailers and pre-movie advertising. The title and trailer of *Miss Peregrine's Home for Peculiar Children* (2016) indicate a pleasant, quirky film with magic and romance. Strange children frolic in a beautiful sunlit garden. It's bizarre, fantastic; there's magic, optimistic music and romance. A young heroine who floats. A handsome boy. Little children with great strength or the ability to grow carrots quickly. A beautiful woman runs the school. There are some glimpses of scary themes, but my partner and I thought we could enjoy it with our children.

In reality, it's a horror movie with 20-foot monsters that kill small children, tear their eyeballs out and eat them. There's graphic violence, including brutal, macabre fight scenes. The heroine Miss Peregrine smokes very obviously.

Yet reviews by *Time, AV Club, Variety* and *The Atlantic* completely fail to mention its violent nature. *Common Sense Media* says 'It's not especially gory' and is suitable for ages 12 plus. *The Atlantic* actually applauds the violence, saying 'Now for some of the good: *Miss Peregrine* has some truly frightening imagery, the kind likely to brand nightmares into the minds of younger viewers.' Others call it 'a perfect match of material for Hollywood's most iconic auteur' and discuss 'Tim Burton's playfully nonthreatening goth aesthetic and outsider sensibility, which should put the director back on the blockbuster charts.' There are supposedly 'deliciously romantic interactions within Goldman's frequently amusing script.'

Only one review is different, claiming that this is 'not the typical young adult fantasy movie. It's a very disturbing and creepy film with horror-like images.' There are also some concerned parent reviews on a site called *Parent Previews,* which use terms such as 'morbid' and 'graphic'. One states that 'throughout the film characters are stalked by scary looking people with white eyes and terrifying monsters that crush, strangle and pluck out the eyes of anyone they catch'. Another says, 'While it was a little creepy before, the screenplay now delves into the disturbing, with characters performing horrific experiments, portrayals of terrifying transformations and ghoulish depictions of creatures feasting on eyeballs. The carcasses of animals and dead people with empty eye sockets are shown.' Another preview states that 'the realism of the action also ups the fright factor.'

Several questions arise here. One is why the reviews of these parents are so different from those of prominent reviewers in journals like *The Atlantic*, one of which applauds the violence instead of being disturbed by it. Are the parents, including myself, over-sensitive? Or have these reviewers become so used to such violence that they don't notice it or even require it to get a buzz out of a film?

The other issue is the deceptive advertising by the film industry. None of this violence was depicted in the trailer, and I was drawn to taking my children to it and then felt very disappointed that I had,, as though I'd been tricked by the film producers. I had experienced this phenomenon earlier, when I saw a poster, reminiscent of Agatha Christie's Miss Marple, for a 1996 film *Fargo* by the acclaimed Coen Brothers, which advertised a 'homespun murder mystery' and seemed to indicate a pleasant Agatha Christie-like film. Instead, it was filled with brutal graphic violence, such as a criminal stuffing his partner's body into a woodchipper. One reviewer echoed many in describing it as a 'modern classic'; another wrote that they 'use humour to present dark and disturbing violence in a light and airy manner [...] These humouristic elements create a light and airy atmosphere in an otherwise dark and disturbing film; for once, viewers can watch a violent noir-esque film with a casual, offhand attitude'. Should not this trend towards making extreme violence casual and humorous ('comedy psycho violence') be a social concern?

Woody Allen's 2016 *Café Society* is similar. The title and trailer seem light and romantic but belie the extreme violence, such as a point-blank shooting in the head. The trailer for the deranged *Banshees of Inisherin* (2023) is another that suggests lightness and humour rather than horrific self-mutilation serving a bizarre, implausible plot. It only makes a semblance of sense as an allegory for the insane internecine violence of the Irish civil war.

You will also rarely see people smoking in the trailers, even in films filled with smoking. Examples from those films include an entirely gratuitous scene of a young woman smoking outside the courthouse in *Denial* (2017), as well as the star, the barrister who wins the case, portrayed as a smoker. Another 2017 film, *Her Finest*, shows the power of film to inspire activism (in this case, resistance to Nazism), yet every major character conspicuously smokes. Even the anti-pollution, anti-cancer crusader *Erin Brokovich* (2000) smokes, while *Monuments Men* has no one smoking in the trailer yet in the film every major character smokes conspicuously and often.

Why Is Our Entertainment So Violent?

Entertainment and economics are closely linked because entertainment is a major global industry. One reason our films are so violent is because violence helps sell them. Filmmakers in a highly competitive market need movies that are sensational, exciting and that attract wide audiences, often by appealing to base emotions such as fear. Even cooking shows, such as *My Kitchen Rules*, are filled with conflict and emotion.

We all like an adrenaline buzz, a bit of a thrill from our books and movies, and this tradition goes back to ancient indigenous stories and books like Homer's *The Odyssey*. But in past decades, it seems that filmmakers have engaged in a race to the bottom – embedding violence into a huge range of films from dramas, thrillers and action movies right down to animated films aimed at children.

This constant increase in violence – such as the horrific glassings in *Mission Impossible* (2018) – is necessary to maintain shock value and novelty. The pervasiveness of entertainment violence is perfectly encapsulated by a Michael Leunig cartoon about a couple about to watch television, where the woman asks her partner: 'What violence do you want? Sporting, military, or random-psychotic?'

Research has shown that 'males watch more violent media than females' and that young males in particular enjoy viewing violent films, often identifying with the protagonist and obtaining stimulation from the sheer physicality that the insistent nature of violence yields.[45] Although there are arguments for an evolutionary basis for this predilection, the uptake of violent media should be seen as a preference rather than a compulsion.

Ratings

Another factor is what children are allowed to watch. Rating discrepancies have allowed more young children to be exposed to extreme levels of violence, and there are ever fewer G-rated films. Drexler examined the change in movie ratings over time, finding that violence allowed in PG-13 movies has tripled since the rating was first introduced and has 'surpassed the levels and amount of violence in films given the R rating [then]'.[46] The people doing the rating are part of a wider culture. If they are inured to violence (e.g. because they have to watch a lot of violent movies as part of their job), their ratings will be different from ones done by people who rarely watch film violence. To give one example, the sci-fi film *Minority Report* (2002), starring Tom Cruise, features severed eyeballs and someone being stabbed in the eye, which many would consider extreme violence, yet it is only rated 'medium level violence'.

Increasingly, ratings are bypassed altogether, such as when Sydney commuters in the underground railway station of Wynyard in 2024 were assailed with a trailer, played on repeat on giant screens just metres away, of the horror streaming series *Fallout* (2024), surrounded by giant billboards advertising the film. This saturation advertising was slick, alluring, seductive and unavoidable, bombarding children and adults indiscriminately, reminiscent of the brainwashing world of George Orwell's novel (and subsequent films) *1984*.

Randal Olson argues that the increase in the number of on-screen deaths within films is not because our cultures are becoming more violent, but partly because film industry advances have enabled massive battles to be filmed in a manner which is more time, cost and energy-efficient.[47] Whereas directors would once have needed to hire thousands of people for battle scenes, now small teams of animators populate them. He also asks: 'Could it be that instead of acting on our violent tendencies, we're sating them with violent films, video games, sports, etc.?' This is a possibility but does not explain the pressures of film corporations selling movies with ever more graphic violence, nor the continuing presence of wars and militarism and their massive costs and impacts.

The Pentagon and Hollywood Connection

Another factor, closely related to militarism, is the pressure by powerful militaries to maintain their power, and by the military-industrial complex to maintain its profits. This is partly achieved through financially and politically supporting nationalistic, pro-war films, which show militaries in the best possible light and help ensure continued military spending by governments.[48] Writing about how Americans are seduced by war, Bacevich[49] notes that '[t]he new American militarism draws much of its sustaining force from myth – stories created to paper over incongruities and contradictions that pervade the American way of life.'

Governments enjoy the narratives created by militaristic stories, told through movies (along with military expeditions overseas), as they posit their country as powerful and try to distract attention from woes at home such as unemployment, poverty and, increasingly, extreme weather events. Militaries want films like *Top Gun* (1986) and *Top Gun: Maverick* (2022) because they make the armed forces seem glamorous, exciting, social and sexy. The military-industrial complex supports them as they maintain cultures favourable towards militarism, 'defence' spending and the purchase of their products.[50]

In *Operation Hollywood: How the Pentagon Shapes and Censors the Movies*, David Robb[51] shows how these films are often given considerable assistance by the US military, such as cheap or free access to billions of dollars worth of military hardware, equipment and locations, such as jet fighters, aircraft carriers and nuclear submarines (all of which are funded by taxpayers). In return, the movies serve as sophisticated and enticing forms of recruitment propaganda.

Hollywood enjoys the collaboration because it lowers the costs of filmmaking, although the loss of intellectual freedom is enormous, as the Pentagon actively suppresses content that is anti-war or critical of military forces. Making a more confronting film about war is much more expensive for the producers, as Francis Ford Coppola found when creating *Apocalypse Now* (1979).

Even sci-fi films like the 2018 *Star Trek*, which presumably didn't need Pentagon support, seem like a recruitment video for the Marines or Air Force. As Tanay observes, 'what we call entertainment is really propaganda for violence. If you manufacture guns, you don't need to advertise, because it is done by our entertainment industry'.[52]

People in the film industry often fail to see the impact of what they do. Matt Damon, for example, visited Australia to shoot a violent, gun-filled *Jason Bourne* film with a white Anglo hero out to rid the world of a crazy, psychopathic Venezuelan. At the same time, he pronounced that he wished that the USA could have gun laws like the Australian ones,[53] apparently ignorant that such films almost certainly reinforce and spread that US gun culture.

Nick Turse argues in his book *The Complex: How the Military Invades Our Everyday Lives* that the military-industrial complex is involved in almost every facet of modern life, from donuts and iPods to Starbucks and Oakley sunglasses.[54] Joint ventures with Marvel Comics and the World Wrestling Federation glamorise war, and video games use a deliberate two-way strategy to draw in recruits to military forces, with the controls of new military vehicles and weapons designed to emulate popular game consoles. We examine video games in Chapter 7, the influence of the military-industrial complex on journalism in Chapter 6, and its impacts on education in Chapter 8.

A Continuum of Films from Gratuitous Violence to Pro-peace

There are nuances to the issue of film violence, of course. Some filmmakers use violence for a particular, considered purpose, with examples including Dennis Rothermel's anti-war films, and the *Handmaid's Tale* (2017), which shines a light on the violence women suffer under patriarchal systems. It is probably prudent to view the issue not dualistically as right or wrong but as existing on a continuum, from films with violence purely to entice and titillate audiences (the majority of violent films), through to films that use violence in order to expose and understand violence in all its forms. Next on the continuum are films that don't use violence at all, and finally there are films which emphatically set out to promote positive peace.

There are countless movies that are supposedly 'anti-war' (such as *Saving Private Ryan*) yet they are filled with violence that is rarely condemned or discouraged. So it is questionable whether they put people off war or condone it and add to people's desensitisation towards entertainment violence.[55]

Other films with a sound objective include the 2015 film *Suffragette*, but they often demonstrate a poor understanding of how social change usually occurs. While *Suffragette* makes some valid points about women's disenfranchisement and oppression, it moves towards a focus on the few and extreme instances of violent protest, probably because these supposedly make for a more exciting film. This, however, obscures the fact that the vast majority of the movement's actions were nonviolent[56] – even though these were often radical and harrowing, such as the hunger strikes of women prisoners, barely covered in the film. Again, it seems that the producers went for the easy options of sensationalism and violence as a solution rather than the story of what was most effective in getting women the vote – mass nonviolent action and shifting narratives.

Are There Solutions or Alternatives?

What can be done to make a more peaceful entertainment culture? One possibility is for parents to set controls on their devices which automatically exclude children from watching certain categories of films – although children are often tech-savvy and can find their way around firewalls. Greater regulation by government authorities is another option. As one *Creating Cultures of Peace* student notes:

> I currently reside in Singapore, which could be classified as a structured and disciplined culture with lower crime rates or acts of violence. Whilst television and other media outlets are somewhat monitored and censored, many expats will still view any desired material through Apple or other pay-for-view arenas. I wonder if the act of censorship (violence included) within Singapore has had an impact upon decreasing the level of anxiety disorders. Singapore's anxiety disorder lifetime prevalence rate is one of the lowest among high-income nations.

However, censorship can lead to a tricky slope, as we saw throughout the McCarthyism era when anything vaguely left-wing or 'subversive' was banned. Similarly, the Taliban's attempts to ban Western movies have been widely resisted.

Giving informed choice through improved classification is perhaps a better option. The Australian Government's classification guide for movies and games for children allows no drug use or nudity; very mild impact themes, sex and language; but mild impact violence. Why, one might ask, is there such a difference? Why is violence the highest permissible category? Why is some violence acceptable for children but no nudity, when nudity is natural – we are all nude under our clothes – but most people are rarely physically violent? (That said, as noted above, movies can also be highly exploitative of people's bodies, particularly those of women.)

We should note that film violence is not just the fault of the industry. Parents in my community regularly allow young children to watch age-inappropriate films, such as letting children much younger than 15 watch M-rated films. As a parent, it's hard to resist the pressure this creates. So, making a stand, even if it's unpopular with your child, is a start, as is discussing the issue in your school and parenting communities (see also Chapter 7).

Furthermore, we can support the many examples of enjoyable films without violence, smoking or extreme body types and behaviour. One very commercial example is the 2017 *Batman Lego* movie. Although the violent crusader Batman is ubiquitous and eternal – he's on t-shirts everywhere from toddlers to teens and beyond – this movie deconstructs the Batman myth in a humorous way by portraying him as a friendless, humourless, macho vigilante.

There are also moves to counter smoking in movies, such as the 2005 movie *Thank You For Smoking,* which portrays a ruthless Big Tobacco lobbyist tasked with spinning even the most heart-breaking child cancer story into favourable public relations for cigarette companies. Another example is the disclaimer which you may have seen: 'No person or entity associated with this film received payment or anything of value, or entered into any agreement, in connection with the depiction of tobacco products'. The World Health Organisation has been lobbying for exactly this, as well as advocating a classification system that takes smoking into account, and asking that filmmakers not feature any tobacco branding in films.[57] In a recent report called *Smoke-Free Movies,* the World Health Organisation[58] moved to have films that glamorise smoking carry an adult rating. The University of California's Smoke Free Media campaign also calls for an R rating and provides a website with research, news, policy solutions, tools and resources for action, and information about which films have or don't have smoking.

Alcohol

There is increasing awareness of the detrimental impact of alcohol on health, with alcohol use linked to several cancers, as well as concerns about alcohol-fuelled violence. In that light, the link between alcohol advertising and televised sport is problematic, embodying the contradiction of linking harmful products with activities which enhance our well-being. Caterina Giorgi, chief executive of the Foundation for Alcohol Research and Education, argues that: 'Saturating sport with alcohol ads, particularly when children are watching, is an appalling marketing tactic to recruit new drinkers'.[59]

There is some resistance to this, however, such as Australian cricket captain Pat Cummins removing bottles of champagne from a celebration of the team's win over England in the 2022 Ashes series so that his Muslim teammate Usman Khawaja could join in.[60] France's star football forward Kylian Mbappé has long taken a stance against the promotion of alcohol, including hiding an alcohol company brand name on a player-of-the-match trophy he'd won in the 2022 World Cup, and refusing to attend post-match interviews. Although he was fined for these actions, the sponsor announced plans for 'alternative, culturally appropriate' arrangements to accommodate what Giorgi claims are growing numbers of athletes who don't want to promote alcohol. She wants stronger action – the removal of alcohol sponsorship from sports, as occurred with tobacco.

Pro-peace Movies

Societies can cultivate cultural peace by supporting, encouraging and promoting exciting or interesting films that actively promote peace while minimising violence. *Joyeux Noel (2005)*, for example, is based on a true story of World War I international camaraderie and has a strong anti-war message without using a lot of violence to convey it[61] (see Chapter 4). A number of films challenge the mainstream narrative of World War II, which so greatly overlooks the prevalence and importance of nonviolent resistance, often led by courageous women.[62] These include *Weapons of the Spirit* (1989), *Miracle at Midnight* (1998), *Among the Righteous* (2010), *The Book Thief* (2013) and German films *Rosenstrasse* (2003) and *Sophie Scholl – The Final Days* (2005). Peace Studies at the University of New England has shown numerous such films, including the 'Force More Powerful' documentary series about significant nonviolent struggles around the world, in its annual Nonviolence Film Festival.

Other films deliberately challenge direct violence, such as *Reckless Kelly*, Australian filmmaker Yahoo Serious's sequel to *Young Einstein*. A 2018 French classic *Le Retour du Héros (Return of the Hero)* has a great deal of humour but also verbally and dramatically describes the horrors of the Napoleonic wars, challenging the narrative of war as heroic and glorious.

One notable mainstream exception to violent film cultures is the long-running British *Dr Who* series, by the BBC, where the lead character hates guns, promotes pacifism and solves gripping dilemmas through evasion and extreme cleverness. There have now been two female Doctors, one of whom was black, and there are LGBTQIA+ and mental health themes, as well as increasingly strident environmental messages. Similarly, the hero of the 2018 movie *Ferdinand* is a bull who loves flowers and refuses to fight.

The brilliant *Paddington Bear* movies oppose bigotry and racism without preaching, and in the second one, Paddington revolutionises a brutal prison into a model institution – humane, colourful, enlightened, gentle and flower-filled. Quietly pro-feminist and without smoking or other product placement, the movie questions hyper-masculinity, promotes yoga and emphasises the possibilities of rehabilitation.

These are vast improvements on traditional children's fare, with *Shaun the Sheep* and Wallace and Grommit's *Curse of the Were-Rabbit* infinitely superior to the crude violence of *Bugs Bunny, the Roadrunner, the Three Stooges* and *Abbott and Costello*, or the sexist violence of many fairy tales, such as the witch-burning in *Hansel and Gretel.* Other exceptions to this rule include educational children's TV such as, in North America, *Sesame Street* and the spin-off *Muppet Show* and movies, and the long-running *Mister Rogers' Neighbourhood,* critically acclaimed for focusing on children's emotional concerns, such as sibling rivalry, school, death and divorce. Exemplary Australian shows include *Play School* and the award-winning contemporary cartoon *Bluey.*

Subverting the Violent Genre

Some films exude a constant tension that something terrible is going to occur (cleverly created through music, plot and dialogue) but then turn this on its head by exposing the threat as nothing frightening at all, getting the viewer to question their assumptions and paranoia. In this vein is *Official Secrets* (2019), featuring Keira Knightley and based on the book *The Spy Who Tried to Stop a War* by Marcia and Thomas Mitchell.[63] With an outstanding (and non-smoking) cast, it involves tension and drama created without violence, is based on a true story of a brave whistle-blower, Katharine Gun, and has a strong message about speaking out against the elite-level corruption and lies which led to the illegal invasion of Iraq in 2003 by the 'Coalition of the Willing'.

Royal Hotel (2023) features two young American women backpackers forced to take work in an outback Australian hotel with a sexist and aggressive drinking culture. Many reviewers had an expectation of violence, with one telling director Kitty Green after watching a scene: 'It looks good, but why do the girls have to die?'. Green responded: 'They don't die.' The reviewer's response was 'Oh, but I just assumed'.[64] Green explains her decision to defy the expectation of violence in this context:

> [It's about] subverting that genre, those expectations. Giving them something different, denying them the violence they're hoping to see, which aggravates some viewers who want that climax. [Reviewers seem to] want that [violent] scene for it to be a movie, that's the bit that's missing. But I can highlight these aspects of behaviour [...] without having a rape scene, without having violence. You never need it: the threat of violence is enough. And it's enough for us to say no, take a stand and not put up with that.[65]

The Lost King (2022) is quietly dramatic, with occasional spine-tingling moments. A beautifully realised dramatisation of the autobiographical book *The King's Grave: The Search for Richard III* (2014), it portrays the real-life story of Philippa Langley, the woman who led the successful search for the remains of England's King Richard III, although the University of Leicester, under pressures of corporatisation and inadequate government funding, allegedly took most of the credit. With no direct violence or smoking, *The Lost King* redresses the injustice and structural violence of the under-recognition of women and their working methods[66] and shows that a combination of hard work and intuition can be effective. It also breaks stereotypes by depicting an amicable post-divorce relationship.

Three Summers (2019), written and directed by Ben Elton, is a light but enjoyable example of a film with no violence and with strong messages about the effects of an arts festival on reconciliation, Australian Aboriginal social justice, alcoholism and biodiversity loss. The latter issue is tackled by a new initiative called Sustainable Screens (www.sustainablescreens.au), which aims to address ecological violence and promote sustainability in the film industry's practices. *The Merger* (2018) is another light-hearted film with a serious message, telling the story of refugees struggling to establish new lives in rural Victoria.

Since the eruption of the Black Lives Matter and #MeToo movements, there is increased diversity in our cultures and the leadership roles of our societies and institutions. Increasingly, LGBTQIA+ relationships are mainstreamed, such as in the gripping political drama *Total Control* (2019–23), a series directed by and starring Australian Aboriginal women (Rachel Perkins and Deborah Mailman, respectively). While some decry this change as 'political correctness', boring, and reducing options, an opposing view is that it allows our narratives to become less monocultural and more quirky and unpredictable. Some scripts, such as the screenplay for *Gravity* (2013) by Alfonso Cuaron and Jonas Cuaron, and the screenplay for *Wild* (2014) by Nick Hornby, feature strong female protagonists and describe male and female characters in similar ways, according to O'Meara.[67] who suggests some simple guidelines for ensuring gender equity on screen. *Belle* (2013), starring Gugu Mbatha-Raw, is a gripping anti-slavery movie set in the eighteenth century and based on a true story. With minimal direct violence and assertive, outspoken female characters, it strongly counters the direct and structural violence of slavery and misogyny.

At least one international collaboration has been formed to intentionally make films that encourage peace. Wim Wenders and Mary Zournazi consider this one of the fundamental questions of our times and believe there's a need to reinvent a visual and moral language for peace (thereby complementing the issues raised in the previous chapter). Inspired by various cinematic, philosophical, literary and artistic examples, they reflect on the need for a change of perception in everyday life as well as in the creation of images.[68]

*

This chapter has examined various types of violence in movies (cultural, structural and ecological, as well as frequent depictions of direct violence). It has covered some of the impacts they can have, how the violence is hidden in the trailers, how movies are reviewed and why there is so much violence. It has also suggested some solutions or alternatives which could reduce the amount of film violence, and discussed some films which deliberately tackle the various forms of violence. There are also many documentaries which are pro-peace. Space hasn't allowed us to consider many, but future research could focus on analysing them and their effectiveness.

In the next chapter, we look at some of the planet's more peaceful societies, nations and regions, and try to find what aspects of their cultures make them more peaceful than others.

Notes

1 Fitzpatrick, Caroline 2018 'Watching violence on screens makes children more emotionally distressed', *The Conversation*, 19 November, https://theconversation.com/watching-violence-on-screens-makes-children-more-emotionally-distressed-106757

2 Mulley, Clare 2012 *The Spy Who Loved: The Secrets and Lives of Christine Granville*, Macmillan, London, p. 360.

3 Strickland, Katrina 2021 'Editor's letter', *Good Weekend*, 18 September, p. 3.

4 Ibid.

5 McArthur, David L., Peek-Asa, Corinne, Webb, Theresa, Fisher, Kevin, Cook, Bernard, Browne, Nick and Kraus, Jess 2000 'Violence and its injury consequences in American movies: A public health perspective', *Western Journal of Medicine*, September, vol. 173, no. 3, pp. 164–168.

6 Lazic, Elena 2018 'Film depictions of sexual violence are increasingly alarming. It has to stop', *Guardian,* 14 March, www.theguardian.com/film/2018/mar/14/red-sparrow-jennifer-lawrence-sexual-violence-films-rape

7 Doebbler, Curtis 2011 *The Illegal Killing of Osama Bin Laden,* JURIST – Forum, 5 May, http://jurist.org/forum/2011/05/curtis-doebbler-illegal-killing-obl.php

8 SBS 2016 'What is Sharia law?', *SBS News,* 28 August, www.sbs.com.au/news/explainer/what-sharia-law

9 Brown, Bob 2012 *Memo for a Saner World,* Penguin, Melbourne.

10 Fitzpatrick 2018.

11 Drexler, Peggy 2014 'Violence in PG-13 movies has tripled', *Huffington Post,* 23 January, https://www.huffpost.com/entry/-study-in-december-pediat_b_4302274

12 Common Sense Media 2019 'Here's how different types of violence in movies affect kids', *Huffington Post,* 1 April, www.huffpost.com/entry/violence-types-movies-affect-kid_l_5c8be246e4b09a8f003fe367

13 Branagan, Marty 2020a 'Tintin: From violent, communist-hating conservative to radical peacenik', *International Journal of Comic Art,* vol. 22, no. 1, Spring/Summer issue, pp. 187–206, https://hdl.handle.net/1959.11/30765; Branagan, Marty 2020b 'Tintin: From violent, communist-hating conservative to radical peacenik (Part Two)', *International Journal of Comic Art,* vol. 22, no. 2, Autumn/Winter issue, pp. 33–63.

14 See Canadian Paediatric Society, Digital Health Task Force 2017 'Screen time and young children: Promoting health and development in a digital world', *Paediatrics & Child Health,* vol. 22, no. 8, December, pp. 461–468.

15 Tanay, Emanuel 2012 'Violence in the media: What effects on Behavior?', *Psychiatric Times,* 6 October, www.psychiatrictimes.com/view/violence-media-what-effects-behavior

16 Drexler 2014.

17 Fitzpatrick 2018.

18 Tanay 2012.

19 Common Sense Media 2019.

20 Drexler 2014.

21 LoBue, Vanessa 2018 'Violent media and aggressive Behavior in children: Does watching violence on TV, in movies, or video games promote aggression?' *Psychology Today,* 8 January,, www.psychologytoday.com/au/blog/the-baby-scientist/201801/violent-media-and-aggressive-behavior-in-children

22 Cited in O'Donnell, Marcus 2016 'As life imitates art, how are we to read terror plots in film and TV?', *The Conversation,* 21 July 21, https://theconversation.com/as-life-imitates-art-how-are-we-to-read-terror-plots-in-film-and-tv

23 Fox, Michael A 2014 *Understanding Peace: A Comprehensive Introduction,* Routledge, New York, p. 41.

24 Winton, Tim 2016 *The Boy Behind the Curtain,* Penguin, Melbourne, pp. 3–15.

25 Tarabay, Chanelle and Warburton, Wayne 2017 'Anger, aggression and violence: It matters that we know the difference', *The Conversation,* 1 September, https://theconversation.com/anger-aggression-and-violence-it-matters-that-we-know-the-difference-82918

26 Kirsh, Steven J., Mounts, Jeffrey R. W. and Olczak, Paul V. 2006 'Violent media consumption and the recognition of dynamic facial expressions', *Journal of Interpersonal Violence,* vol. 21, no. 5, May, pp. 1–14.

27 Boyse, Kyla 2010 'Television and children', *University of Michigan Health System*, 1 November, www.med.umich.edu/yourchild/topics/tv.htm
28 DeMille, Nelson and Block, Thomas 1998 *Mayday*, Grand Central Publishing, New York.
29 Trend, David 2003 'Merchants of death: Media violence and American Empire', *Harvard Educational Review*, vol. 73, no. 3, pp. 285–308.
30 Campbell, Eric 2005 *Absurdistan*, Harper Collins, Pymble, pp. 29–31.
31 Jacks, Timma 2018 'Time to rethink your SUV? Australia's cars among the dirtiest, new report warns', *Sydney Morning Herald*, 12 June, www.smh.com.au/business/the-economy/time-rethink-your-suv-australia-s-cars-among-the-dirtiest-new-report-warns-20180611-p4zkqy.html
32 Hasham, Nicole 2017 'Diesel cars help drive Australia's energy emissions to highest level, report shows', *Sydney Morning Herald*, 29 September, www.smh.com.au/politics/federal/diesel-cars-help-drive-australias-energy-emissions-to-highest-level-report-shows-20170928-gyqfbq.html
33 'Criticism of coca-cola', 2021 *Wikipedia*, 7 October, https://en.wikipedia.org/wiki/Criticism_of_Coca-Cola
34 Lincoln, Kevin and Bramesco, Charles 2016 'You can blame soda brands for the rise of product placement in Entertainment', *Vulture*, 26 October,, www.vulture.com/2016/10/80s-kick-started-modern-product-placement.html
35 Cited in Mughrabi, Maher 2018 '"People still believe in Syria": Searching for a shattered nation', *Sydney Morning Herald*, 17 June, www.smh.com.au/world/middle-east/people-still-believe-in-syria-searching-for-a-shattered-nation-20180613-p4zl5r.html
36 Common Sense Media 2019.
37 O'Meara, Radha 2017 'How to reduce sexism in screenplays', *The Conversation*, 4 July, https://theconversation.com/how-to-reduce-sexism-in-screenplays-80142
38 Boboltz, Sara and Yam, Kimberley 2017 'Why on-screen representation actually matters', *Huffington Post*, 24 February, https://www.huffpost.com/entry/why-on-screen-representation-matters_n_58aeae96e4b01406012fe49d
39 Rodenburg, Cassie 2013 'Grand theft auto V makes it cool to pick up – even kill – prostitutes', *Guardian*, 27 December, www.theguardian.com/commentisfree/2013/dec/27/grand-theft-auto-v-prostitutes-killed
40 World Health Organisation 2021 'Tobacco', *WHO Newsroom*, 26 July, www.who.int/news-room/fact-sheets/detail/tobacco
41 BBC 2008 'Hollywood "paid fortune to smoke"', *BBC News*, 25 September, http://news.bbc.co.uk/2/hi/health/7632963.stm?source=post
42 Donohoe, Rose 2016 'The movies the UN doesn't want your kids to see', *NewDaily*, 2 February, https://thenewdaily.com.au/entertainment/movies/2016/02/02/smoking-in-movies/
43 Jhunjhunwala, Ankit 2023 '"Wicked Little Letters" review: Olivia Colman and Jessie Buckley spar in diverting little triffle [sic]', *The Playlist*, 17 September, https://theplaylist.net/wicked-little-letters-review-olivia-colman-and-jessie-buckley-spar-in-diverting-little-triffle-tiff-20230917/t
44 Truth Initiative 2017 'How tobacco companies have used women's history and equality struggles to sell cigarettes', 13 March, https://truthinitiative.org/research-resources/targeted-communities/how-tobacco-companies-have-used-womens-history-and-equality
45 Kirsh et al 2006.

46 Drexler 2014.

47 Olson, Randal S. 2013 'Violence has been on the rise in the film industry', 31 December, www.randalolson.com/2013/12/31/violence-has-been-on-the-rise-in-the-film-industry/

48 Fleischer, Jeff 2004 'Operation hollywood', *Mother Jones*, 20 September, www.motherjones.com/politics/2004/09/operation-hollywood/

49 Bacevich, Andrew J. 2013 *The New American Militarism: How Americans Are Seduced by War*, Oxford University Press, Oxford.

50 Turse, Nick 2008a 'The golden age of the military-entertainment complex', *Tomgram*, 20 March, www.tomdispatch.com

51 Robb, David 2004 *Operation Hollywood: How the Pentagon Shapes and Censors the Movies*, Prometheus, Amherst, NY.

52 Tanay 2012.

53 Thomas, Sarah 2016 'Jason Bourne star Matt Damon on gun control: "I wish that could happen in my country"', *Sydney Morning Herald*, 4 July, www.smh.com.au/entertainment/movies/jason-bournes-matt-damon-on-gun-control-i-wish-that-could-happen-in-my-country-20160704-gpy4cb.html

54 Turse, Nick 2008b *The Complex: How the Military Invades Our Everyday Lives*, Metropolitan Books, New York; see also Stone, Andrew 2008 'The complex: Book review', *Socialist*, May, www.socialistreview.org.uk

55 Moore, Sam 2014 'Lone Survivor: Just because a film shows the ugly side of war, doesn't mean it's an anti-war film', *New Statesman*, 24 November, www.newstatesman.com/culture/2014/11/lone-survivor-just-because-film-shows-ugly-side-war-doesnt-mean-its-anti-war-film

56 Lakey, George 2020 'A century later, the women's suffrage movement offers a timely lesson on how to win through escalation', *Waging Nonviolence*, 30 July, https://wagingnonviolence.org/2020/07/19th-amendment-womens-suffrage-movement-alice-paul-escalation/

57 Donohoe 2016.

58 World Health Organisation 2015 *Smoke-Free Movies: From Evidence to Action*, WHO, Geneva.

59 Giorgi, Caterina 2022 'Athletes break the link with alcohol, so let's just do it', *Sydney Morning Herald*, 26 December, www.smh.com.au/lifestyle/health-and-wellness/athletes-dare-to-break-the-link-between-alcohol-and-sport-so-let-s-just-do-it-20221223-p5c8jd.html

60 Matthey, James 2022 'Pat Cummins' classy post-Ashes act goes viral for all the right reasons', *News.com.au*, 17 January.

61 Moore 2014.

62 Branagan, Marty 2022a 'Women and nonviolent resistance to WWII Nazism (Part One)', *Social Alternatives*, vol. 41, no. 3, October; Branagan, Marty 2022b 'Women and nonviolent resistance to WWII Nazism (Part Two)', *Social Alternatives*, vol. 41, no. 4, December.

63 Mitchell, Marcia and Mitchell, Thomas 2008 *The Spy Who Tried to Stop a War: Katharine Gun and the Secret Plot to Sanction the Iraq Invasion*, Marcia Mitchell, PoliPointPress, Sausalito.

64 Bunbury, Stephanie 2023 'New twist on outback thriller', *Sydney Morning Herald*, 19 November, p. 33.

65 Ibid.

66 See Branagan 2022a,b and Branagan 2021 'Women in environmental nonviolent action', in K. Standish, H. Devere, A. Suazo and R. Rafferty (eds) *The Palgrave Handbook of Positive Peace*, Palgrave Macmillan, Singapore.

67 O'Meara 2017.

68 Totaro, Paola 2014 'Wim Wenders and Mary Zournazi's peace mission', *The Saturday Paper*, www.thesaturdaypaper.com.au/culture/books/2014/04/12/wim-wenders-and-mary-zournazis-peace-mission/1397224800#.VAfzCvmSx8E

Chapter 4

PEACEFUL CULTURES ALREADY EXIST

Peace is neither naïve idealism nor utopian fantasy. There are people living in relative peace, with minimal armed conflict, all over the world. Although there is a great deal of direct, structural and cultural violence, most of our planet's eight billion population engage daily in peaceful interactions, trade, communication and cultural exchange.

High levels of social, inner and ecological peace occur in small communities such as the Penan people of Borneo and the Hopi Native American community; in temporary ones such as the 2014 Bentley blockade against coal seam gas in northern New South Wales, Australia; in entire countries such as Iceland, regarded as the world's most peaceful nation;[1] and in long-term communities such as pacifist religious groups of Jains, Quakers, Bruderhof and Mennonites. The latter groups often engage in brave actions such as being conscientious objectors in times of war, although you will also find some forms of violence in many of these communities, such as the structural violence of patriarchy. Some peace communities never engage in war; others only engage in acts of war outside the boundaries of their community.

Peace systems, involving communities with peace deeply embedded in their cultures, policies and practices, can occur on a large scale, although they are rarely recognised or celebrated as such. The five Nordic nations, for example, have not warred with each other for more than two centuries.[i] Similarly, the creation of the European Union (EU) has led to 446 million people across 27 countries now living without war in their region. This shows that, even though creating peace systems has many challenges, new and major initiatives are possible:

---

i Although it could be argued that this is because the nations in that region are fairly homogeneous, they have plenty of differences too, including separate languages and indigenous peoples. All people share more similarities than differences. The Nordic bloc has chosen to focus on similarities – such as a shared desire for peace – rather than on differences.

> creating a pan-continental peace system had never been attempted until the EU was implemented [...] Ridding the continent of war, the central purpose of European integration, has been a resounding success.[2]

Similar ideas continue to be put forward. For example, in October 2023, the prime minister of Fiji was reported as advocating a zone of peace to de-escalate tensions between the United States and China and to set an example to other countries and regions.[3]

Peace is also a process rather than a static state of affairs. What we choose to believe and project onto society can lead us to think that the eternal presence of violence is our destiny, leading to a self-fulfilling prophecy. Alternatively, we can view humanity as having a choice to learn from the many examples of peacefulness and cooperation and spread that peace more widely and deeply, extending it to all our interactions and to the highest levels of national and international governance and law.

Philosopher Michael Fox[4] shows that it's not inevitable that societies are violent, pointing to many examples of existing peaceful societies in the past and present. Fox discusses what a real-life peaceful society looks like, which is useful because it's helpful knowing what to aim for and having a detailed picture of what is possible, if we are to move towards such a society.

The pursuit of peace, as an overarching objective, is a distinguishing measure of these communities. These societies are generally egalitarian, individuals self-identify as peaceful, and decisions are made by consensus. The extremely low levels of physical violence between the adult populations also define them. Children are raised with little or no violence, and being peaceable is embedded into their psyche via their language and culture.[5]

Long-term peace in the Nordic countries occurred over time through numerous conscious actions:

> Gradually non-warring norms, values, and practices developed, as reliance on discussion and negotiation, mutual respect, collaboration in many spheres, and faith in the rule of law became embedded in the interactions among the Nordic countries.[6]

Reassessing Violence and Peace

It's also worth thinking about the societies most of us live in. The majority of our person-to-person interactions, right across the world and every minute of every day, are not directly violent – and this is something to celebrate and build on. If we're *mostly not violent*, it's not too hard to imagine a much more peaceful world.

However, as we saw in the first chapter, even if there is no overt physical violence, there is often hidden violence – such as domestic violence, psychological violence, structural violence, cultural violence or ecological violence. The UK, and 'the West' more generally, often consider themselves the epitome of civilisation and peace, beacons for other nations to look up to. Samuel Huntington, for example, claims that the Muslim world:

> lacks the core political values that gave birth to representative democracy in Western civilization: separation of religious and secular authority, rule of law and social pluralism, parliamentary institutions of representative government, and protection of individual rights and civil liberties as the buffer between citizens and the power of the state.[7]

The UK has certainly been involved in international peacebuilding, with both advances and backward steps in recent years,[8] but increasingly it is realised that its wealth and institutions, as historian Zoë Laidlaw observes, have been built on a long history of colonialism, dispossession, slavery and exploitation.[9] While claiming a commitment to 'minimum force' and operating among the people as 'we frame ourselves as a more mature, less "cowboy-like" international power', it continues to be one of the main sites of the global military-industrial complex.[10] The United Kingdom and the United States are the biggest investors in countries such as Australia[11] despite narratives, partly based on xenophobia, about Chinese dominance.[ii]

Even the symbolism of the UK remains deeply embedded in militarism, as exemplified by the funeral of Queen Elizabeth II, where every aspect of the funeral processions was dominated by all manner of military personnel – naval, airforce, army, Heraldic troops, Beefeaters, Grenadier guards, mounted bands, pipers, marching bands and foreign troops such as Australian and Canadian mounted police, at a cost to the UK government of £162 million[12] and millions more to nations who sent representatives and held ceremonies. The queen's coffin was borne on a gun carriage. Much of the royal family, including the new monarch, was in military uniform – intimating that this is the most formal or respectful form of dress. Considering the UK's colonialist history, it could be viewed as a disturbing spectacle of past, ongoing and potential military violence, yet this militarism was largely unquestioned amidst images of a rapturous public outpouring of royal mania.

ii Nor are Chinese investors driving up Australian house prices, as widely suspected (see Zhou, Naaman 2021 'More than 80% of Australians mistakenly believe Chinese investors are driving up house prices', *Guardian*, 8 July, www.theguardian.com).

Contrast this with Western media images of North Korea, a country which is often shown only through images of massed, uniformed troops goosestepping. The result, whether conscious or not, is to show the country as a frightening militaristic society full of mindless automatons ready for battle. In contrast with the UK, rarely are more sympathetic images shown of close-ups of ordinary citizens or people partaking in ordinary civilian pursuits, coverage which might encourage an understanding of shared humanity.

Our Complicity

We may also be unwittingly contributing to violence in other countries, as well as structural, cultural and ecological violence. For example, our taxes may be supporting militaries who are killing civilians in another country. Our land clearing or frequent plane use may be adding to global warming, which is causing floods on Pacific islands and more droughts in Africa. The banks, superannuation funds[iii] and corporations we invest in might be supporting the nuclear weapon industry or tobacco, armaments, uranium, animal testing, gambling, fossil fuels or industries which breach human rights or labour standards.

In the *Political Economy of Peace*, Franklin suggests that the task of peacemakers is to develop a culture involving nonviolent means to achieve 'goals based on sustainable development. Such development would focus on social needs that minimally embrace health, education, and human rights'.[13] We can use our economic power – where we spend and invest – to make a more peaceful, equitable and sustainable world.

Cultivating peace, therefore, requires taking the big picture into account, recognising how interconnected the world is now and planning accordingly for a more peaceful world. Peace systems do not automatically represent groups that are free from conflict and aggression. Peacefulness and peacebuilding must be seen as a dynamic process that requires proactive participation utilising peacemaking dialogue.[14] Again, one might suggest that the values of peace systems comprise a language of peacefulness. Peace is the preferred outcome of every negotiation; tolerance, human rights and social cohesion are goals in their own right.[15]

---

iii Superannuation is a compulsory system in Australia and elsewhere of placing a minimum percentage of your income into a fund to support your financial needs in retirement.

Freedom to Choose Peace

A key element that underlies much of our acceptance of militarism and our ruling out of nonviolence is the assumption that violence is inherent in human nature, and therefore that war and competition are an inevitable part of human society. Yet this is contrary to the entire history of human survival and evolution, which has generally been one of cooperation, intelligence and planning.

Following from the discourses and narratives discussed in the first topic, evolutionary biologist David P. Barash challenges the common assumption that humans are naturally violent and warlike, arguing that the 'war is in our genes' perspective is not only scientifically invalid but ethically suspect.[16] This was also affirmed by 'the Seville Statement' by neurophysiologists, psychiatrists, geneticists, psychologists and other scientists at a 1986 UNESCO conference.[17]

While there is a tendency towards interpersonal violence under certain circumstances (such as alcohol-fuelled football crowds), war is 'a quite different phenomenon, typically involving elaborate cognitive processes, extensive planning, and (ironically, perhaps) substantial social cooperation, at least among those on the same side'.[18] War[iv] is a comparatively recent cultural addition to human society, acquired within about the last 10,000 years as a result of factors such as the invention of agriculture, urban hierarchies and the accumulation of material resources which can be stolen as well as defended.

Human evolution has at the same time promoted constructive social activities and inclinations, including 'altruism, empathy, and numerous aspects of social coordination for learning, handicrafts and tool-making, constructing homes, animal enclosures, food storage systems, crop-raising, as well as animal domestication, organizing daily as well as migratory movements of people'.[19] Barash concludes by reiterating that the presumption that our species is biologically doomed to unceasing violence is 'cynical, self-deceiving, and indeed scientifically unsupportable'.[20]

Now that the problems humanity faces are on a global scale, we need to think big and holistically with regard to our perceptions of society:

> To the extent that we don't consider ourselves one global population and try to help each other out – to the extent we see 'us' in competition with 'everybody else' – the world's going to become a very difficult place to live in.[21]

---

iv 'War' is defined in Chapter 1 (footnote 1).

Jeremy Rifkin[22] demonstrates that humans have created ever more complex societies that heightened empathic sensitivity and expanded human consciousness but, ironically, this has relied on an ever-greater consumption of the Earth's resources, resulting in a dramatic deterioration of the health of the planet. To survive, we need rapid changes in human consciousness itself and 'an unprecedented level of mutual understanding among diverse peoples and nations'.[23] He describes the evolution of empathy and the profound ways that it has shaped our development and suggests that we are more inclined towards empathy than aggression.

Peace Is Growing

To counter another myth: if we exclude ecological violence, and that's a big 'if', the world is not getting more violent all the time. Stephen Pinker[24] argues that violence in the West has declined in both the short and long term, mainly because of education but also because of UN and NGO peacebuilding interventions. Not everyone agrees with his figures, and it's clear that levels of violence fluctuate, such as with the Russian invasion of Ukraine in 2014 and escalation in 2022, and the renewed extreme violence in Palestine/Israel in 2023.

Others support Pinker's premise, however, with Joshua Goldstein observing that we are 'winning the war on war',[25] and Roser et al. noting that '[c]onflicts between states have almost ceased to exist'.[26] Northern Ireland is one remarkable success story in virtually ending a seemingly intractable conflict (see Chapters 9 and 10), while Japan moved from a highly militaristic past to a country with a pacifist constitution that formally renounces war and is filled with peace museums and education (Chapters 5 and 8). Although it is currently increasing its militarism at the United States's behest and has sexist elements (Chapter 9), in my experience it remains a safe, orderly, quiet, friendly country, so trusting that people regularly leave handbags and laptops on tables in busy cafés while they use the restrooms.

Other studies indicate significant falls in both the extent and intensity of war in all forms of political conflict and violence, with a dramatic decline in the average number of deaths per conflict.[27] Conflict-prevention and peacebuilding efforts were found to be both more numerous and more effective, and the increasing weight of globalised opinion, interventions and legal institutions such as the International Court of Justice are having an impact on warlords who previously felt few constraints on aggression, war-making and human rights abuses.

Peaceful First Nations

Pinker's work does, however, perpetuate a modernist paradigm – the idea that so-called primitive societies were very violent and that we are naturally progressing towards a better state, which contradicts the evidence of many peaceful societies throughout human history, who often honed their cultures over thousands of years to make them peaceful. Good examples include the sophisticated and highly effective governance, creative story-based education and oral history traditions of the Nhunggabarra people in north-western New South Wales, described in the book *Treading Lightly*.[28] Another is the Iroquois Confederation of Native Americans in the United States, in which women had equality and great power, speakers at meetings weren't allowed to be interrupted, and some leaders were elected and could be impeached. It influenced the United States's founders in their choice of a system which was much more democratic than any British or European one of the time.[29]

These generalisations about what makes a 'civilised' society continue to find traction. One review of the literature about the emergence of civilisation questions some of these assumptions while continuing others, such as by contrasting hunter-gatherer societies with 'complex' ones, defined by some in terms of technologies of violence, control and extraction and by others as 'socially stratified with powerful leaders and the rapid invention of writing, money and new technologies'.[30] The first definition, taken to its logical extension, means that nuclear-armed, repressive and environmentally rapacious states are the apex of 'civilised' society, which most peace, human rights and environmental advocates would find highly problematic. Regarding the second definition, anarchist theorists from Emma Goldman to Randall Amster would dispute that social stratification and powerful leaders make a society more complex or better; rather their view is that these erode egalitarianism and equity and lead to a hierarchical state which requires violence to enforce its rules and boundaries.

Furthermore, despite not using writing or money, there has traditionally been great complexity in Australian Aboriginal societies in terms of their multilingual capacities, kinship systems that ensured genetic health and diversity, and cultural and philosophical traditions deeply embedded in sustainability and connection to Country. Their intricate oral history traditions were globally unique, able to accurately pass on information dating back to 13,400 BP, far longer than the supposedly superior written traditions.[31] Their lack of materialism was the envy of sadhus. Eschewing money, they had steady-state (rather than growth-based) economies and populations, and generous, cooperative trade systems that spanned the continent and connected the nations, rather than being competitive and serving minority private interests.[32] Similar systems (such as LETS and the Community Exchange Network [www.communityexchange.net.au]) are now advocated by contemporary environmentalists and post-growth theorists.

Finally, 'new technologies' are not in themselves beneficial, with the nuclear bomb being a prime example which has made humanity live under a cloud of fear for more than 75 years. Aboriginal people are often regarded as not having had modern, technological societies, yet they pioneered 'appropriate technology'[33] – well-suited to their needs – demonstrating early aerodynamic expertise in the woomera and boomerang, and engaging in detailed astronomical observation 30,000 years ago[34] which sometimes resulted in carved star-maps.[35] They created one of the world's first musical instruments, the yidaki (also known as the 'didgeridu'), and their art involved the world's oldest known use of reflective pigment.[36] They were the first to bake bread, 36,000 years ago, well ahead of other civilisations,[37] and the first to make edge-ground axes, nearly 50,000 years ago,[38] and perhaps 15,000 years earlier than that.[39] At Brewarinna, they built one of the biggest aquaculture systems in the world, which some scientists believe is the oldest human construction on Earth.[40] In North Queensland, they used partial dams on rivers to catch fish when needed, in sustainable amounts.[41]

So, as David Wengrow from University College, London, argues, we need to reconsider the whole concept of social complexity and be more cognisant of the benefits to peace and sustainability of indigenous societies:

> We might instead choose to define complexity in terms of kinship systems, ecological resilience and artistic creativity. In which case, the Indigenous islanders of Ambrym [in Vanuatu] would come out somewhere near the top, and European societies would be pretty low down.[42]

To give some more examples, the Semai people in Malaysia live in small autonomous villages valuing equality over typically masculine characteristics, such as bravery, strength and aggressiveness. They maintain peace through two main mechanisms: an 'internalised' fear of committing violence, and 'rigorous self-control'.[43] 'Goodness' is defined in terms of nurturance, while 'badness' relates to aggression and violence. Major disagreements are resolved through meetings which continue until the problem is solved, and through gift-giving.

The Xingu River Basin Tribes of Brazil keep peace through inter-village trade, inter-marriage, ceremonial interconnections and shared values. Every tribe produces items for trading, with the Wauja making pottery, the Yawalapiti creating shell decorations and the Trumai producing salt. This trading requires trust, since items presented may not be reciprocated for months. Similar to the Semai, peace is regarded as moral, while war and violence are seen as immoral. They too place high value on self-control, with individuals gaining prestige, social approval and respect through demonstrating restraint.[44]

Two Choices

Humans have two ancient and conflicting philosophies. One is the peaceful resolution of conflict, taught to children in homes, schools and churches, and which guides most of our daily interactions. The other is the extreme, premeditated violence of war, where (primarily) young, working-class men are ordered to kill strangers using ever more powerful technology.[45]

There's a good illustration of these two contrasting paradigms in the true story of the Christmas Truce of 1914, fictionalised in the 2005 film *Joyeux Noel*. This story shows that even in the midst of the carnage of World War I, ordinary soldiers on both sides, supposed enemies, were able to find common ground in the religious and cultural traditions of Christmas, in shared love of food, drink and football. They began to forge connections and understandings, to make agreements and cooperate for mutual benefit.

Many of the opposing troops spontaneously declared a truce in the fighting for the Christmas period, initially just for practical reasons such as burials and fixing their trench homes in the bitterly cold winter.[46] In all, 100,000 took part, some playing football, others singing together or to each other, attending religious services jointly, and exchanging pleasantries, mail, newspapers, food and alcohol. One German veteran, Richard Schirrmann, wrote that

> they visited each other through disused trench tunnels, and exchanged wine, cognac, and cigarettes for Westphalian black bread, biscuits, and ham. This suited them so well that they remained good friends even after Christmas was over.[47]

(A similar story is told by Australian musician Normie Rowe in his self-titled autobiography[48] of his time in the Vietnam (or 'American') war, where the Australian soldiers would relax in steam baths in Vung Tau next to Viet Cong soldiers they'd been shooting at the day before.)

The Christmas Truce built upon complicated local truces and agreements not to fire at each other, which were developed by men along the front throughout the war. These often began with agreements not to attack each other at tea, meal or washing times, and in some places became so developed that whole sections of the front would see few casualties for extended periods of time. This system, historian Tony Ashworth argues, 'gave soldiers some control over the conditions of their existence'.[49] The December 1914 Christmas series of truces were not unique, but a dramatic example of non-cooperation with the war that included refusal to fight, unofficial truces, mutinies, strikes and peace protests. It seemed that, despite orders from above, *peace was breaking out.*

There was some discussion of this in the news, mainly in Great Britain and to a lesser extent in Germany, but there was censorship in France. Soldiers were reminded that fraternising with the enemy was treason, and military commanders tried to prohibit and prevent any further truces and agreements.

Later, however, there were memorials created as well as books, novels, songs, a music video by Paul McCartney, plays and radioplays, and movies, such as *Joyeux Noel.* German veteran Richard Schirrmann, who had founded the first youth hostel in 1912, became an even stronger proponent of hostels after the war. Inspired by the Christmas Truce, he envisaged hostels as places where youth of different nationalities could meet and socialise – 'bridges of peace' to foster international understanding. In 1919 he founded the German Youth Hostel Association, and in 1922 retired from teaching to dedicate himself to building the association into an international movement which is thriving today.

Similarly, an au-pair scheme was founded after World War I to foster peacetime European collaboration, writes Lucy Lethbridge. It was designed as an exchange programme to encourage the learning of languages and to experience other cultures. Bed and board were offered in exchange for light childcare, although the experience for many was mixed.[50]

Characteristics of Peaceful Communities

Eight criteria for defining a peaceful society are as follows:

1. The society has no wars fought on its territory;
2. The society is not involved in any external wars;
3. There are no civil wars or internal collective violence;
4. There is no standing military-police organisation;[v]
5. There is little or no interpersonal physical violence;
6. There is little or no structural violence;

v Some forceful policing resources may always be necessary, such as to deal with violent offenders. However, police need not be lethally armed (UK police rarely carry guns) but can rely on non-lethal or non-killing technologies, despite issues with these (see Centre for Global Nonkilling, https://nonkilling.org/center/).

7. The society has the capacity to undergo change peacefully; and
8. There are opportunities for idiosyncratic development.[51]

Peaceful societies typically demonstrate positive attitudes of trust, cooperation, respect for human rights, sustainability and social norms. A peaceful society is a community that works together to avoid aggression and violence and values harmony and peace. Large-scale examples which have all or most of the eight characteristics include Switzerland, Bhutan, New Zealand, Costa Rica and Norway.

Each of these communities has shown a commitment to both achieving and maintaining peace while preserving their own cultural identities and beliefs. Through an understanding of how peaceful societies turn away from aggression and violence, modern societies may come to accept that violence is neither normal nor necessary. As cultural peace pioneer Elise Boulding said in a keynote lecture:

> We can point to a few small societies that live in isolated circumstances, indigenous people who have beautiful peaceful ways. We can say, that's a peace culture. But mostly in our very complex society, we identify pieces of peace culture, elements and sectors. Our challenge is how to build out from what we already have and to have a deep appreciation of human difference.[52]

Let's have a closer look at some of these societies which are more peaceful than average.

New Zealand

New Zealand has a history of global leadership in the suffragette movement which gained women the vote. It also stood up to the United States in the 1980s and continues to refuse to let nuclear-armed US warships into its harbours. It also has a treaty and reasonably good relations between the original Maori inhabitants and the later colonists. More recently, New Zealand has been in the news for compassion towards refugees and reducing ecological violence by granting legal personhood status to a river.[53]

Its wealth relative to other countries is probably a factor. That is, if it can afford to minimise structural violence, it's likely to have less direct, visible violence. This does not explain, however, why it is more peaceful than other countries with comparative wealth. One factor is the long tradition of Maori nonviolence (commencing well before Gandhi) explored in Chapter 6. Their comprehensive peace education system is another factor (see Chapter 8).

San Jose de Apartado – Colombia

The small Colombian town of San Jose de Apartado is comprised of 32 villages totalling approximately 3,000 citizens in a remote mountainous location in Colombia. In 1997, San Jose declared itself a 'Peace Community'. From 1970 to 1996, it was far from peaceful, being surrounded by the military and guerrilla fighters and frequently under attack.[54] Colombia has endured generations of violent civil wars that have claimed thousands of lives and left many more without land or livelihoods. The citizens of San Jose, a small farming community, retained hopes for a peaceful society and, with the assistance of international religious, educational and peace organisations, sought to declare their territory a 'neutral zone'. However, the term 'peace community' was more effective in gaining recognition and respect from both the military and guerrillas, and gradually San Jose began to create a sustainable and peaceful future.

The entire community committed to work together to create and enforce regulations to drive out the armed forces. Using cooperation, defined as fundamental for sustainability and survival,[55] the citizens of San Jose were able to resist war and violence and create a peace community, classified as one that has 'workable strategies' to resolve conflict nonviolently.[56] San Jose's protection strategies included a ban on selling alcohol within the town, a ban on supplying goods or information to soldiers and a veto on carrying weapons or participating in military activity. Simple but effective security measures to protect each other included warning bells, always travelling in groups, and hiding from attackers.[57] Importantly, they strategically internationalised their cause, gaining protection for San Jose from the Inter-American Court of Human Rights and from Peace Brigades International, who gave them support and international publicity. Despite many attacks, San Jose's commitment to peace has endured.

Sarvodaya Shramadan – Sri Lanka

Similarly, the peoples of Sri Lanka have experienced decades of 'civil' war but sought peace through their own positive courses of action. A long history of political power struggles, internal conflict and violence within the many ethnic and religious groups of the mainland and islands of Sri Lanka has resulted in the deaths of tens of thousands of people as well as creating mass displacement and economic crises.[58]

In the midst of this, however, the Sarvodaya Shramadan movement has been a peaceful current flowing in the opposite direction for more than 60 years. Sarvodaya is translated as 'the awakening of all', and the well-organised movement is synonymous with a society that embraces trust, nonviolence and human rights. Sarvodaya tries to build peace by enabling communities to develop a self-sufficient and sustainable future. Their vision is to create a society without poverty or inequality, and which supports the rights of all people.

Sri Lanka has a predominantly religious culture made up of Buddhists, Muslims, Hindus and Christians, so it is logical that the peace activities of Sarvodaya incorporate spiritual healing and meditation in their initiatives. A mass peace meditation in 2002 attracted 650,000 people to a single event. In 2004, on International Peace Day, 200,000 people came together to meditate. Other events have included peace marches, peace talks and youth peace camps, and ongoing initiatives are offered that promote trust and friendship between villages such as village-to-village and people-to-people exchange programmes. A workshop series coordinated by the movement created an opportunity for 800 people from diverse backgrounds to speak freely of their experiences and hopes for a peaceful future. With many people doubting that the government and political system in Sri Lanka can provide a means to a peaceful future, Sarvodaya Shramadan offers hope and envisions a future of 'constructive consensual politics'.[59]

La Paz – Mexico

The United Nations lists a number of conditions necessary for a culture of peace, including gender equality, human rights, understanding, tolerance and education.[60] The community of La Paz is an internally peaceful society, embracing all these conditions in their daily lives. It places a high value on the importance of women and has a culture that favours peace in education and socialisation, and a social order based on tolerance and respect.

La Paz, located in Mexico in the valley of Oaxaca, is one of 34 communities that have existed in the area since the 1500s.[61] Despite being a small subsistence farming community, La Paz has come to prominence as a model of a peaceful and unique culture, with gender equality and an emphasis on mutual respect, cooperation and nonviolent behaviour.[62]

Women have contributed to the La Paz economy for generations by creating and selling their pottery and passing their skills on to their daughters. The men have great respect for the contribution and abilities of these women, and this mutual harmony flows through to their marriages, relationships and families.

Avoiding physical violence or aggression is also part of the La Paz culture; instead, children learn through discussion, instruction and by example. Avoidance is the preferred response in La Paz to any confrontation, with it considered more practical to retreat than try to control the situation.[63]

If conflict cannot be avoided, local authorities will listen to the case, no matter how minor. The people of La Paz generally respect their authorities and accept their rulings. La Paz maintains its peaceful community through cooperation, tolerance and a commitment to a system of beliefs and values that cherish family values and their way of life.

The existence of such communities is all the more remarkable given that the current situation of violence between drug-trafficking organisations and a growing military in Mexico 'can only be described in terms of international law as a non-international (or internal) armed conflict'.[64] La Paz is recognised by the International Cities of Peace organisation, an all-volunteer, non-profit association dedicated to facilitating the establishment of Cities of Peace worldwide (www.internationalcitiesofpeace.org).

The Nordic Region

The Nordic Region is made up of Iceland, Norway, Sweden, Finland and Denmark, modern, technologically advanced and wealthy countries with a large combined population that lives as a peaceful region. The people of the Nordic area take great pride in their nonviolent history and, despite all the graphic 'Nordic noir' novels and films, their low rates of violent crime.[65] At the beginning of World War II, the Nordic countries declared themselves neutral, and their geographical location in northern Europe provided them with a modicum of insulation from World War II that consumed Europe.[66] Denmark was occupied by Nazi Germany (as was Norway), but most of Denmark's Jewish population were hidden or smuggled to safety in neutral Sweden, and widespread nonviolent resistance, including general strikes, denied Germany much material benefit from the occupation, drew troops away from the war frontlines and made Denmark virtually ungovernable by August 1944.[67]

Regional peace has been aided by their similar cultures, religions and belief systems, their common history and similar languages, and a preference for avoidance rather than confrontation in hostile situations.[68] Their internal political policies have focused on conflict resolution, solidarity and respect for the law; these are reflected in their foreign policies that promote the peaceful settlements of disputes.[69] Nordic countries have a higher-than-average number of women in senior positions in parliament, and gender equality is valued.

However, Sweden is a major arms exporter on a per-capita basis, and its government and companies gave substantial material support to the Nazi regime.[70] In response to Russia's invasion of Ukraine, Sweden abandoned its long-held policy of international neutrality and joined the North Atlantic Treaty Organisation military alliance in 2024 (Finland had joined in 2023).

Sweden has had a substantial rise in income inequality since the mid-1980s, whereas Norway is the most equal country on Earth. Other countries bucking the global trend and taking strong action to reduce inequality include Costa Rica, New Zealand, Barbados and, until armed conflict intensified in 2023, the Occupied Palestinian Territories.[71]

Costa Rica

Demilitarisation, along with tolerance and cooperation, is an important element in creating a culture of peace.[72] Costa Rica is a world leader in demilitarisation, having successfully existed – and prospered – without an army since 1948.

The decision to replace their army with a much smaller security force made up of paramilitary, civil guard and border police was made by the government at a time when the 'military was weak and low in status'[73] in order to stop a recurring cycle of the military starting coups to overthrow existing regimes.

The citizens of Costa Rica supported the decision of their government for both the financial benefits to the community and their commitment to a peaceful future, which has maintained a neutral, non-confrontational, democratic society that is still flourishing more than 70 years later.[74] Since 'Abolition Day', Costa Rica has successfully resisted or minimised external threats through a number of mechanisms, such as cultivating good relations with its neighbours. It also enjoys some protection from the international community, membership of the Inter-American Reciprocal Defence Treaty, international law and UN rules against invasions. The fact that it has created numerous international links through its UN-mandated University of Peace, unique in the world, is another beneficial factor. However, the pressures of economic refugees, and drug smugglers passing through the country on the way to the lucrative North American markets, create multiple problems.

The enormous savings it has made from cutting military spending have been ploughed into social welfare, education, water security, sanitation, human development, social activities, sport and preserving most of its rainforests.[75] Costa Rica has topped the Happy Planet Index and the World Database of Happiness, despite a relatively low per-capita gross domestic product. Although its population is small, Costa Rica is the most successful national football team in the history of Central America, reaching the quarter-finals of the Football World Cup in 2014.

Many other countries, such as Fiji, could follow Costa Rica's lead in abolishing their military forces to end the recurring cycle of military-sponsored coups. In the last century, far more people were killed by their own government's forces than by militaries from another country. This includes regimes from both the left and right, such as those led by Hitler, Stalin and Mao. That is, internal repression and what R.J. Rummel calls 'democides' ('public murders' by governments) killed more than war did.[76] While wars killed about 37 million people in the twentieth century, government forces killed 262 million of their own citizens in the same period[77] – people they were meant to be protecting. One could presume from this that *abolishing armies is the simplest way to cut down the global premature death rate.*

Twenty-two other member states of the United Nations do not have a standing army: Andorra, Dominica, Grenada, Haiti, Kiribati, Liechtenstein, the Marshall Islands, Mauritius, the Federated States of Micronesia, Monaco, Nauru, Palau, Panama, Samoa, San Marino, the Solomon Islands, St Lucia, St Vincent and the Grenadines, Tuvalu, Vanuatu and the Vatican.[78]

Bhutan

Another country with minimal defences is Bhutan. It has no navy as it is a landlocked country. It has no air force, and an army of only 8000, although it does rely on India for military training, arms supplies and air defence. Bhutan is striving to be a zero-carbon country, and its moves towards equity, sustainability and peacefulness are extraordinary, reflecting a vibrant culture, educated populace and strong but enlightened government. Doing this as one of the poorest nations on Earth makes this even more remarkable.

Influenced by Buddhism, they initiated the notion of Gross National Happiness (GNH), which measures prosperity through formal principles and the spiritual, physical, social and environmental health of its citizens and natural environment.[79] This belief that well-being should take precedence over material growth has remained a global oddity for decades. But now, amidst rising concern about global environmental crises, gross inequity and precarious financial systems, this state's approach is attracting attention and gaining traction. In 2011, the UN adopted Bhutan's call for a holistic approach to development, a move endorsed by 68 countries. A UN panel is now considering ways that Bhutan's GNH model can be replicated across the globe.

Bhutan's principles have been set into policy through the GNH index, based on equitable social development, cultural preservation, conservation of the environment and promotion of good governance. In just a quarter of a century, Bhutan has doubled life expectancy, enroled almost 100 per cent of its children in primary school and overhauled its infrastructure. At least 60 per cent of its landmass will remain under forest cover in perpetuity. It has banned export logging and has instigated a monthly pedestrian day that bans all private vehicles from its roads.

However, the nation is not perfect. Tightened citizenship laws since the mid-1980s have forced an exodus of about one-sixth of its population, nearly all of them of Nepalese origin. They had been declared illegal immigrants, even though many of them had lived in Bhutan for several generations.[80]

Intentional Communities

Another example of peaceful communities, albeit dispersed, is the intentional community movement. In the 1960s and 1970s, many youth in Western nations engaged in a mass exodus back to the land, led by anti-war countercultural events such as the 1969 Woodstock festival in the United States – advertised as 'three days of peace and music' – and the 1973 Aquarius Festival in northern New South Wales (NSW), Australia, organised by university students from the University of New England and elsewhere. They set up communes where they tried to live self-sufficiently and outside of mainstream society, which they considered dominated by war, militarism, greed, inequity and unsustainable practices.

Although often derided as dropouts, their aim was to create alternative models of living which opposed, undermined and might eventually replace the outmoded old ones. Rather than being anti-technology, most were in favour of the 'appropriate technology' which Schumacher[81] advocated, with groups such as the Rainforest Information Centre in the northern NSW town of Lismore leading the use of the internet for environmental campaigning on an international scale. These communes were all different, and none were perfect. Some came and went, but many survived and thrived and have been joined by new ones and multiple occupancies. The Northern Rivers region in northern NSW, or 'Rainbow Region', has one of the largest concentrations of these intentional communities in the world.[82]

The hippies didn't invent the concept, however, and there are examples of such communities throughout history. A major eruption of them occurred in India during the time of Mahatma Gandhi, as he advocated that people should 'live simply so that others can simply live'.[83] He set up communities that are still going, dedicated to creating positive examples of peaceful living. Other such communities have sprung up in India such as Auroville (https://auroville.org), whose mission statement is 'to be a universal town where men and women of all countries are able to live in peace and progressive harmony above all creeds, all politics and all nationalities'. Formerly independent and thriving, Auroville is currently subject to intense pressures, repression and co-option by the conservative Modi government, but with international support, it may survive and thrive again.

Conclusion

Peace is a concept which is both relative and undervalued. Although there are always terrible examples of violence, it is clear that there is also a great deal of peace in the world, some of it deliberately cultivated. There are many examples of peaceful communities, some of which are actively trying to spread peace outwards. The mere existence of tribes, nations, regions and other social systems comprised of non-warring neighbours shows that living without war is possible. As Fry and Souillac write:

> A systematic study of peace systems may hold valuable lessons about how to promote transborder cooperation desperately needed to meet the threats of climate change, pandemics, ecological collapse, and ticking nuclear catastrophe.[84]

The many peaceful societies that exist today demonstrate that it is possible to achieve harmony in most aspects of daily life. The core values of human rights, gender equality, tolerance, trust and cooperation are evident within the peaceful communities examined above. They engage in non-conflict strategies such as avoidance, demilitarising, egalitarianism, consensus decision-making, positive socialisation (see Chapter 7), peace education (Chapter 8), and refusing to accept or condone violence and aggressive behaviour. Using these cultures as an example, and with the inclusion of transparency, low levels of corruption, the free flow of information, diverse media and peace journalism (see Chapter 6), peace could be achievable in many other societies too. In the next chapter, we'll examine how this could be aided by a realignment of our histories, memorials and public spaces.

Notes

1. Carlström, V. 2017 'Iceland is the most peaceful country in the world', *Business Insider,* http://nordic.businessinsider.com/iceland-is-the-most-peaceful-country-in-the-world-2017-6/
2. Fry, Douglas P and Souillac, Geneviève 2021 'Peaceful societies are not Utopian fantasy. They Exist', *Bulletin of the Atomic Scientists,* 22 March, https://thebulletin.org/2021/03/peaceful-societies-are-not-utopian-fantasy-they-exist/
3. Brennan, Dechlan 2023 'During Australia visit, Fijian Prime Minister calls for "Ocean of Peace"', *Diplomat,* 19 October, https://thediplomat.com/2023/10/during-australia-visit-fijian-prime-minister-calls-for-ocean-of-peace/
4. Fox, Michael A. 2014 *Understanding Peace: A Comprehensive Introduction,* Routledge, New York.
5. Fox 2014, pp. 86–88.
6. Fry and Souillac 2021.

7 Inglehart, Ronald and Norris, Pippa 2003 'The true clash of civilizations', *Foreign Policy*, no. 135, pp. 63–70.

8 Ramsbotham, Alexander and Dumasy, Teresa 2021 'A "Force for Peace"? UK peacebuilding and peacemaking and FCACs', *Foreign Policy Centre*, https://fpc.org.uk/a-force-for-peace-uk-peacebuilding-and-peacemaking-and-fcacs/

9 Laidlaw, Zoë 2014 'Imperial complicity: Indigenous dispossession in British history and history writing', in Catherine Hall, Nicholas Draper and Keith McClelland (eds.), *Emancipation and the Remaking of the British Imperial World*, Manchester University Press, Manchester, pp. 131–148.

10 Blain, Harry 2015 Confronting Britain's military-industrial complex', *Open Democracy*, 1 May, www.opendemocracy.net/en/opendemocracyuk/confronting-britains-militaryindustrial-complex/

11 Australian Government 2022 'Foreign investment statistics', *Department of Foreign Affairs and Trade*, www.dfat.gov.au/trade/trade-and-investment-data-information-and-publications/foreign-investment-statistics/statistics-on-who-invests-in-australia

12 Adams, Charley 2023 'Queen Elizabeth II: Funeral and 10 days of mourning cost government £162', *BBC News*, 18 May, www.bbc.com/news/uk-65636772

13 Franklin, Ray L. 2009 'Political economy of Peace', in Joseph de Rivera (ed.), *Handbook on Building Cultures of Peace*, Springer, p. 27.

14 Fox 2014, p. 8.

15 Fry, Douglas P., Bonta, Bruce T. and Baszarkiewbcz, Karolina 2009 'Learning from extant cultures of peace', in Joseph de Rivera (ed.), *Handbook on Building Cultures of Peace*, Springer, pp. 19–20.

16 Barash, David P. 2014 'Are human beings naturally violent and warlike?' *Philosophy Now*, vol. 105, https://philosophynow.org/issues/105/Are_Human_Beings_Naturally_Violent_And_Warlike

17 Adams, David et al. 1991 *The Seville Statement on Violence: Preparing the Ground for the Construction of Peace*, UNESCO, https://unesdoc.unesco.org/ark:/48223/pf0000094314

18 Barash 2014.

19 Ibid.

20 Ibid.

21 Tim Kohler, cited in Marshall, Michael 2023 'Rethinking civilisation', *New Scientist*, July, p. 39.

22 Rifkin, Jeremy 2010 *The Empathic Civilization: The Race to Global Consciousness in a World in Crisis*, Polity Press, Cambridge.

23 Ibid.

24 Pinker, Steven 2011 *The Better Angels of Our Nature: Why Violence Has Declined*, Viking, New York.

25 Goldstein, Joshua S. 2011 *Winning the War on War: The Decline of Armed Conflict Worldwide*, Dutton, New York.

26 Roser, Max, Hasell, Joe, Herre, Bastian and Macdonald, Bobbie 2016 'War and peace', *Our World In Data*, https://ourworldindata.org/war-and-peace

27 La Franchi, Howard 2005 'A welcome surprise: War waning globally', *Christian Science Monitor*, 18 October, www.csmonitor.com

28 Sveiby, K. E. and Skuthorpe, T. 2006 *Treading Lightly: The Hidden Wisdom of the World's Oldest People*, Allen & Unwin, Crows Nest, NSW.

29 Little, Becky 2023 'The native American Government that helped inspire the US Constitution', *History*, 12 July, www.history.com/news/iroquois-confederacy-influence-us-constitution
30 Marshall, Michael 2023 'Rethinking civilisation', *New Scientist*, July, pp. 37–38.
31 Reid, Nicholas, Nunn, Patrick D. and Sharpe, Margaret 2014 'Indigenous Australian stories and sea-level change', *Indigenous Languages: Their Value to the Community.* Proceedings of the 18th FEL Conference, Foundation for Endangered Languages pp. 82–87.
32 Sveiby and Skuthorpe 2006.
33 See Schumacher, E. F. 1973 *Small is Beautiful: A Study of Economics as if People Matter,* Blonde and Briggs, London.
34 Knox, Judy Kaye (Gomeroi traditional custodian) 2016 presentation, Beyond Coal and Gas conference, Myuna Bay, 10 April.
35 Branagan, David and Cairns, Hugh 1994 'Marks on sandstone surfaces – Sydney region, Australia: Cultural origins and meanings?', *Journal and Proceedings of Royal Society of NSW*, vol. 126, pp. 125–33.
36 Clarkson, Chris, Marwick, Ben, Wallis, Lynley, Fullagar, Richard and Jacobs, Zenobia 2017 'Buried tools and pigments tell a new history of humans in Australia for 65,000 years', *The Conversation*, 20 July, https://theconversation.com/buried-tools-and-pigments-tell-a-new-history-of-humans-in-australia-for-65-000-years-81021
37 Wood, Alecia 2016 'Were indigenous Australians the world's first bakers?' *SBS*, 6 October, www.sbs.com.au/food/article/2016/10/06/were-indigenous-australians-worlds-first-bakers
38 Young, Emma 2016 'Scientists find ice age art in the Kimberley', *WA Today*, September, www.watoday.com.au/wa-news/scientists-find-ice-age-art-in-the-kimberley-20160905-gr8u2z.html, accessed 14 October 2016
39 Clarkson et al. 2017.
40 Marlow, Karina and Mandybur, Jerico 2017 'Not Hunter-gatherers: Bruce Pascoe on storytelling, history and cultural pride', *NITV*, 12 August, www.sbs.com.au/nitv/article/not-hunter-gatherers-bruce-pascoe-on-storytelling-history-and-cultural-pride/q6exaeir5
41 Pascoe, Bruce 2018 'Historical and national significance of Myall Creek Massacre', Keynote Address, Myall Creek and Beyond symposium, Oorala Aboriginal Centre, UNE, 8 June.
42 Cited in Marshall 2023, p. 39.
43 Fox 2014, p. 87.
44 De Rivera, Joseph (ed) 2009 *Handbook on Building Cultures of Peace,* Springer, New York, p. 12.
45 Schell, Jonathan 2003 *The Unconquerable World: Nonviolence and the Will of the People,* Metropolitan Books, New York.
46 Slayton, Nicholas 2022 'The complicated truth about the famous "Christmas Truce" of World War I', *Task and Purpose*, 27 December, https://taskandpurpose.com/history/christmas-truce-world-war-1-history/
47 Cited in Reyes, Rudy 2009 *Hero Living: Seven Strides to Awaken Your Infinite* Power, Celebra, Penguin Publishing Group, New York, p. 109.
48 Rowe, Normie with Ed Nimmervoll 2013 *Normie: The Normie Rowe Story*, New Holland, Sydney, p. 100.
49 Ashworth, Tony 1980 *Trench Warfare 1914–1918: The Live and Let Live System, Pan Grand Strategy,* Macmillan, London.

50 Lethridge, Lucy 2013 *Servants: A Downstairs History of Britain from the Nineteenth Century to Modern Times,* WW Norton and Co, New York, pp. 303–304.
51 Fabbro, David 1978 'Peaceful societies: An introduction', *Journal of Peace Research,* vol. 15, no. 1, pp. 67–83.
52 Boulding, Elise 1999 'Elise Boulding keynote', *Ikeda Centre,* www.ikedacenter.org/resources/elise-boulding-peace-cultures-and-living-difference
53 Kramm, Matthias 2020 'When a river becomes a person', *Journal of Human Development and Capabilities,* vol. 21, no. 4, pp. 307–319.
54 Anderson, Mary B. and Wallace, Marshall 2013 *Opting Out of War: Strategies to Prevent Violent Conflict,* Lynne Rienner, Boulder, p. 129.
55 Fox 2014, p. 96.
56 Bonta, B. 2013 'Peaceful societies prohibit violence', *Journal of Aggression, Conflict and Peace Research,* vol. 5, no. 3, p. 128.
57 Anderson and Wallace 2013, p. 135.
58 Ariyaratne, V. 2006 'Building a culture of non-violence and peace: The Sarvodaya experience in Sri Lanka', in S. Toh and V. Cawagas (eds.), *Cultivating Wisdom, Harvesting Peace: Educating for a Culture of Peace Through Values, Virtues and Spirituality of Diverse Cultures, Faiths and Civilizations,* Griffith University, Brisbane, p. 87.
59 Ariyaratne 2006, p. 93.
60 Mayton, D. M. 2009 'Cultural and societal perspectives of nonviolence', in D. M. Mayton (ed.), *Nonviolence and peace psychology: Intrapersonal, interpersonal, societal, and world peace,* Springer, New York, p. 134.
61 Bonta 2013, p. 117.
62 Fry, Douglas, P. 2003 'Multiple paths to peace: The "La Paz" Zapotec of Mexico', in G. Kemp and Douglas P. Fry (eds.), *Keeping the Peace: Conflict Resolution and Peaceful Societies around the World,* Routledge, New York, p. 22.
63 Fry, Bonta and Baszarkiewicz 2009, p. 22.
64 Bermúdez,José Antonio Guevara2022 'Mexico: A country at war?' *Peace in Progress,* vol. 40, May, www.icip.cat/perlapau/en/article/mexico-a-country-at-war/
65 Bonta 2013, p. 118.
66 Archer, C. 1996 'The Nordic area as a "Zone of Peace"', *Journal of Peace Research,* vol. 33, p. 459.
67 Ackerman, Peter and Duvall, Jack 2000 *A Force More Powerful: A Century of Nonviolent Conflict,* Palgrave, Hampshire, pp. 207–31.
68 Bonta 2013, p. 120.
69 Archer 1996, p. 464.
70 Cohen, Roger 1997 'The (Not So) neutrals of World War II', *New York Times,* 26 January, section 4, p. 1.
71 Oxfam 2022 'Global index shows Sweden worst in the Nordic countries at fighting inequality', 11 October, https://oxfam.se/en/nyheter/globalt-index-visar-sverige-samst-i-norden-pa-att-bekampa-ojamlikhet/
72 Fry, Bonta and Baszarkiewicz 2009, p. 11.
73 Harris, Geoff 2004 'Central American demilitarisation: A model for small countries?' Harris (ed.), *Achieving Security in Sub-Saharan Africa: cost effective Alternatives to the Military,* Institute for Security Studies, South Africa, p. 196.
74 Fox 2014, p. 56.
75 Vargas-Araya, Armando 2020 'Costa Rica abolished its military. Other countries can too', *Canberra Times,* 3 December, www.canberratimes.com.au/story/7038431/costa-rica-abolished-its-military-other-countries-can-too/

76 Rummel, R. J. 1994 *Death by Government*, Transaction Publishers, New Brunswick, www.hawaii.edu/powerkills/DBG.CHAP2.HTM
77 'Murderous Governments' 2009 *Development Education*, https://developmenteducation.ie
78 Ibid.
79 Kelly, Annie 2012 'Gross national happiness in Bhutan: The big idea from a tiny state that could change the world', *Guardian*, 2 December, www.theguardian.com/world/2012/dec/01/bhutan-wealth-happiness-counts
80 Mishra, Vidhyapati 2013 'Bhutan is no Shangri-La', *New York Times*, 28 June, www.nytimes.com/2013/06/29/opinion/bhutan-is-no-shangri-la.html
81 Schumacher 1973.
82 Bible, Vanessa 2018 *Terania Creek and the Forging of Modern Environmental Activism*,, Springer, Cham.
83 Gandhi, Mohandas K. 1927 *Gandhi: An Autobiography*, Navajivan Publishing House, Ahmedabad.
84 Fry and Souillac 2021.

Chapter 5

PEACE HISTORY: MUSEUMS, MEMORIALS, PARKS AND GARDENS

History is an important aspect of culture and its transmission. Ranging from the distant past to the present moment, it is often passed on through museums and memorials which can be found in a diversity of places, from great palaces such as Versailles to humble sheds, from parks, statues and fountains in town squares down to small plaques. More subtly, it can also be encapsulated in the names of towns, streets and parks. Although often purporting to tell the objective truth, subjectivity usually exists in the choice of what narratives are portrayed, what stories are minimised or ignored, who tells those stories and how they are told. History and its institutions can support militarism, colonialism, racism, sexism, homophobia, transphobia, ageism and ableism. Alternatively, they can actively strive to counter them and to create positive peace. This chapter will explore these issues, firstly through an Australian lens before expanding to an international perspective to examine pro-peace museums, memorials, parks and gardens, and find lessons which are globally applicable.

The Militarisation of History

It has been argued that Australia's major cultural institutions are in crisis and its history is being militarised.[1] History and culture writer Paul Daley claims that while there is no shortage of funding for upgrades to the Australian War Memorial, and more than $100 million is available for 'a questionable ANZAC [Australian and New Zealand Army Corps] "interpretive centre" in France', a number of Australia's national cultural institutions, such as the National Museum of Australia, National Portrait Gallery, Museum of Australian Democracy, National Film and Sound Archive, National Gallery of Australia and National Library, have faced major funding cuts. This, Daley argues,

> all alludes, of course, to an ever-increasing militarisation of Australian history at the expense of other narratives – the peaceful transition to a federation, the murders of tens of thousands of Indigenous Australians, the significant role of women, for example – that also define national foundation.[2]

The ANZAC myth continues to play a major role in Australian society. On 25 April 1915, Australian and New Zealand soldiers (ANZACs) formed part of an allied (Entente) expedition that attempted to capture the Gallipoli peninsula from the Ottoman Empire. After eight months of fighting, the expedition was abandoned in January 1916, with approximately 250,000 casualties on each side. Despite its ineffectiveness and high cost to human lives, the expedition is remembered on ANZAC Day, celebrated annually in Australia and New Zealand. The ANZAC story has changed over time, from one of horror at the carnage of World War I, deep sadness and grieving, anger at British leadership incompetence and Australian obedience, and revulsion of war. Now it is a story that glorifies the ANZACs and posits them as a vital part of Australia's emergence as a nation.[3]

A very different narrative to the current one – an anti-war narrative – emerged after World War I but was gradually drowned out by powerful forces such as the Returned Service League. Massive resources have been thrown at maintaining and deepening the current dominant narrative, such as the controversial redevelopment of the Australian War Memorial, strongly opposed by the Medical Association for Prevention of War.[4]

Aboriginal Stories

This resourcing is to the detriment of numerous other stories that could be told about Australia – such as depictions of Aboriginal resistance to dispossession, like the nonviolent Gurindji land rights struggle movingly depicted in the classic song 'From Little Things, Big Things Grow', by Kev Carmody and Paul Kelly, a song now widely used to support nonviolent struggles.

One Australian case study is that of Wiradjuri leader Windradyne (c. 1800–1829). Named 'Saturday' by the colonial authorities, he was a resistance leader who, after the massacres of many of his relations, led a proud and dignified delegation of Wiradjuri warriors in late December 1824 to the early colonial settlement of Parramatta to call for peace.[5] He addressed the governor, calling for an end to the killing and wearing a hat with 'peace' written in English on it. Despite the dispossession of their land and major impacts on their lives, some traditions which the Wiradjuri were able to maintain include consensus decision-making and conflict resolution without reference to outside forces such as the police. Wiradjuri people were also active in the Aborigines Progressive Association which challenged the living conditions of Aboriginal people in New South Wales (NSW). They lobbied the government and churches for Aboriginal rights for citizenship and education, and they helped organise the first Day of Mourning in Sydney on 26 January 1938.[6]

Dinawan Dyirrabang, otherwise known as Uncle[i] Bill Allen, a Wiradjuri Elder and a direct descendant of Windradyne, as well as a former soldier in the Australian Army, continues this advocacy today. He argues that because of the wars of extermination directed against Aboriginal people across the continent, 'my family and all of us descendants afterwards [...] have all lost out on [our] birthrights. Our rights to learn to speak our language properly, know where our cultural sites are and learn more about our culture'.[7] On 25 April, ANZAC Day, Dyirrabang and the Wiradjuri people continue to remember Windradyne as a 'true patriot', and Dyirrabang believes that indigenous people who fought in frontier conflicts across the nation should be acknowledged on ANZAC Day.

Other Overlooked Histories

Is there racism in forefronting the story of Gallipoli rather than those of Windradyne and other resistance leaders such as Pemulwuy, Jandamarra or the Gurindji? Why aren't more resources devoted to celebrating the suffragette movement, which ensured that Australia was one of the first countries to secure voting rights for women? Why is there such little recognition of Australia's environmental movements, which have often led the way internationally, such as the first forest blockades, the introduction of active resistance (such as tripods and burials), successful resistance to uranium mining at Jabiluka or the successful nonviolent campaign to save the Franklin River in which more than a thousand people were arrested?

All these have contributed immensely to the makeup of Australia yet are far less well-known and don't have national holidays or dedicated, well-funded chunks of the school curricula. They also tend to involve nonviolence, so the privileging of histories of violent actions over nonviolent ones reinforces popular perceptions that violence is acceptable, important and effective (despite Gallipoli being a military disaster), whereas nonviolence supposedly doesn't work or is unimportant. (Maciej Bartkowski's *Recovering Nonviolent History*[8] gives a detailed discussion of this issue internationally.)

---

i 'Uncle' is a term denoting an Australian Aboriginal Elder (senior community member and co-leader).

The Perils of Critiquing Militaristic Paradigms

This is a sensitive issue that often provokes savage personal attacks on social media. Some argue that ANZAC Day should be an apolitical day of respect and remembrance, while others such as former SBS[ii] presenter Scott McIntyre claim that the 'cultification of an imperialist invasion of a foreign nation that Australia had no quarrel with is against all ideals of modern society'.[9]

McIntyre was fired after posting a series of comments about Anzac Day on Twitter, which referred to some Australians marking Anzac Day as 'poorly read, largely white, nationalist drinkers and gamblers'. To his 30,000 followers, he talked about

> Remembering the summary execution, widespread rape and theft committed by these 'brave' Anzacs in Egypt, Palestine and Japan. [...] Not forgetting that the largest single-day terrorist attacks in history were committed by [the USA] & their allies in Hiroshima & Nagasaki.[10]

Writer Yassmin Abdel-Magied also outraged some Australians by publishing an Anzac Day Facebook post under the title 'Lest We Forget', suggesting that Australians should also remember the suffering occurring on Nauru and Manus Island, where asylum seekers have been detained for years, and the violence and oppression in Syria and Palestine. The backlash was such that she felt forced to leave Australia.[11]

Given that Australia's wars overseas are supposedly to defend democracy and free speech, is there a contradiction in that comments such as those by Abdel-Magied and McIntyre resulted in censure, abuse and sacking? Or is there some line in the sand which they crossed?

On the other hand, small gestures can be significant cultural shifts. One *Creating Cultures of Peace* student noted that:

> A simple example of how a gesture of reconciliation can pave the way for positive peace is the way that the incoming Prime Minister Anthony Albanese directed that all his press conferences would include the Indigenous Flag alongside the Australian Flag in the background. The cultural significance of this decision is potentially far-reaching and transformative, paving the way for the acceptance of more substantial reforms in this policy space.

---

ii SBS (Special Broadcasting Service) is an Australian multicultural broadcaster in television, radio and online.

War Memorials

War memorials impact on different people in different ways. A memorial may, for some people, inspire them with thoughts of the bravery and self-sacrifice shown by many military personnel and lead them to enlist in the armed forces. For others, the same memorial may lead to great sadness about the human condition, resulting in despondency and even depression. Still others may come away with a determination to work in peace education to reduce the incidence of wars.

In some cases, the work may be subtle, allowing viewers to draw their own conclusions. In others, the architect of the memorial may have wanted audiences to have a particular emotion or thought – and this is where an architect or artist who has engaged in peace education or at least considered how their work may lead to peace could influence viewers over the life of the memorial.

Sometimes the communities where the memorial is to be sited will have a say in the creation of the memorial. They may even have initiated it as a grassroots project, such as the memorial to the Myall Creek massacre of Australian Aboriginal people by settler colonists.

This messaging will often involve a delicate balancing act. Can a memorial (such as a sculpture) impart a peace message without being too obvious or didactic? Will some people miss the message, and does this matter? Some of the best artworks can be very subtle, requiring the viewer to do some work until they get a 'lightbulb moment' and come away inspired by the artist's understated cleverness and vision. Some examples include Aboriginal artist Michael Brogan's artworks on blankets, which represent Aboriginal poverty following paternalistic dispossession, or some of the pieces in a touring '*Bimblebox: art – science – nature*' multimedia exhibition, which critique the ecological violence of coal mining near a nature reserve.[12]

Militarised Central Public Spaces

War memorials are often in the geographical centre of towns, and this has symbolic significance in that local authorities seemingly deem them a central part of our lives. This practice seems much less prevalent in some countries, such as France, Japan and Ireland, but Australian examples include a prominent statue of a soldier at the crossroads in the NSW regional town of Dorrigo, and a memorial garden in the centre of Central Park in Armidale, the city where the University of New England is situated. In Hyde Park in Sydney's central business district, the War Memorial is a mammoth structure that dominates the southern part of this popular park. 'The Bullets' sculpture by Australian Aboriginal artist Tony Albert, installed in 2015 on the west side of the War Memorial, may be seen as maintaining a culture of militarism, but it is also an important recognition of the many Aboriginal servicemen and women who engaged in courageous, dedicated military service for Australia yet were given little recognition afterwards, and in many cases were barred from ex-services clubs until recently.

The highway between Sydney, Australia's economic powerhouse, and Canberra, the nation's capital, is called 'Remembrance Driveway', with its rest stops dedicated to war heroes. All were men. This militarised road to the capital is further emphasised by the siting of the new and former parliament houses in line with the Australian War Memorial and its avenue. Why is there no road recognising suffragettes or activists for land rights, social justice, environment and peace? In Canberra, most suburbs and many buildings are named after men, such as previous prime ministers. (Australia has had one woman prime minister, Julia Gillard, who endured extraordinarily sexist jibes, such as by then Opposition Leader Tony Abbott. Her response was a powerful speech known as 'The Misogyny Speech', voted in 2020 by readers of *The Guardian Australia* as the most unforgettable moment in Australian TV history.)

Militarism and National Leadership

Many of the nation's governors-general and the states' governors, usually men, have been military personnel, although occasionally these men speak against the militaristic status quo. For example, an ANZAC Day speechby Peter Underwood, governor of Tasmania,[13] gave a strongly pro-peace viewpoint that challenged orthodox views of the ANZAC legend and advocated spending less on 'the ANZAC festival' and more on Peace Studies. It's important when such prominent figures (including novelist Richard Flanagan) voice such views, particularly when there is often such vehement and even vitriolic opposition to those views, such as in online forums. Even governors, however, are not immune to tabloid attacks.[14]

The Australian Army was utilised for a widely criticised 'Intervention' in remote Aboriginal communities in the Northern Territory and later tasked to lead COVID-response teams – the implication being that militaries can be trusted and are good organisers and leaders. As we saw in Chapter 2, legendary novelist Ursula Le Guin argues the opposite.

Alternative 'Landscapes of Remembrance'

An article titled 'The Landscapes of Remembrance' argues that:

> So often with conventional sites of mourning associated with war, there is highly selective remembering. The frequently reiterated secular prayer of nationalism about 'Lest we forget' is about remembering those who have sacrificed their lives on the battlefield. It is rarely about prompting celebrations about human capacities to work together to transcend destructive conflicts. That is why, from a peace education perspective, it is important to create wherever possible, whether within the formal classroom context or outside, opportunities for creative dialogue on nonviolent pathways and inclusive learning environments.[15]

The article investigates some alternative 'landscapes of remembrance' or 'sites of conscience', such as the grassroots-driven memorial site for the Myall Creek massacre, and Canberra's SIEVX memorial, which remembers the 2001 drowning of 353 refugees between Indonesia and Christmas Island. Other sites discussed also memorialise terrible events but all of them have a dedication to reconciliation, cultivating peaceful relations across cultures, building peace, forging bonds of friendship and aiming for a world free of war. The authors emphasise 'the importance of resisting militarizing "mental maps" [because] such "maps" imply inevitability about future wars'.[16] Instead, they advocate:

> finding constructive ways to respond to the relative silence about peace culture. [...] the value of working with the idea of 'sites of conscience' [...] exploring sites of alternative history that give possible insights, for example, about nonviolent activism and the value of empathetic imagination.[17]

Fabio Carbone proposes that war museums could be considered as local infrastructures for peace, a platform binding together tourism and post-conflict peacebuilding. Acknowledging that just showing the horrors of war is not enough to persuade audiences of the need for peace, he asserts that through the application of a 'forgiveness model', a new kind of war museum narrative could be created, resulting in 'inclusive, participatory experiences aimed at locals and tourists, particularly when the latter come from countries that took part in the conflict as opponents of the former'.[18]

A Changing Cultural Landscape

Peace movements have been a dissenting voice in the militarisation of history, challenging it and providing alternative narratives. For example, the Medical Association for the Prevention of War vocally opposed the Australian War Memorial's sponsorship deals with big global weapons manufacturers, such as BAE and Lockheed Martin, claiming these impede the objectivity of its programmes and blur the 'distinction between commemoration [...] and entertainment'.[19] Others have called for governments to stop spending millions on the dead and focus on living veterans.[20]

Penrith Regional Gallery and other galleries have hosted a 2016–2019 national touring exhibition *Black Mist, Burnt Country,* which tells the story of British nuclear testing in Australia, its impact, and protests about it. Around 110,000 visitors saw the exhibition during this period, and many more experienced it online and through the media. Feedback indicated that visitors were shocked, moved and sometimes brought to tears hearing about the suffering of the Aṉangu Aboriginal people.

> [M]any visitors were surprised to learn about the ongoing long-lasting contamination of the land, continuous health issues affecting Aboriginal communities and nuclear veterans; the persistent and increased threat of nuclear weapons; and repeated attempts to make the Maralinga lands and other parts of Aboriginal country the location for the storage of Australia's (highly radioactive) nuclear wastes.[21]

War museums occasionally feature anti-war perspectives, such as 'Peace', a Shrine of Remembrance exhibition in Melbourne (2012–13). London's Imperial War Museum in 2017 mounted *People Power: Fighting for Peace* [sic], a show about the British anti-war and peace movement. Reaching beyond the activist world, the international art magazine Apollo noted that:

> It's this graphic – in every sense – response to war that defines so much protest art, most notably in the macabre, skull-laden creations of the brilliant anti-nuclear campaigner Peter Kennard, whose early works hang next to a banner painted by Kenneth Hockney (father of the celebrated artist David Hockney). This reaches a climax with David Gentleman's anti-Iraq art in 2002, with its ubiquitous and casual splatter of blood like something from *Reservoir Dogs*. It feels like the industrialisation of peace, a passive aggressive conclusion to a thoughtful and moving exhibition.[22]

Is there value in these small 'voices in the wilderness', or are they drowned out by the noise of the wealthier militarists? How could these voices for peace grow?

More Cultural Shifts towards Positive Peace

In 2020, the killing of African American George Floyd by a US police officer sparked a global upsurge in the 'Black Lives Matter' movement, with major cultural implications. As well as calls for stronger regulations and less funding for police, numerous statues of people who made their wealth and fame through exploitation (such as Cecil Rhodes at Oxford University) have been torn down or are being reconsidered. Some believe that these statues are important historically and should be preserved in museums rather than destroyed, albeit with a fuller and more honest story presented.

Another alternative to simply tearing down offensive statues and monuments which portray outdated or racist views of history is to engage in 'dialogical memorialisation' which does not erase other versions of history but respectfully disputes and counters them, 'where one view of the past takes issue with another and history is seen, not as some final statement, but a contingent and contested narrative'.[23]

Meanwhile, the state flag of Mississippi is being redesigned to remove the confederate flag, and the names of the Dixie Chicks band and some Disney World rides are changing, as is Wiltshire Street in Alice Springs, Central Australia, named after a renowned murderer and sexual predator of Aboriginal people. A number of TV programmes deemed racist have been removed, including Netflix pulling four series by Chris Lilley. Some people, such as Vanessa Thorpe, argue, however, that 'panic-erasing' distracts from what really matters: employing more ethnically diverse people on and off screen.[24]

Although, sadly, it was the death of a man that led to these changes, there has been a significant international cultural shift in a very short time. However, much cultural and structural violence remains.

Name Changes

The momentum for these changes had been building for some time. Chapter 2 noted the importance of language, and in recent years, there have been moves to change event and place names to make Australia more inclusive or to remove things that are offensive to some groups of people. For example, Ayers Rock reverted to the Aboriginal name Uluru in 1993, while recently Aboriginal people and supporters have successfully changed the name of an inner Melbourne electorate from Batman to Cooper, arguing that Melbourne's founder John Batman was accused of involvement in the massacre of Aboriginal people. 'Cooper' instead commemorates Yorta Yorta activist and leader William Cooper.[25]

In Woolgoolga, NSW, some organisations, such as the Wiigulga Sports Complex, are reverting to the more phonetically correct *Wiigulga*, a Gumbaynggirr word for the black apple tree found locally, after which the town is named.[26] The Australian Wildlife Conservancy's newest wildlife sanctuary is acknowledged as 'located on the Traditional Lands of the Worimi

Nation', and they are consulting with the Local Aboriginal Land Council on an appropriate name.[27] A 2023 ABC documentary, *Australia's Wild Odyssey*, narrated by Aboriginal actor Deborah Mailman, features Aboriginal Elders such as Uncle Micklo Jarrett detailing Gumbaingirr names for places within his traditional lands.

There are calls to rename other places, such as Coutts Crossing, NSW (named after an alleged mass murderer), which has sparked fierce online debate.[28] Some claim that these incidents happened a long time ago and don't really matter now, and that 'Leaving it as it is acknowledges history'. An opposing comment is: 'Imagine your family were murdered and the place they were murdered was named after the murderer? It's that simple! Have some respect! The past is only the past if it didn't directly affect you!!! Murder resonates for generations.' From this viewpoint, it is 'not just about a name change – it's about learning our history and reconciling with Aboriginal people'.

Another example of this growing movement is the decision to move Triple J radio station's 'Hottest 100' programme away from 26 January, currently known widely as 'Australia Day' but by Aboriginal people as 'Invasion Day'. Former federal communications minister Mitch Fifield said he was 'bewildered' by the decision: 'The ABC shouldn't be buying into this debate. Australia Day is our national day. The ABC should honour it and not mess with the Hottest 100'.[29] Aboriginal songwriter Dan Sultan, however, welcomed the announcement: 'To have it on a day that essentially celebrates genocide is disgusting and it's embarrassing. And for me, as an Indigenous person, it's hurtful and it's harmful'.[30]

Peace Museums

As we've seen, history and memorials can either perpetuate militarism, structural and cultural violence or help to cultivate peace. We now turn our focus to an important way of creating cultures of peace – peace museums. These generally share a commitment to making the world a more peaceful place, but they may go about it in quite different ways. For example, the rationale of the World Peace Museum (www.amsterdam.info/worldpeace) in Amsterdam is

> apolitical, points to dangers of nationalism and isolationism, explains the causes of war and violence of all kinds and focuses on the peace-making moments in Europe's history. The Museum points to the necessary change in education for future generations.

There's also a subtle challenge to capitalism in their admissions policy, which states:

> You may decide yourself about the admission price, any contribution, even the smallest one will be accepted. Also, a small object which expresses the feeling of peace, will be taken by the museum as your admission donation. Many of these items are exhibited in the museum's reception hall.

Museums for peace are usually non-profit educational institutions that promote a culture of peace through collecting, displaying and interpreting peace-related material. Museums for peace inform the public about peace and nonviolent action using illustrations from the lives of individuals; the work of organisations; campaigns; and historical events. One of the strengths of museums for peace is that they can reach out to and involve a broad general public, many of whom might not be involved in the peace movement per se. Every museum for peace tells its own story, displays different peace-related artefacts and focuses on different periods and places in the history of peace.

There are peace museums around the world, with notable ones in Bradford, Teheran and Hiroshima. Many African countries, such as Namibia, Kenya, Tanzania, Rwanda and Sierra Leone, have a Peace Museum, as do Sri Lanka, Bangladesh, Cambodia and Lithuania. The Czech Republic, Netherlands, Germany, Korea, Taiwan, China and United States all have multiple peace museums, but Japan is the world leader in terms of sheer numbers, with 68 listed in a listing of 'Museums for Peace Worldwide' by Kazuyo Yamane and her colleagues.[31]

The Hiroshima Peace Museum

The Hiroshima museum is probably the best known of these, telling the horrific story of the impact of the first nuclear bomb used in war, which was dropped on 6 August 1945 on a civilian population of an entire city. Hiroshima had some military targets, and the museum has little on Japan's militarism that led it to invade Manchuria in 1931 (parodied by Hergé in the Tintin comic *Le Lotus Bleu*) and to attack Pearl Harbour on 7 December 1941. However, with an estimated death toll of 140,000 people,[32] only a few thousand of whom were Japanese Army soldiers, the bomb blast also killed more than 130,000 civilians, including women and the elderly, who had little to do with the war. The most heartbreaking stories were of Hiroshima's babies and children, who had *nothing* to do with the war. *They were entirely innocent victims of the violence of adults, taken to extremes by military-industrial technology.*

Some died instantly; others in agony in the following days and weeks; many more died years later from cancers. This targeting of innocent people en masse could be considered a war crime, but 'victors' justice' – where the winners of a war decide how post-war justice will be meted out – ensured that no prosecutions have occurred. The exhibitions suggest that the bombs were dropped on Hiroshima and Nagasaki (a less well-known but equally horrific story) when Japan was already virtually defeated and suing for peace, and they were more about an anti-Soviet exercise in geopolitical power by the United States, and using a new weapon developed at great public expense.

Although the museum is popular and there is a constant, long queue at the entrance, the exhibitions are harrowing and there is little to inspire faith in humanity, apart from some material at the end on movements to outlaw nuclear weapons. More positively, there is a flame in the surrounding park which will burn continuously until there are no more nuclear weapons.

> No-one can see the flame in the Hiroshima Peace Memorial Park [...] without realizing with new urgency that nuclear weapons must be abolished from the face of the earth. No one can visit No Gun Ri [...] without understanding in a new way the cruelty of war. No one can visit Auschwitz without feeling tremendous grief, but also new energy to promote education and understanding among peoples.[33]

The Hiroshima Peace Memorial's work is ably supported by the nearby Hiroshima Museum of Art, also built on the ruins of the bomb and 'intended to solace the minds not only of the citizens of Hiroshima but also of the public in general, and also to offer a prayer for the repose of the souls of the victims of the Atomic Bomb'.[34] With a small but world-class collection, including some exquisite gems of post-impressionism by Cezanne, Van Gogh and Seurat, its theme is 'For Love and Peace'. This work is also supported by other institutions internationally, such as India's No More Hiroshima, No More Nagasaki Peace Museum, which warns of the dangers of nuclear weapons, exacerbated by the regional arms race between India and Pakistan, and reminds people of the fragility of peace.

Other Peace Museums

The Tehran Peace Museum (tehranpeacemuseum.org) is housed within the historic City Park. A member of the International Network of Museums for Peace, it is both a museum and an interactive peace centre, coordinating a peace education programme and hosting conferences and the Iranian secretariat for the international organisation Mayors for Peace. It has workspaces and a peace library complemented by online resources on its website. Within an overall context of promoting peace and raising awareness of the devastating impacts of war, it focuses on the health and environmental impacts of chemical weapons.

The Peace Museum in Bradford (peacemuseum.org.uk) aims 'to be seen as a national resource that educates and inspires people for peace, using a unique collection of artefacts and stories. The Peace Museum explores the history and the often untold stories of peace, peacemakers, social reform and peace movements.'

This uncovering of untold stories is an important way of countering museums and historical practices that privilege militarism by focusing entirely or mainly on 'great' battles and leaders. By contrast, subaltern museums and histories often examine the quieter achievers, the people who work for peace in ways that don't always attract headlines at the time or even afterwards but that nevertheless may create a significant impact on society. This impact may not be obvious until long afterwards, but it may be more lasting than headline-grabbing violence.

Peace Museums may be constructed to:

- remember and honour the innocent victims of a war or massacre,
- provide solace to survivors and bereaved families,
- reveal the truth about a war, genocide or massacre,
- promote peace and human rights,
- prevent and abolish war and military forces,
- challenge militaristic cultures,
- outlaw nuclear weapons and other weapons of mass destruction,
- contribute to the making of a more just, sustainable and peaceful world,
- prevent historical traumas or conflicts caused by war from taking place in societies today, and
- educate people about nonviolent activism, peacemaking, peacebuilding, reconciliation and conflict transformation.

They usually try to do this from a perspective that is constructive, future-oriented and peace-promoting. Other examples of peace museums include one in Sierra Leone (www.slpeacemuseum.org) and The Australian Living Peace Museum, an online museum that presents narratives of peacemaking, nonviolent social change and alternative forms of resistance to war and violence. Artistic elements include drawings and photographs of both war and pioneering peacemakers (www.livingpeacemuseum.org.au).

Mexico maintains a Museum of Memory and Tolerance (www.myt.org.mx) in Mexico city. The museum is well-balanced in that the 'memory' section remembers genocides and crimes against humanity such as in Rwanda and

Guatemala, while the 'tolerance' section is more positive, solutions-oriented and forward-looking, addressing issues such as dialogue, empathy towards all humanity, human rights, the power of the media and the benefits of diversity. It aims to engender a sense of responsibility, respect and consciousness in every visitor, who is then invited to be a generator of change through social action.

Alternative World War II Memorials

In Austria, there is now a memorial for World War II deserters, some of whom deserted for conscientious reasons, yet were criminalised by the Nazis (and executed if they were caught), and were still officially deemed traitors by Austria as late as 2009, when the Austrian parliament finally agreed to rehabilitate their reputations.

Across France are museums dedicated to World War II resistance, much of which was nonviolent and women-led (see Chapter 9). The one in Lyon is exceptional but in places chilling, being situated in a former Gestapo headquarters. The exhibitions are encapsulated in the book *War in a City,*[35] published in English and French. Lyon's museum and numerous others also memorialise the deportations to death camps, in which so many French people were complicit.

One such museum is particularly inspiring. Situated in the village of Le Chambon-sur-Lignon, it celebrates the extraordinary bravery of its inhabitants in World War II, when they opened their homes and their hearts to Jewish children and other refugees. They sheltered them in the village under the noses of convalescing German *Wehrmacht* soldiers and on the remote farms and forests of this central plateau of France. The discretion, courage and solidarity of the community were unbreakable. Although some of the protectors lost their lives, the community hid around 800 refugees, with perhaps 3,000 passing through.[36] The memorial has sections on civil, spiritual and armed resistance, pedagogical activities for schools, a bilingual book, and creative, innovative and engaging multimedia exhibitions, including the 2023 exhibition of drawings titled *Cabu: Dessins de la Rafle du Vel D'Hiv*. The village is one of only three places named as 'Righteous Among the Nations' by the Yad Vashem Institute in Jerusalem.

These museums are valuable sites of peace education.

> [O]ur museums do much more than give us pleasure. They also teach us. They teach us to appreciate talent, to marvel at greatness, to remember tragedy, to reflect on the past. In a world where we spend more and more time in front of a computer, seeing virtual representations of life, a museum is doubly important, because it presents us with tangible items: the rough surface of a painting, the desk of a great writer, the shoe of a Holocaust victim.

> Museums have as much power to educate as any university. They have as much power to interpret history as any book. They have as much power to inspire as any speaker. And because of this, they can affect the future. Museums are much more than storehouses of history. They shape the way we think, and the way we act. That is precisely why it is so essential to build museums and memorials to celebrate peace. The delicate balance of a peace negotiation requires just as much control and mastery as the brushstrokes of Monet. The pen that signs a peace treaty must be held with just as much confidence as Michelangelo's chisel. And the peacemaker faces just as much controversy and criticism as the men and women who are more usually celebrated in traditional museums – public figures, generals, scholars and artists. Museums that present to humanity the history of violence, and of nonviolence, are essential to building a better future.[37]

Internationalising Peace Museums

Peace museums are becoming more organised as a global network able to share information and resources, collaborate, support each other and build synergies. One sign of this is the growing strength and sophistication of the International Network of Museums for Peace (INMP), which began in Bradford, England, in 1992 at the first International Conference of Peace Museums, with a topic of 'Bringing Peace to People'. INMP now has more than 100 member institutions, including museums, peace gardens, libraries and galleries that work for peace. In 2022, INMP celebrated its thirtieth anniversary with a hybrid webinar, and the abstracts were later printed in a booklet accompanied by QR codes that enable access to each speaker's presentation video.

This initiative could also be viewed as ineffectual voices in the wilderness. Alternatively, it can be seen as a growing network of inspirational institutions working towards common goals of peace education (see Chapter 8), persevering against tremendous militaristic and economic forces. Given more support, they could grow as torch bearers spreading peaceful light, kindling imaginations and inciting nonviolent fervour, illuminating the world with a gentle but persistent anti-war flame.

Peace Parks

One alternative to parks which celebrate, condone or perpetuate war and militarism is the phenomenon of peace parks. A prime example is the Hiroshima Peace Memorial Park, where the Hiroshima Peace Memorial Museum is situated (see Figures 5.1 and 5.2). The park is filled with poignant sculptures, the

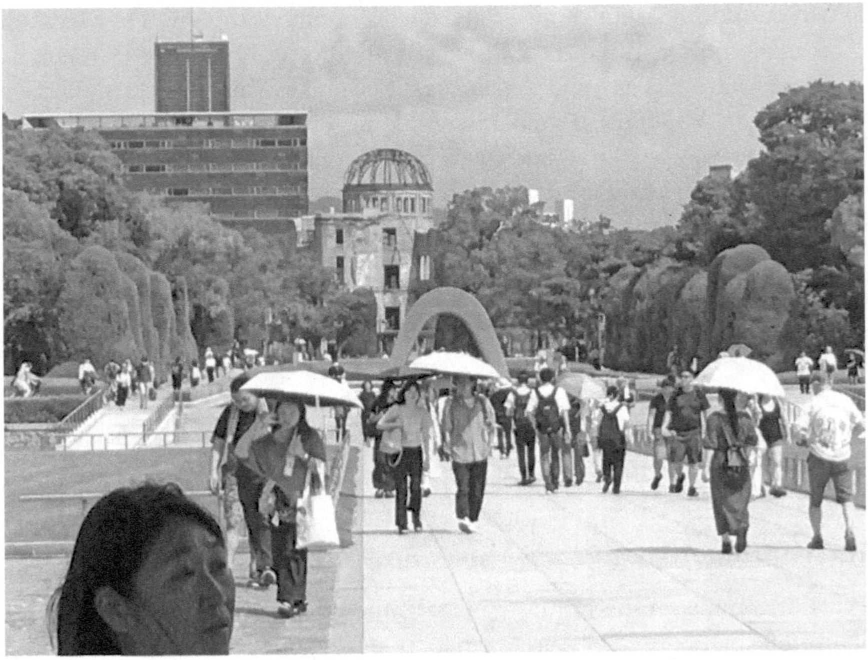

Figure 5.1 Hiroshima Peace Park with Genbaku Dome in background.

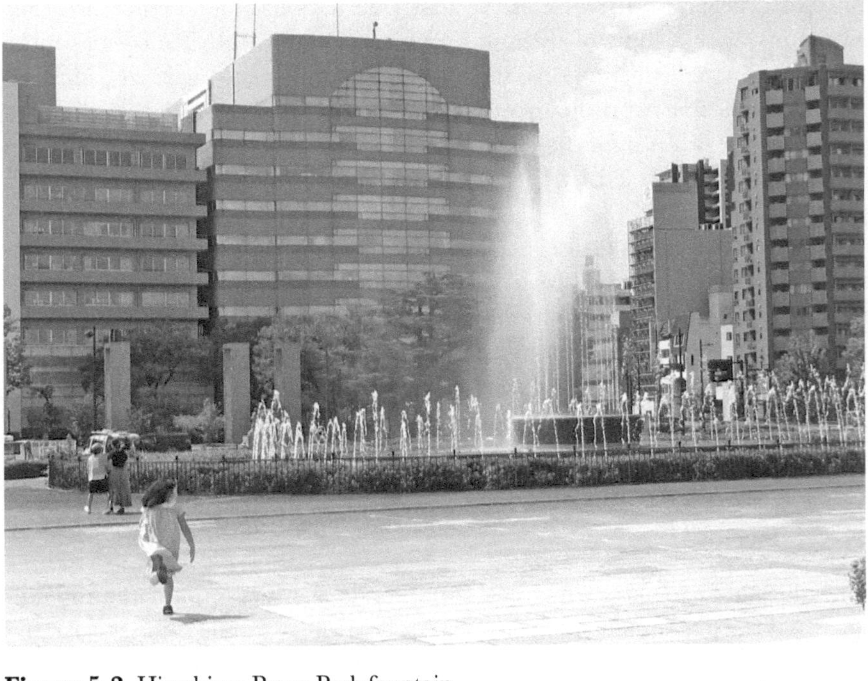

Figure 5.2 Hiroshima Peace Park fountain.

Genbaku Dome (the only structure left standing in the area where the atomic bomb exploded), dynamic fountains and a bell where prayers can be offered for peace and for the souls lost in the bombing. There's also a shop with many items promoting peace and remembrance.

As with histories and museums, parks and gardens are contested spaces. Frequently, they are used to remember wars and those who died in them – usually the fallen soldiers, and much less often the civilian victims of war, including women and children. As noted above, central to many of Australia's public parks, such as Armidale's Central Park, are war memorials. Other parks memorialise pioneer movements or logging, such as Armidale's McDonald Park; these tend to emphasise the male side of history, as well as ignoring or glossing over unpalatable aspects of that history, such as the dispossession and massacres of Aboriginal people that occurred at the same time as and enabled those European pioneer movements.

Much more rarely are there parks that commemorate the countless people who have engaged in advocacy and nonviolent action to make the world a better place, such as through unionism and other social change movements. One exception in Armidale is a small but beautiful corner of a park dedicated to the memory of environmentalist, land rights advocate and poet Judith Wright, and planted with native trees and shrubs. Such parks are all the more remarkable because, unlike war memorials, which are usually well-supported by governments and ex-services organisations, peace and nonviolence parks tend to have less political, institutional, corporate and financial support.

Sometimes there are public gardens and walks designed explicitly for peace. Often, these also aim to recognise the hard work and sacrifice that many people have put into making more peaceful cultures yet have rarely been acknowledged for this. Some examples include the Wellington Peace Heritage Walk and the Auckland Peace Heritage Walk.

Peace parks may be created for numerous purposes and include protected areas crossing borders or used sympathetically across boundaries. They may exist for nature preservation or protection from the drastic damages that war and military exercises can bring. Cross-border cooperation for environmental reasons builds sustainable peace,[38] and so the creation of such parks can lead to increased peace between countries[39] especially when both countries work together for broader environmental purposes, such as global warming mitigation and adaptation. One of the first such parks was created between the states of Alberta (Canada) and Montana (USA) in the hope of promoting cohesive park management.[40] These trans-boundary protected areas continue to increase in number and size in some countries, acting as biological refuges along international boundaries and benefitting the public rather than minority private interests. They promote negotiation, compromise and cooperation between countries, especially in areas of ecotourism, giving locals a chance at an alternative livelihood, for example through jobs as rangers, caretakers or tour guides. Antarctica, with its treaty system, can also be viewed as a peace park for tourism, ecological and scientific research purposes. Each country that has signed the treaty cooperates within the various aspects of the 'park'.

Far from a peace park, the demilitarised zone between North and South Korea nevertheless preserves an uneasy truce between these countries which share a language and traditional culture. Although strewn with around two million land mines, there is plenty of wildlife living precariously, as well as blue-painted UN huts where the two sides have occasionally met for talks during rare periods of détente. In 2018, both sides cancelled their border propaganda broadcasts, and a no-fly zone has been established. Clearing of mines has commenced as part of their recent tension-reduction steps.[41]

Peace Gardens

Gardens, like parks, have long been viewed as places of refuge from the trials of the world, from the traffic noise and 'foetid air and gritty of the dusty, dirty city', in the words of poet A. B. 'Banjo' Paterson's classic 1889 poem *Clancy of the Overflow*. They can provide an escape and a place to recharge physically, mentally and spiritually.

Gardens can, paradoxically, be both fragile and resilient and can be found even in war zones or the most difficult of times. During World War I, soldiers built gardens along the trenches, and in World War II, gardens, grown for food resources, distraction, comfort and aesthetic purposes, could be found in ghettos and prisoner-of-war camps.[42] Gardens can even be a form of defiance and resistance, with Jaafar Hamid al Ali, the parks supervisor of Baghdad, saying that he and his team would plant something for every life lost in armed conflict; one worker remarked that: 'when you take care of gardens you forget the war'.[43]

Gardens are calming, therapeutic and hope-inducing. Gardens are valued in Bogota's squatter settlements in war-torn Colombia. One refugee from the violence, Luis Antonio Medina, grows a rooftop garden filled with plants from his native province of Boyaca: 'it serves both as a reminder of his former rural home and a place of solace and activity in the city'.[44]

Just as the Peace Museum in Hiroshima is surrounded by a Peace Park, the Memorial museum in Le Chambon-sur-Lignon in France has a 'Jardin de la Memoire' (Garden of Remembrance' (Figure 5.3)). This serene garden was designed by French landscape architect Louis Benech and donated by a

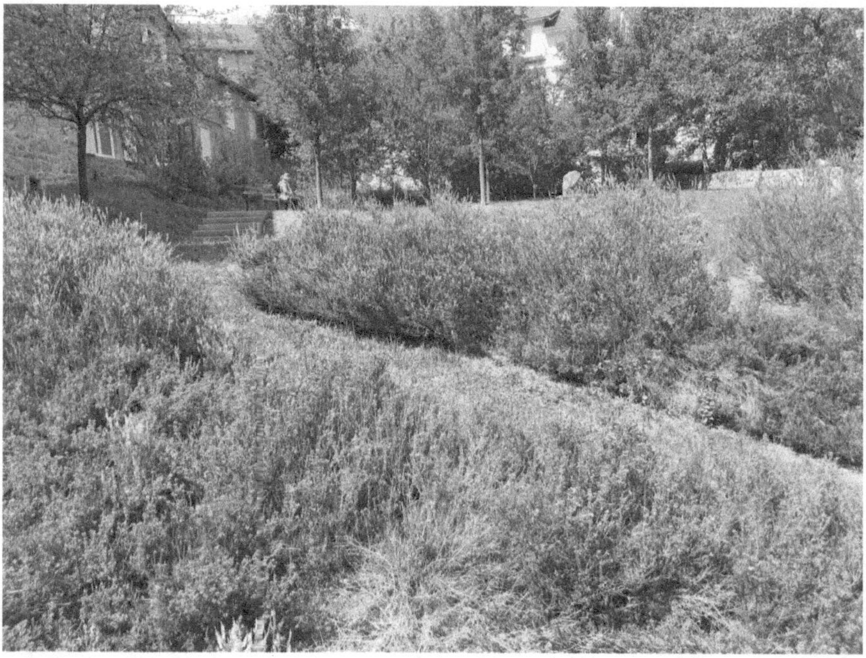

Figure 5.3 'Jardin de la Memoire' (Garden of Remembrance) in Le Chambon-sur-Lignon, France.

private sponsor whose mother was sheltered in Le Chambon in World War II. With colourful flowers, ancient walls and modern sculpture, it encourages reflection on the bravery that whole communities can show in the face of widespread racism, oppression, unthinking obedience and cowardice.

Gardens can also be a site of subtle resistance, positivity and Gandhi's 'constructive programme', which aims to build a better and more peaceful world. As Lalage Snow writes in her book *War Gardens: A Journey through Conflict in Search of Calm*:

> To garden in a time of crisis and conflict is to escape to 'a world within a lost world'. It is to rise above the 'horrid wilderness' – to treat war as an inconvenience. It is a refusal to accept a world defined by violence and destruction but instead create life.[45]

Radical Gardening

Reviewing George McKay's 2011 book *Radical Gardening: Politics, Idealism and Rebellion in the Garden*, Dianne Dentice at first wonders: 'how can gardening be radical and what does gardening have to do with politics?'[46] McKay shows, however, that even the most dismal human circumstances can be uplifted by a garden and that 'notions of utopia, of community, of activism for progressive social change, of peace, of environmentalism, of identity politics, are practically worked through in the garden, in floriculture, and through what Paul Gough has called "planting as a form of protest"'.[47] Rather than merely a suburban leisure activity, gardening can be a radical centre of what McKay calls *horticountercultural politics,* such as through the evolution of London's network of public peace gardens from the initial hope symbolised by the 'Peace' rose of 1945.

The most radical form of gardening is known as 'guerrilla gardening' although, unfortunately, militaristic terms permeate this quiet but important international movement, such as 'green-fingered vigilantes', 'seed bombs', 'arsenals of seeds' and 'activist call to arms'. Nevertheless, it reduces ecological violence by transforming public space into oases of colour and life, boosting biodiversity and growing food locally with minimal 'food miles'. It can also bring communities together and, by seizing local control of our shared environment and cherishing it, makes political statements about neglectful land ownership and anarchistic, nonviolent direct action.[48] In my experience of replacing exotic (foreign) creekland vegetation with more suitable co-evolved natives, better suited for endangered native fauna, it can also be physical exercise that is spiritually satisfying and therapeutic. Even the insecurity of these plantings, while stressful at times, encourages detachment. Ellen Miles enthuses that:

> From scattering wildflower seeds onto road verges to building community allotments on vacant lots, these peaceful acts of rebellion are where flower power meets people power.[49]

Permaculture

Permaculture (permanent agriculture) is a design system for ecological and sustainable living, involving the harmonious integration of landscape and people, providing their food, energy, shelter and other material and non-material needs in a self-sufficient and sustainable way (see Figures 5.4 and 5.5). It draws inspiration from nature to develop synergetic farming systems based on crop diversity, resilience, natural productivity and sustainability.

The founders of the permaculture system of gardening, Bill Mollison and David Holmgren, and leading teachers such as Robyn Francis also view gardening as a political and economic act of resistance, transformation, creativity

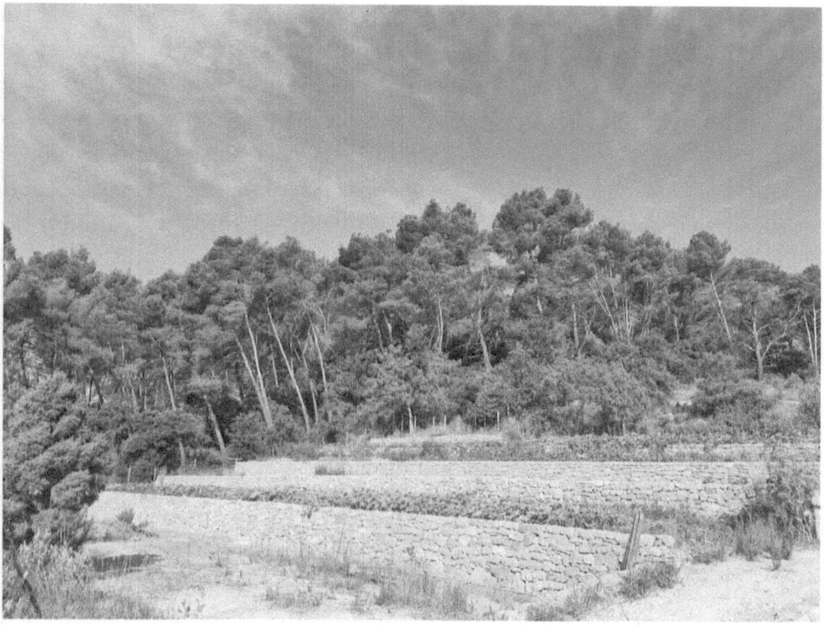

Figure 5.4 Permaculture farm 'Les Papillons Verts' in Provence, France.

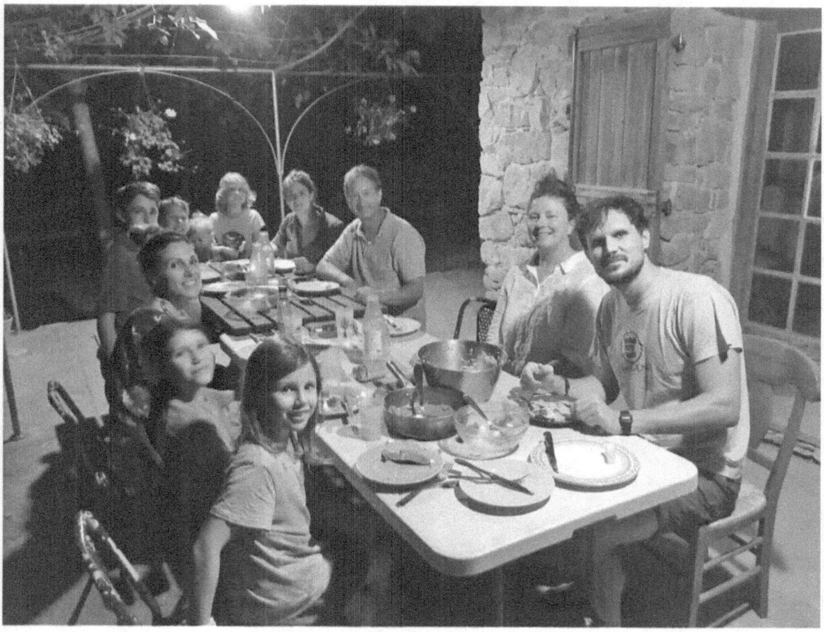

Figure 5.5 French, Italian and Australian permaculturists at 'Les Papillons Verts', Provence.

and positive change. For them, growing one's own food provides an alternative to industrialised corporate-controlled agribusiness, whose corporations (such as Dow Chemicals and Monsanto) have long had close associations with war. Large-scale use of herbicides, for example, has occurred in both massive monocultural agriculture projects and in the American war on Vietnam, to defoliate forests to reduce hiding places for combatants. There, carcinogenic herbicides such as Agent Orange were sprayed on almost 1.5 million hectares of forests and crops, causing famine, malnourishment and starvation. Four million Vietnamese people, as well as many American and Australian soldiers, were exposed to the chemicals, resulting in generations of horrific health effects.[50]

Permaculture is a localised response to the economic forces of globalised consumerism and ecological violence. It is grassroots seizure of an essential aspect of culture: food. As a holistic philosophy, drawing together food, water, local economies, homes and work into a radical synthesis with humans and nature at the centre, rather than corporations, it has much in common with bottom-up peacebuilding:

> [P]ermaculture is a holistic peacebuilding model that addresses war-induced environmental damage and post-conflict structural violence. Permaculture impacts multiple dimensions of practitioners' lives, functions as sustainable livelihood education, contributes to the eco-localisation of economies, and builds community between individuals while also creating a relationship of agency between natural environments and permaculture practitioners.[51]

Friendship Gardens

Madhu Suri Prakash supports such moves through a celebration of what she terms 'Friendship Gardens', which embrace the best ideals of Victory Gardens (gardens established to feed a nation during times of war). These go further, however, 'collapsing the dualisms separating victors from losers', turning enemies and strangers into friends and neighbours, as 'local grassroots initiatives continue flowering and blossoming' into community-supported agriculture, and replacing paradigms of growth and ecological and structural violence with alternative paradigms such as Gross National Happiness.[52]

> Friendships that transcend differences and honour diversity are among the many fruits and organic gifts harvested and shared in the commons created by Friendship Gardens. [...] It also joins many millions whose dreams are already taking flight while getting grounded: seeking to transform all our toxic lawnscapes into foodscapes; ending the disease

of billions going to bed starving amidst the mountains of food wasted for growing Wall Street profits in the twenty first century.[53]

*

This chapter has examined the perpetuation of militarism through mainstream histories, war museums and militarised public spaces. It has also shown that there are many pro-peace museums, memorials, parks and gardens which produce counter-narratives challenging war, militarism and all forms of direct, cultural and ecological violence. Each of these endeavours could be seen as a seed – small and seemingly insignificant. If, however, following the parable recounted in Matthew 13:20, the seed is planted in fertile soil rather than rocky ground, and watered with tears of grief, hope, determination, joy and solidarity, its descendants might be legion, fruitful and long-lasting.

Notes

1 Daley, Paul 2016 'Our major cultural institutions are in crisis – and our history is being militarised', *Guardian*, 22 February, www.theguardian.com/australia-news/postcolonial-blog/2016/feb/22/our-major-cultural-institutions-are-in-crisis-and-our-history-is-being-militarised

2 Ibid.

3 Donaldson, Carina and Marilyn Lake 2010 'Whatever happened to the anti-war movement?' in Marilyn Lake and Henry Reynolds with Mark McKenna and Joy Damousi (eds.), *What's Wrong With ANZAC? The Militarisation of Australian History*, University of NSW Press, Sydney, pp. 71–93.

4 See Wareham, Sue 2018 'How the Australian War Memorial has lost its way', *Pearls and Irritations*, 23 May, https://johnmenadue.com/sue-warehan-how-the-australian-war-memorial-has-lost-its-way/

5 Bathurst Regional Council n.d. 'Wiradjuri country, culture and heritage', *The Wiradjuri People*, p. 8, www.bathurst.nsw.gov.au/community/community_mm/aboriginal-people/92-community/aboriginal-people/190-wiradjuri-people.html

6 Bathurst Regional Council n.d., p. 9.

7 Cited in Knowles, Rachael 2022 'Should Frontier War heroes like Windradyne be recognised on ANZAC Day?' *NITV News*, 25 April, www.sbs.com.au/nitv/article/should-frontier-war-heroes-like-windradyne-be-recognised-on-anzac-day/z20phv7od

8 Bartkowski, Maciej J. 2013 *Recovering Nonviolent History*, Lynee Rienner Publishers, Boulder.

9 'SBS presenter sacked over "disrespectful" Anzac tweets', 2015 *BBC*, 26 April, www.bbc.com/news/world-australia-32476479

10 Ibid.

11 Stuart, David Douglas 2022 'Five years on from lest-we-forget Anzac Day controversy, Yassmin Abdel-Magied says she was "ahead of my time"', *ABC News*, 6 June, www.abc.net.au/news/2022-05-31/yassmin-abdel-magied-says-drama-finds-me-/101112186

12 Semmler, Erin 2019 'Bimblebox 153 birds art exhibition takes aim at coal mining, highlights environmental issues', *ABC News*, 14 March, www.abc.net.au/news/2019-03-14/bimblebox-153-birds-exhibition-takes-aim-at-coal-mining/10886712

13 Underwood, Peter 2014 'ANZAC day speech by Peter Underwood, Governor of Tasmania' 2014, *Social Alternatives*, vol. 33, no. 4, pp. 6–7.

14 See, for example, Bolt, Andrew 2014 'Tasmanian Governor Peter Underwood enters hall of shame over Anzac Day speech', *Herald Sun*, 28 April, www.heraldsun.com.au/news/opinion/tasmanian-governor-peter-underwood-enters-hall-of-shame-over-anzac-day-speech/news-story/08a10b618a5fb661925b203f19cc4bc5

15 Herborn, Peter J. and Hutchinson, Francis P. 2014 'Landscapes of remembrance and sites of conscience: Exploring ways of learning beyond militarising "maps" of the future', *Journal of Peace Education*, vol. 11, no. 2, pp. 131–149.

16 Herborn and Hutchinson 2014, p. 146.

17 Ibid.

18 Carbone, Fabio 2022 '"Don't look back in anger". War museums' role in the post conflict tourism-peace nexus', *Journal of Sustainable Tourism*, vol. 30, no. 2–3, pp. 565–583.

19 Whyte 2018 'War Memorial should ditch weapons manufacturers: Anti-war organisation', *Canberra Times*, 22 May, www.canberratimes.com.au/story/6017422/war-memorial-should-ditch-weapons-manufacturers-anti-war-organisation/

20 Daley, Paul 2015 'Australia's lavish spending on Anzac memorials cloaks a more distasteful reality', *Guardian*, 11 November, www.theguardian.com/australia-news/postcolonial-blog/2015/nov/11/lavish-spending-first-world-war-commemorations-cloak-distasteful-reality

21 Black Mist, Burnt Country n.d.Exhibition tour wrap-up, https://blackmistburntcountry.com.au/index.php/2019/03/30/exhibition-tour-wrap-up/

22 Watts, Peter 2017 'A show of pacifism at the Imperial War Museum', *Apollo*, 4 April, www.apollo-magazine.com/a-show-of-pacifism-at-the-imperial-war-museum/

23 Scates, Bruce Charles 2017 'Monumental errors: How Australia can fix its racist colonial statues', *Conversation*, 28 August, https://theconversation.com/monumental-errors-how-australia-can-fix-its-racist-colonial-statues-82980

24 Thorpe, Vanessa 2020 'Censoring old films and TV shows misses the point, say BAME leaders', *Guardian*, www.theguardian.com/world/2020/jun/13/censoring-old-films-and-tv-shows-misses-the-point-say-bame-leaders

25 Wahlquist, Calla and Karp, Paul 2018 'Melbourne electorate of Batman renamed after indigenous activist', *Guardian*, 20 June, www.theguardian.com/australia-news/2018/jun/20/melbourne-electorate-of-batman-renamed-after-indigenous-activist

26 Pembroke, Kate 2021 'Gumbaynggirr name for Wiigulga sports complex', *Coffs Harbour City Council Newsroom*, 11 February, www.news.coffsharbour.nsw.gov.au/2021/02/12/gumbaynggirr-name-for-wiigulga-sports-complex/

27 alHolland, Greg, Hoggett, Aled and Brennand, Hannah Sheppard 2022 'New sanctuary for New South Wales', *Wildlife Matters*, Issue 44, November, p. 6.

28 Charles, Caitlan 2018 'Heated discussion over renaming of Coutts Crossing', *Daily Telegraph*, 31 May, www.dailytelegraph.com.au/news/nsw/grafton/heated-discussion-over-renaming-of-coutts-crossing/news-story/38c1d3a1893e521890ed56cdf60d216e

29 Donoughue, Paul 2017 'The Hottest 100 won't be held on Australia Day next year, triple j says', *ABC News*, 27 November, www.abc.net.au/news/2017-11-27/hottest-100-wont-be-held-on-australia-day-triple-j-says/9197014

30 Ibid.

31 Yamane, Kazuyo, Katsura, Ryotaro and Anzai, Ikuro (eds) 2020 *Museums for Peace Worldwide*, Anzai Science & Peace Office, Kyoto, Japan.

32 Wellerstein, Alex 2020 'Counting the dead at Hiroshima and Nagasaki', *Bulletin of Atomic Scientists*, 4 August, https://thebulletin.org/2020/08/counting-the-dead-at-hiroshima-and-nagasaki/

33 Attributed to Oscar Arias Sánchez.

34 Hiroshima Museum of Art n.d, exhibition guide.

35 Doré-Rivé, Isabelle 2013 *War in a City,* Fage, France.

36 Moorehead, C. 2015 *Village of Secrets: Defying the Nazis in Vichy France*, HarperCollins, New York, p. 336.

37 Attributed to Oscar Arias Sánchez.

38 Amster, Randall 2015 *Peace Ecology*, Routledge, London.

39 Fuller, S. 2004 'Parks for peace', *Alternatives Journal,* vol. 30, no. 4, p. 27.

40 Hines, S. 2008 'Can parks promote international peace?' *Landscape Architecture*, vol. 98, no. 3, pp. 36–45.

41 Kim, Hyung-Jin 2018 'AP explains: Removal of mines from Korean Demilitarized Zone', *AP News*, 2 October, https://apnews.com/general-news-a6da46cf967b430987d04ab6ad4a4c18

42 Helphand, Kenneth I. 2010 'Gardens and war', *SiteLINES: A Journal of Place*, vol. 5, no. 2, pp. 11–13.

43 Ibid.

44 Ibid.

45 Snow, Lalage 2018 *War Gardens: A journey through conflict in Search of Calm,* Quercus, London, p. 355.

46 Dentice, Dianne 2015 'Radical gardening (Book Review)', *Social Movement Studies*, 12 September, https://doi.org/10.1080/14742837.2015.1083851

47 McKay, George 2011 *Radical Gardening: Politics, Idealism and Rebellion in the Garden*, Frances Lincoln Ltd, London.

48 Reynolds, Richard 2014 *On Guerrilla Gardening: A handbook for gardening without boundaries,* Bloomsbury, London.

49 Miles, Ellen 2023 *Get Guerrilla Gardening: A Handbook for Planting in Public Places*,, Dorling Kindersley, New York.

50 Blakemore, Erin 2017 'Agent Orange wasn't the only deadly chemical used in Vietnam', *History*, 29 August, www.history.com/news/agent-orange-wasnt-the-only-deadly-chemical-used-in-vietnam

51 Felix-Romero J. 2010 *Harvesting Peace: Permaculture as Peacebuilding*, PhD dissertation, George Mason University, USA; see also Chapter 11.

52 Prakash, Madhu Suri 2015 'Our friendship gardens: Healing our mother, ourselves', *Cultural Studies of Science Education*, vol. 10, p. 183.

53 Ibid.

Chapter 6

PEACE JOURNALISM AND WRITING

Journalism, and the news media it supplies, is a vital part of our societies' cultures. Although it often purports to be neutral and objective and is widely perceived as such, it's actually a varied and complex phenomenon that is affected and shaped by many factors, including power and corporate influence. It is sometimes called the 'fourth estate', which supposedly acts as a guardian of the public interest and as a watchdog on the activities of government, a role that is important to a functioning democracy. While some do this consistently, others regularly betray the Fourth Estate principles because they represent the economic interests of the powerful:

> In our modern world, the interest of 'the nation' is no more than the collective interest of those who wield political and economic power. Today, the state is the executive branch of the ruling class. [...] When a newspaper claims to speak to and for the nation – that is, to and for the people – but instead appears to speak for the government, it abandons any claim it may have had to independence of thought and action.[1]

The Military-Industrial-Media Complex

Commercial media in the private sphere is a prime example. If a company involved in the arms industry owns a media company, such as General Electric's ownership of the NBC TV network (and ties to Mobil) until 2013, it's almost inevitable that its editorial policies and the general thrust of its media stories and coverage will be unsympathetic towards and probably critical of any peace activism, if it covers it at all. It's also likely to be supportive of continuing high levels of defence spending because this benefits the corporation's profits.

Linked to this is usually support for hawkish foreign policies, military interventions in foreign countries, and militaristic solutions to problems such as terrorism.[2] It will probably run positive stories on visits of politicians and entertainers to war zones, and will portray 'our troops' in a favourable light and 'theirs' in a negative light, contributing to a view of foreign peoples as 'others' or outsiders, and a threat to 'our' values and way of life, even if more objective studies show that most ethnicities share similar values.

Major US TV networks with global influence, such as CBS, ABC, Fox and CNN, tend to be owned by some of the world's largest corporations, with members of their boards of directors also sitting on the boards of weapons manufacturers and military-linked companies such as Boeing, Texaco, Chevron, JP Morgan Chase and Honeywell.[3] Being integrated into the military-industrial complex means that those networks often celebrate major new military projects and purchases such as a new fleet of fighter planes, submarines or warships, with little discussion of how much this will cost, what else the money could have been spent on and what societal benefits the new hardware will bring (if any).

It is also rare to see prolonged discussion of the problems that past purchases have had, such as the $6 billion 'Collins-Class' submarines, six diesel-electric submarines built in Australia for the Royal Australian Navy and designed by Swedish shipbuilder Kockums, with propulsion units provided by a French engineering firm. Originally meant to be $3.9 billion, the construction programme was:

> beset with poor planning, lack of client-shipyard coordination, lack of performance vision, and poor craftsmanship from the builder Kockums. On the operator's side, this resulted in immense reliability and performance problems, had leaks, inadequate propellors, an incorrect sound signature and a staffing shortage.[4]

Propulsion system problems of Australia's two largest naval ships meant that when there was a real need for them, they weren't able to join the emergency response for Cyclone Debbie in 2017, a repeat of the situation with Cyclone Yasi in 2011, when none of Australia's main amphibious landing vessels was operational. Another issue with little coverage concerns Australia's $17 billion purchase of 72 F35 Joint Strike Fighters, which have been plagued by significant delays, cost blowouts, hundreds of deficiencies such as overheating problems and cybersecurity vulnerabilities,[5] and they 'can't hit moving targets such as cars'.[6]

Media can also be influenced by think-tanks sponsored by arms companies and 'defence' departments. For example, the Australian Strategic Policy Institute, which has numerous defence-related sponsors, framed the narrative and laid the groundwork for the 'Red Alert' series of fearmongering front-page articles in Australia's 'Nine' newspapers, which argued for greater defence capabilities to resist a supposedly imminent war with China.[7]

Whitewashing War

In New Zealand, citizens concerned that US warships, refusing to confirm or deny that they were nuclear-armed, were visiting cities such as Auckland, took to the waters en masse to blockade and protest those ships. A supportive Labour government in 1984 banned nuclear-powered or nuclear-armed ships from using New Zealand ports or entering their waters. This ban has endured despite dire warnings at the time about the dangers of upsetting the United States and its alliance with New Zealand.

Elsewhere, however, corporate media outlets tend to celebrate visits of warships to cities with no mention that they're nuclear-powered and possible nuclear targets in the centres of major population congregations. They will run warm and fuzzy stories about the sailors having a great time ashore and boosting local economies[8] without mentioning prostitution, violence and drug use,[9] or intra-service issues such as bullying, sexual violence and the silencing of victims which Joanna Bourke analyses in the *Journal of War & Culture Studies*.[10]

At the same time, these media outlets are also showing a lot of the movie violence that we discussed in Chapter 3 – not necessarily as part of a pro-military viewpoint – but as a way of maintaining ratings. These movies complement war coverage, such as the 24-hour-a-day coverage (sponsored by Exxon and General Electric) of the 1991 Gulf War.[11] The cumulative effect is the widespread acceptance of militarism as 'normal'.

As Helen Johnson summarises, we now have a

> military-industrial-media complex, in which the corporate media does not provide a check on government use of military power, but rather influences our perception of war so as to manufacture support for the military apparatus that drains our nation's resources, perpetuates endless war and violence and profits [from] death and destruction.[12]

Concentration of Ownership, and Militaristic Narratives

This is exacerbated by the dramatic consolidation of the corporate media industry over the last few decades, with the number of dominant US media corporations shrinking from 50 in 1983 to just five today:

> These five conglomerates own about 90 percent of the media in the United States, including newspapers, magazines, book publishers, motion picture studios and radio and television stations. As of 2020, the five media giants are AT&T (Time Warner, CNN, HBO), Comcast (NBC Universal, Telemundo, Universal Pictures), Disney (ABC, ESPN,

Pixar, Marvel Studios), News Corp (Fox News, Wall Street Journal, New York Post), and ViacomCBS (CBS, Paramount Pictures).[13]

This, writes Johnson, leaves 'the power to control the majority of messaging and information in the hands of a very few'.[14] She notes Ben Bagdikian's observation, in his book *The New Media Monopoly,* that '[t]his gives each of the five corporations and their leaders more communications power than was exercised by any despot or dictatorship in history'.[15]

The selective presentation of information to the public by the mass media includes minimal reporting on the long-term toxicity of 'depleted' uranium, the 'revolving door' of politicians and arms executives, or the glaring omission of militarism (and its close links to oil companies) from global warming negotiations.

Chapter 2 discussed the importance of narratives in cultivating peaceful cultures. Over time, the repetition by politicians, pro-military think-tanks and journalists of a narrative such as the 'War on Terror' embeds it in our psyches and predisposes us towards nationalism while simultaneously normalising the idea of violence as the only solution to non-state terrorism. Staking a claim for 'national security', it is actually a linguistic cross-current that legitimises military aggression and revenge.[16] Research drawing on neuro and cognitive science shows a correlation between language and identity which poses a challenge for peace journalism.[17] In order for peace journalism to be effective, it first needs to address the way we use language and the fact that terms like 'War on Terror' are underpinned by notions of 'Us' and 'Others'. This is cultural violence which serves war and has little to do with sustainable security or peace.

Media and Ecological Violence

Another issue involving privately owned media is that it is heavily reliant on advertising revenues from other major corporations, so it will be reluctant to run any stories critical of those corporations. In many cases, media companies are part of larger business conglomerates. It's inevitable that someone like Kerry Stokes, who is both a mining magnate and the chairman of Seven West Media, Australia's largest diversified media business, with an extensive presence in broadcast television, radio, print and online publishing, will discourage any reporting that is critical of his mining interests and mining in general. The Seven Group, its largest shareholder, itself has shares in multi-billion-dollar oil and gas projects[18] so it will naturally tend to pressure editors and producers to avoid or downplay stories about the link between fossil fuels and global warming.

This corporate influence and Australia's concentrated newspaper ownership have a significant effect on how climate science is covered. Although there is a consensus position in climate science, that human beings are major contributors to global warming, accepted by 97 to 98 per cent of climate scientists and every major national and international scientific body (with a couple of neutral exceptions), one-third of articles in Australia's major newspapers don't accept that consensus position. Two-thirds of the coverage of climate science by News Corp's *Herald Sun,* owned by Rupert Murdoch, does not accept the scientific consensus, and prominently runs stories counter to the science and often funded by fossil fuel interests, thereby obfuscating the issue and creating doubt in the minds of the public.[19] This sort of coverage of perhaps the major news story of our times is a major reason why almost 90 per cent of Americans don't know that there is (unprecedented) scientific consensus on global warming.[20]

If we look at another medium, radio, the cash-for-comment scandals that periodically arise give a glaring example of how talkback radio hosts such as John Laws and Alan Jones, while supposedly giving fiercely independent views, were in fact being paid to put certain points of view.[21]

In recent years, news broadcasts began to devote a large percentage of time to finance news, in what could be described as a triumph of neo-liberal capitalism over public narratives. Many people in the West have shares through their superannuation funds, and many have mortgages, but one has to wonder why this practice was introduced, as it forefronts finance and excludes other topics that could be considered more important or of broader interest. Given that there's no economy without a stable environment, and we're in the midst of the greatest environmental changes for at least 65 million years, perhaps there should also be segments on greenhouse gas emissions and species extinctions, and practical steps towards reducing these. Given the international impacts on economies and food security caused by wars such as in Ukraine, perhaps global peace indicators could be regularly shared. Social capital indicators pertaining to equality or even happiness, as in Bhutan's Gross National Happiness (discussed in Chapter 4), could also be added for balance and diversity.

*

All of this means that privately owned media tends to be supportive of both militarism and various forms of direct, structural, cultural and ecological violence. You may expect public media to be more objective, and there are certainly many quality journalistic programmes produced by public broadcasters such as the BBC, PBS, Australian Broadcasting Corporation

(ABC) and SBS. However, these broadcasters are constantly at the mercy of the sitting government, so they may self-censor in order to avoid its wrath (and that of conservative media) lest it leads to further restrictions and funding cuts.[22] As it is, the global acceptance of neo-liberal paradigms of privatisation, smaller government departments, and less spending (at least towards social services, which often leads to spending increases for police, jails and militaries) means that there are ever fewer resources and staff with which to engage in objective, quality journalism that gets to the root of issues. There is still plenty of intelligent, courageous media; people can support it by buying or subscribing to reputable, independent news and analysis sources.

Pressures on Journalists

In repressive regimes, journalists have very real fears that if they run stories that criticise the regime, they are likely to lose their jobs, get arrested and possibly even be murdered. About a third of the world's journalists who are in jail are in Türkiye, according to the *Committee to Protect Journalists* and *Amnesty International*, with hundreds of academics, journalists and writers viewed as critical of the government being jailed or undergoing criminal investigation, prosecution, intimidation, harassment and censorship; at least 180 media outlets have been shut down.[23]

There is also pressure to produce a lot more copy to satisfy the voracious needs of 24/7 news stations like ABC News Radio and ABC News TV, and there's competition from a range of sources, including social media, to get stories out ever faster, leaving less time to do in-depth research for stories.

Public media is also subject to ratings and critics, so there may be biases towards more sensational stories. Violence is sensational and fairly easy to write about in a shallow way. Getting to the causes of that violence, on the other hand, involves more work, and the stories aren't as adrenaline-filled and attention-grabbing. Showing a lot of violence and very few of the less sensational stories of good news, successful peacebuilding, and incremental improvements in crime reduction also leads to an imbalance between what is prominently reported and thus widely believed, and what is really the case.[24] It creates an impression that the world is an overwhelming and frightening place that is ever more violent, and this can lead to fear, despair, apathy and feelings of powerlessness in the populace, rather than active, positive, empowered and forward-looking citizens.

Even the grammar used by journalists to describe violent events can be problematic, writes linguistics professor Annabelle Lukin,[25] while Tanya Hopwood is investigating psychological illness caused by too much bad news and 'prolonged immersion in the minutely-documented violence, suffering and uncertainty being transmitted through modern communications networks'.[26] It's important to be informed, especially by relying on in-depth research into root causes and possible solutions, but it's also healthy to have regular breaks from the news.

Other Factors Affecting Journalism

Poor coverage of militarism and violence may also occur because of ingrained respect for authorities, fear of positing minority viewpoints or upsetting powerful interests, ignorance, poor teaching of journalism or simply laziness – it is easier to cut and paste from official statements than to seek out alternative views or views from war's victims. Even for public broadcasters, their idea of balanced coverage of 'defence' spending usually just involves statements by the government and the opposition, who usually share a pro-military viewpoint.[27] Peace experts, activists and advocates are rarely consulted. Similarly, media 'embedded' within Western militaries get unprecedented access to the militaries, but their coverage tends to be very one-sided.

Covering Nonviolent Protest

Journalists may also be impacted by unconscious bias, such as significant preconceptions against nonviolent protest as deviant, irrational, irresponsible, ineffective and involving marginal subcultures.[28] Where violence occurs, it is presumed that the demonstrators, and not the police, initiated it. Even when violence does not occur, protests are often described through military metaphors and as 'naturally violent', with the audiences implicitly encouraged to identify with the police and other state and corporate representatives as fellow rational actors.[29]

Yet protest against the state is a fundamental right in a democracy. Thomas Paine and other intellectuals of the eighteenth and nineteenth centuries who formulated the conception of the Fourth Estate as a civil watchdog also argued that the public citizenry and the nation-state need to be seen as two separate entities with differing interests, and that 'we may have just cause to overthrow the state if it is seen to be no longer acting in our interests'.[30]

Coverage of Black Lives Matter (BLM) protests is a useful case in point of the demonisation of protest. The Armed Conflict Location & Event Data Project reports that 93 per cent of BLM protests, in over 2,400 locations, have not engaged in violence or destructive activity and, in the violent demonstrations, there were reports of *agents provocateurs* – or infiltrators – instigating the violence to discredit the protest.[31] Despite this, politicians such as Donald

Trump and media outlets like *Fox News* repeatedly portrayed the protests as extremely violent and destructive.

Often in conflicts, there is asymmetric reporting which prioritises the views of the more powerful side, such as Israel and its US backers, while there is minimal coverage of Palestinian grievances about Israeli direct and structural violence, for fear this coverage might be termed anti-Semitic. Critics respond that the international boycott, divestment and sanctions campaign that helped end South Africa's Apartheid regime was not anti-white but directed at a particular regime based on systemic, racist discrimination.

Similarly, there is little coverage of nonviolent actions such as a mass strike in 2021, when millions of Palestinians downed tools and walked out of their workplaces to protest Israeli violations and airstrikes.[32] More coverage of nonviolent actions might reduce the incidence of deplorable and counter-productive acts of violence designed to achieve equality and justice.

Media Gender Imbalance

Another factor mitigating against positive peace in the media is gender imbalance. As mentioned in Chapter 3, talkback radio hosts still tend to be mainly male, an imbalance lampooned in comedian Kitty Flanagan's autobiographical book *Bridge Burning and Other Hobbies*.[33] There are often two men on a radio show, occasionally a man and a woman, but rarely two women. Commercial radio trios are usually two men and one woman (e.g. *Nova*'s Ricki-Lee, Tim and Joel in 2023), although occasionally one of those men is openly gay. Those minority women are often overruled, not heard, talked over, targets of teasing or are the 'emotional', caring ones compared with 'realistic' hard-nosed men. Some programmes make no attempt at gender balance, such as *Triple M*'s 'The Rush Hour', featuring 'Gus, Jude and Wendell' (although former football star Wendell Sailor, backgrounded in the station's publicity photo, is of South Sea Islander and West Indian descent). There's also less coverage of women's sport, although some shifts are occurring here.

Men have long dominated British television shows such as *Mock the Week, the IT Crowd, Black Books* and *Would I Lie to You*? There's some ethnic and sexual diversity, but white middle-aged males dominate the conversations. Australian shows *Mad as Hell* and *The Weekly* also feature brilliant, hilarious satire but exhibit similar patterns of male dominance, as have children's shows such as the 'Bananas in Pyjamas', 'Hooley Dooleys' and 'Wiggles', although the recruitment of Emma Watkins in 2013 and Tsehay Hawkins, a female Ethiopian-born teenager, in 2021 added some diversity to the latter. There are mainstream exceptions, of course: from 'I Love Lucy' and 'The Golden Girls' to 'Sex and the City', 'Friends', and Namila Benson, a woman with Papua New Guinean heritage who is the flamboyant host of ABC TV's 'Art Works'. However, even 'all-women panels' on International Women's Day programmes often have at least one male.[34]

Peace Journalism

Many journalists may simply have never considered how to approach journalism from a peace perspective. Probably few have been taught the principles of peace journalism, a form of journalism that is explicitly oriented towards positive peace and away from supporting violence in any form. It involves careful consideration of how any reporting on a conflict will impact on it, with the aim to reduce violence rather than inflame it.

This involves seeking out a wide variety of sources of information, from all levels of society – from multiple, small minority groups to large, powerful institutions – to form a deep understanding of the conflict and its root causes. As peace scholar John Lederach notes, '[t]here are people who have a vision for peace, emerging often from their own experience of conflict and pain', but these are often unheard 'because they do not represent official power [...] or because they are written off as biased'.[35]

Inoue Yasuhiro argues that the journalistic tenet of objectivity should be shifted towards a proactive role of the media in peacebuilding, given the media's 'central role in international affairs and violence'. He argues that the media can exacerbate conflict and even cause war through its obsession with objectivity, by contributing to fear, constructing and reinforcing stereotypical and negative views, and producing 'war journalism' that is ethnocentric and in fact far from objective.[36]

Peace journalism ideally requires reporters to have a broad Peace Studies education in order to understand the international, regional and national contexts in which conflicts arise, including political-economic, geographical and historical factors and the influences of globalised neo-liberal capitalism, post-colonialism and global warming. They should understand peacemaking, peacebuilding and conflict transformation strategies. They should understand nonviolent action, including its history and how it works. Peace journalism is also solutions-oriented rather than just presenting critiques, and therefore has commonalities with the emerging field of 'solutions journalism'.[37]

Mainstream reporting on wars often exhibits biases towards violence and rests on the conceptual belief that 'conflict' equals 'war'. Some level of conflict, however, is inevitable whenever two or more people get together for an extended period, and conflict can be considered an opportunity to search for a new harmony between the parties involved. According to Johan Galtung and former BBC journalist Jake Lynch, other key principles of peace journalism include:

1. Exploring how a conflict has formed: who are the parties involved; what are their goals; what is the sociopolitical and cultural context of the conflict; what are the visible and invisible manifestations of violence?
2. Avoiding the dehumanisation of the parties involved, and highlighting their concerns, needs and interests;
3. Offering nonviolent responses to conflict, and alternatives to militarised/violent 'solutions'; and
4. Reporting nonviolent initiatives occurring at the grassroots level, and following the resolution, reconstruction and reconciliation phases.[38]

Covering Stories from the Global South

In our globalised world, there is a tendency for coverage of news events that are easily accessed by journalists and passed around the world, while events and processes in more remote places, such as the forests of Borneo or the desert communities of Western Australia, tend not to be covered.

A pioneer of fearless reporting in remote locations was the journalist Wilfred Burchett, probably the first Western journalist to enter Hiroshima after the atomic bomb and report on the 'atomic plague' afflicting the inhabitants. American authorities attempting to suppress information about fallout dismissed his story as pro-Japanese propaganda. Burchett began to question 'the morality of untrammelled American military might'[39] and would become a diplomat, activist and advocate as well as covering wars and peace negotiations around the world, including national liberation struggles in southern Africa and Vietnam, and the genocide in Cambodia. Although a dedicated communist, he was perspicacious enough to question the nature of the Soviet form and the crumbling of China's socialist ideals.

Controversial and Little-Known Stories

Sometimes, films are not picked up by government broadcasters because of their 'controversial' content, such as documentaries which 'challenge Australia's silence on West Papua'[40] and expose nefarious activities in Australia's close neighbourhood. Hughes describes a long-term conspiracy of silence between Australia and Indonesia and the refusal of Australian television to finance or, in the case of the critically acclaimed *Strange Birds in Paradise: A West Papuan Story*, to even screen such documentaries. He argues that 'Australian public broadcasters – whose legitimacy rests with their integrity in providing a venue for minority voices, and Australian independent creative work – seem increasingly afraid to step outside the diminishing square of their own creation'.[41] Another film, *Hope in Slingshot*, about Palestine, was similarly barred by the ABC. Peace Studies, at the University of New England, showed it in our 2013 Nonviolence Film Festival.

Under-reported stories include the atrocities being perpetrated by the military junta in Myanmar, which usurped power from a democratically elected government and proceeded to violently suppress nonviolent protests and to wage war on the Rohingya population. The use of boycotts, divestment and sanctions (BDS) in combatting such regimes is also under-reported, even though its use has been pivotal in past campaigns, such as the one which ended South Africa's Apartheid regime.[42]

So, a peace journalism perspective might include a story on 'Justice for Myanmar', a group which is not using violent, largely ineffective resistance but works as 'covert activists using research, data visualisation, and reporting to expose the companies and criminals profiting from brutality, war crimes and mass-scale suffering'.[43] An intelligent key strategy is providing information about and calling for boycotts of entities which support the regime with military equipment, taxes or conferring legitimacy by continuing with business-as-usual in Myanmar. According to 'Justice for Myanmar', these entities include ASEAN; Austrian, Russian and Indian arms companies; Israeli surveillance company Cognyte; French and Australian banks; a Japanese railway project; the Adani Group; and the Heineken and Carlsberg companies.

A similar group, Burma Campaign UK (burmacampaign.org.uk), argues that most of the estimated two million people who have been forced to flee their homes since the military coup have fled because of airstrikes or the threat of them. They state: 'Without aviation fuel the jets can't fly. If they can't fly, they can't bomb. Tell the British government to sanction aviation fuel now.' They urge Finland and Switzerland to stop lending legitimacy to Myanmar's military junta, and they publish 'The Dirty List', which names international companies (including Toyota and Chinese corporations) doing business with the military in Myanmar or involved in projects with human rights violations or environmental destruction.

Understanding Nonviolent Civil Resistance Histories

In the last chapter, we discussed how historians can research and publish more on nonviolence and grassroots stories and less on military and elite ones. Journalists could amplify this trend by writing about little-known stories, such as the extraordinary New Zealand Maori leader Te Whiti, ably supported by his relative and fellow spiritual leader Tohu Kākahi, whose effective nonviolent civil resistance strategies long predated Gandhi's. In the second half of the nineteenth century, they led a lengthy campaign against the theft of their land by ploughing it – choosing the settlers' tool (and religious symbolism of turning swords into ploughshares) to assert their right to participate in the modern economy on land taken in contravention of the government's own word. Hundreds were imprisoned and fined exorbitantly, but when threatened with military violence, the community responded with cultural resistance and kindness.

> The 1500 Armed Constabulary soldiers and volunteers, weighed down with ammunition, encircling the village, expecting violence but greeted instead by singing, skipping children and women who had baked 500 loaves of bread to feed their visitors.[44]

The protesters were vilified by most contemporary journalists, although two defied a news embargo on the action above, with one writing that:

> The whole spectacle was saddening in the extreme; it was an industrious, law-abiding, moral and hospitable community, calmly awaiting the approach of the men sent to rob them of everything dear to them.[45]

The relentless dispossession by the colonial government continued, with the village destroyed, sexual assaults and rapes, and more than 1,500 men, women and children being forcibly removed and abandoned. However, unlike with violent resistance elsewhere, a total bloodbath was avoided and nonviolent lobbying continued over the next century and a half, leading eventually to the Taranaki iwi Deed of Settlement, signed on 27 February 2021. It returns land of cultural significance and contains reparations and a sincere 400-word apology from the Crown – 'a full-throated admission of wrongdoing, not an evasive expression of "regret"'.[46]

Kennedy Warne's article 'Why Wasn't I Told?', complemented by historical photographs, is a great example of contemporary writing to revive lost nonviolence stories of significance.

> It is inconceivable that an Indian child growing up today would not know about Gandhi, just as it is impossible to imagine a child in the United States not knowing about Martin Luther King Jr, or a South African child Nelson Mandelà. Yet generations of New Zealand children have grown up in ignorance of a man whose message and practice of peace and nonviolent protest preceded theirs by decades.[47]

Positive News Stories

Much mass media focuses on direct violence because it is obvious, often frightening, and usually sensational. With this dominating the news, it can create or amplify negativity in the populace – a feeling that violence is everywhere, is part of human nature, is a massive problem, and there's little that can be done about it. Consequently, little *is* done about it.

However, there are always positive currents in the tides of human affairs, and some writers and journalists believe in giving these more prominence. One example is Jesse Richards' *The Secret Peace: Exposing the Positive Trend of World Events*.[48] Working at the intersection of culture, design, writing and technology, Richards examined thousands of sources to research the world's positive trends. More recently, he reflected in his blog:

> When I published *The Secret Peace* in 2009, the headlines looked bad. The world was mired in the worst global economic crisis since the Great Depression. But all the underlying data, the long-term data, told a different story: Sure, the world is a terrible place, but it used to be much worse. Slowly, inexorably, through the cumulative day-to-day efforts of millions of people, it keeps getting better.[49]

To support his argument, he cites a number of facts from journalistic sources printing good news stories.

- Every day, the number of people around the world living in extreme poverty (less than about $2 a day) goes down by 217,000.
- Since 2000, global malaria deaths have declined by 60 per cent. Since their peak a decade ago, AIDS-related deaths have fallen by 45 per cent.
- The essential finding of Steven Pinker's 2011 book *The Better Angels of Our Nature* is that we are living in history's most peaceful era, with violence of all kinds – from deaths in war to schoolyard bullying – in steep decline.
- Shooting incidents involving students have been declining since the 1990s. [...] More kids are killed each year from pool drownings or bicycle accidents.
- A study on the crime decline in six American cities concludes: 'As the degree of violence has fallen, the gap between the neighborhoods of the poor and non-poor has narrowed'.
- American gun ownership has dropped to the lowest rate in nearly 40 years.[i,50]

Other authors draw similar conclusions, saying that despite 'widespread resistance to the idea that things have improved [. . .] it's so spectacularly clear

---

i However, there was a spike prior to the 2020 US elections when Donald Trump falsely intimated that the election would be rigged, and widespread violence was predicted.

that life is much better now than it was'.[51] In Australia over the last 50 years, there have been vast improvements across the board, including in sewage and communication systems, gun control, crime rates, corruption, bullying, life expectancy, litter, outdoor dining and the opening of Sunday activities.[52] The poor are also getting richer, although there is greater economic inequality in many countries, and this can have implications for the physical and mental health of societies, education outcomes and violence.[53]

Some media outlets are making an effort to include positive news stories in daily segments, or celebrating National Bird Week by encouraging audiences to engage in citizen science observations and reporting. One ABC News Radio promotion (16 October 2022) observed that you don't need aggressive questioning to get the facts.

There's a radio station that broadcasts peace songs day and night: Peace Sounds Radio (https://peacesounds.us), which describes itself as 'an internet radio/webpage dedicated to the music of peace and positive social change' and includes global music and peace songs for choirs by the Movement for the Abolition of War.

Writing Peace

'Change is hard', writes Symon Hill, Campaigns Manager of the Peace Pledge Union. 'Even radical activists can struggle to envisage a world without established institutions and practices. Perhaps this is why most anti-war campaigners stop short of calling for the abolition of military forces'.[54]

Exceptions include Jørgen Johansen and Brian Martin, with their highly accessible 2019 book *Social Defence*. Another writer who wanted armies abolished and refused to compromise his belief that war is immoral was Leo Tolstoy, author of *War and Peace* (first published serially beginning in 1865), and a major influence on Mahatma Gandhi. The sick sadism of Stieg Larsson's 'Nordic noir' books and films can be contrasted with Tolstoy's writings and life. Tolstoy explained his complete aversion to war in the simplest of terms – murder always remains murder. He was adamant that no one, politician or otherwise, can commit to both war and being a Christian, with the two being completely contradictory. Writing 30 years after he had begun *War and Peace*, Tolstoy observed that:

> 'Thou Shalt Not Kill' is enjoined on all Christians, and either governments claiming to be Christian must accept and disband their armies, or they do not deserve the support of their citizens.[55]

As Hill observes, 'Armed forces are not there to protect us, but to preserve the power of the powerful. Let's have the courage to say so'.[56] Many people have had the courage to speak out against war and conscientious objectors have gone further by refusing to join armed forces when ordered, often enduring jail, opprobrium, financial sacrifice and sometimes execution. Writers who have documented such people include Nicholas Gillett's *Men against War*[57] and Lyn Smith's more gender-balanced *Voices Against War: A century of protest.*[58] The latter provides fascinating accounts by conscientious objectors, pacificists and anti-war activists of their resistance to war. Other powerful writing by a non-violent activist and global south feminist is Arundhati Roy's *The Ministry of Utmost Happiness*, published in 2017 after 20 years of activism about massacres, paramilitary attacks, nuclear power, inappropriate dams and dispossession of the poor had halted her fiction writing. This book covers all those issues while bringing in discourses on industrial pollution and transgender issues. It contains the deep insights of both a courageous activist and a woman who experienced a difficult childhood and then extreme poverty.[59]

Anti-War Fiction

Fiction has long been used to promote peace and oppose war and other forms of violence. One example is the classic anti-war novel *All Quiet on the Western Front* (1929), by Erich Maria Remarque, a German veteran of World War I. Later made into a famous film, it described the soldiers' physical and mental trauma during and after the war, and how their lives were thrown away by indifferent commanding officers stationed safely away from the front. Blind nationalism is another theme, with much of the blame for the disastrous and pointless war being laid at the feet of arms dealers and industrialists. After the rise of the Nazis, the book was one of the first burnt as 'degenerate', and it was banned in other European countries such as Austria, Czechoslovakia and Italy.

Neville Shute's haunting *On The Beach*[60] is another classic, this time following World War II, and also made into a high-profile film, starring Gregory Peck, Ava Gardner, Fred Astaire and Anthony Perkins. *On the Beach* is dystopian and post-apocalyptic, with the people of the northern hemisphere wiped out from nuclear war, and those of the southern hemisphere waiting for the radiation to sweep south and kill them too. It is a deeply sobering book (which unsettles one's consciousness for months after reading), warning of the all-too-real consequences of the use of nuclear weapons.[ii] It has been echoed in

ii On learning these consequences, ironically on a military cadet course, Monty Python's Eric Idle became 'violently pacifist' and, still a schoolboy, took part in the 1962 Campaign for Nuclear Disarmament march from Aldermaston to London.

children's fiction, such as Katherine Paterson's *A Midnight Clear*,[61] where hallucinations of mushroom clouds haunt a young boy.

Cli-Fi

One of the fastest growing genres of fiction is cli-fi (climate fiction), led by prominent authors such as Barbara Kingsolver, Ben Elton, Margaret Atwood, Corey Doctorow and Maja Lunde. Cli-fi adopts many forms, ranging from 'distant future imagining' (originally pioneered in sci-fi by Frank Herbert's *Dune*) to 'near future imagining' such as in *The Water Knife* by Paolo Bacigalupi. Much cli-fi consists of dystopian stories that act as cautionary tales about the extreme weather and climate injustices resulting from anthropogenic global warming, with examples being Jennifer Mills' brilliant but disturbing *Dyschronia* or Tim Cadman's *The Changes* series. While dystopian fiction has a role in exposing possible futures and possibly inspiring environmental action, there is a danger that it may have the opposite effect and add to already high levels of eco-anxiety, fear, despair or a sense of hopelessness. As Sally Adee writes, 'doom is booming' and 'planning for the end of the world just hastens its arrival'.[62]

People fail to engage in activism for numerous reasons, including a belief that power lies outside them, only existing in governments and wealthy elites. Many believe that their own actions will have little or no effect, and that individuals only have power if they are charismatic leaders such as Gandhi. Some are paralysed by fear already, so no amount of dystopian writing or fearmongering campaigning will galvanise them into action, unless the action is explosions of random, wild, angry, desperate or violent acts (think Black Bloc or those keen on 'revolutionary violence') that have little positive impact and plenty of negatives.

Utopian and Solarpunk Fiction

Utopian fiction, on the other hand, can be holistic, encouraging action and showing what's possible. It can suggest solutions, ways forward, visions for a peaceful and sustainable future. It can encourage people to act, and in a particular direction – nonviolent, productive, constructive, effective. In this way, fiction can be a form of prefigurative politics, modelling the qualities that make us human, such as hope, joy and humour.

Naomi Alderman's *The Future*[63] is in the utopian 'solarpunk' camp, which envisions what the future might look like if we live in harmony with nature in a sustainable and egalitarian way.[64] A literary and artistic movement, solarpunk imagines dramatically different systems of transport, energy delivery and essential services, integrated with nature and community. It's an optimistic vision that rejects climate doomism and embraces renewables and post-capitalist, decolonial counter-culture. *The Future* is 'glorious [...] because Alderman has the imagination (including moral imagination) to take us out of the doom loop. May it inspire many copycats'.[65]

Jacqui Svenson's highly engaging *Direct Action* and this author's *Locked On!* explore the role that activism can play in resisting major polluters and promoting the socioeconomic changes required to effectively address global warming. *Direct Action* shows how difficult this activist work can be, while *Locked On!* is a book of fan fiction, the 'seventh and most illegal in the Hitchhiker's Guide trilogy'. Douglas Adams agreed with fans that his last *Hitchhiker's Guide to the Galaxy* novel was too bleak, and he wanted to end the series with a more positive book, saying in an interview prior to his untimely death: 'I would love to finish Hitchhiker on a slightly more upbeat note'.[66] *Locked On!* uses Adams' characters and aims to create a glimmer of hope, striving to be optimistic and solution-oriented. The novel shows the power of ordinary people acting together at a grassroots level and seeks to inspire collective direct action. It even suggests that people can live happily without cities, governments, high technology and mass consumption, reassuring readers that the possible climate-induced collapse of modern civilisation may not be catastrophic for everyone. However, as solarpunk art teacher Michelle Tulumello says,

> If we wish to survive and keep some of the things we care about on the earth with us, it involves a necessary fundamental alteration in our world view where we change our outlook completely from competitive to cooperative.[67]

Both *Direct Action* and *Locked On!* encourage nonviolent direct action and protest for immediate emissions reductions, as advocated by climate scientists and groups like Extinction Rebellion and Blockade Australia, rather than incremental reformist change as banks and superannuation funds claim to be doing.

In a similar vein, but aimed at children, *The Big Book for Peace*[68] edited by Ann Durell and Marilyn Sachs encourages peace through outspoken and flamboyant protests. It was written after a librarian was outraged that other librarians were enthusing over a new 'war' book for children, with photographs of World War II German tanks.

Kim Stanley Robinson, the author of works like *Pacific Edge* and *The Mars Trilogy*, uses both dystopian and utopian fiction, advocating rewilding, changes in the processes by which decisions with environmental implications are made, controls on individual aggrandisement and changes in social practices and attitudes, including race and gender equality, which are not always directly linked to ecological issues. Such 'intersectional' changes are necessary to create a social fabric strong enough to support sensible environmental policies:

> [F]iction can link human social structures and larger ecologies while rejecting both permanent despair and cruel optimism. [...] Robinson's indignation about our climate emergency drives his focus on economic exploitation and species extinctions. [...] Relying on both concrete realism and subtler allegory, these novels prepare readers for climate devastation that spans many decades, features painful splits, and demands bold maneuvers. They invite readers to empathize with climate victims both familiar and distant and to pursue long-term transformations, not rhetorical band-aids.[69]

Poetry and Positive Peace

Bundjalung woman Evelyn Araluen's *Dropbear* (2021) is significant given the complete absence of Black poets in many previous Australian poetry anthologies. It grapples with the contradictions of survivors of colonialism using the language of colonisers to assert sovereignty: 'It is hard to unlearn a language to unspeak the empire,/ to teach my voice to rise and fall like landscape,/ a topographic intonation'.[70] Incorporating 'lyric meditations, memoir and pastiche with equal facility',[71] it is also a clever counter-narrative to two centuries plus of Australian myth-making, repurposing Biblical themes, Australiana kitsch and settler-colonial tropes. It is a 'deeply nuanced, sophisticated and self-aware book of poetry that, in challenging colonial persistence, also provides an array of entry points into understanding and perception for non-Aboriginal as well as Aboriginal readers'.[72] Another element is that it balances protest with paeans of love and hope for a decolonial future:

> It is easy to say an activist book is full of 'fury' or 'anger', but that is too easy and even reductive. This book is intense in many different ways. It's also a book of love and respect – of ancestors, family, community, a partner, and the power of language and country.[73]

Pommy Granita is a recent book of politically charged peace poetry by peace journalism academic Jake Lynch. The Patron of BDS Australia, Lynch won a case in the Federal Court to establish his right to implement the academic boycott of Israel. *Pommy Granita* contains pithy commentaries on issues of struggle and resistance including: the AUKUS partnership[iii] and Australia-China

iii See Chapter 8.

tensions; justice for Palestinians; an independent Australian Republic; protest for decisive action to curb global warming, and Britain's vote to Brexit.

*

This chapter has explored how conventional journalism and mass media tend to perpetuate militarism and war because of military-industrial-media influences, concentration of media ownership, militaristic narratives, pressures on journalists, gender imbalance and other factors. They also contribute to ecological violence and tend to misrepresent nonviolent struggles. Peace journalism, on the other hand, is normatively pro-peace, solutions-oriented, uses a greater diversity and covers global south and lesser-known stories. It embraces positivity, as does utopian cli-fi and solarpunk writing. In the next chapter we change direction, to examine how parenting is vital for peacebuilding and how domestic peace can be achieved through pro-peace parenting.

Notes

1 Hirst, Martin 2013 'Right to know: The "nation", the "people" and the Fourth Estate', *Conversation,* 11 December, https://theconversation.com/right-to-know-the-nation-the-people-and-the-fourth-estate-21253

2 Goodman, Amy and Goodman, David 2004 *Exception to the Rulers: Exposing America's War Profiteers, the Media that Love Them and the Crackdown on Our Rights,* Hyperion Books, New York.

3 Johnson, Helen 2021a 'The (Im)Proper meshing of the corporate media and the military-industrial complex', *Transcend Media Service,* 17 May, www.transcend.org/tms/2021/05/the-improper-meshing-of-the-corporate-media-and-the-military-industrial-complex/; Andreas, Joel 2004 *Addicted to War: Why the U.S. Can't Kick Militarism,* 3rd edition, AK Press, Oakland, p. 58.

4 Green, Robert 2019 'Australia's *collins*-class submarines enter a 20th year of trouble', *Diplomat,* 16 February, https://thediplomat.com/2019/02/australias-collins-class-submarines-enter-a-20th-year-of-trouble/

5 Deutrom, Rhian 2018 'Australia's biggest defence mistake that will cost us billions,' *News.com.au,* 23 October.

6 Burgess, Aiden 2017 'F-35 joint strike fighter can't hit moving targets such as cars', *Manufacturer,* 29 March, www.themanufacturer.com/articles/f-35-joint-strike-fighter-cant-hit-moving-targets-such-as-cars/

7 Barton, Ainsley 2023 'ASPI takes exception to media scrutiny', *Pearls and Irritations,* 25 March, https://johnmenadue.com/aspi-takes-exception-to-media-scrutiny/

8 See, for example, Hauptman, Max 2022 'US sailors, marines in Greece exhausted a town's supply of eggs, meat, and tattoos', 4 August, https://taskandpurpose.com/news/marines-sailors-greece-eggs-tattoos/; '1,400 US sailors coming ashore', 2004 *Greenock Telegraph,* 25 October, www.greenocktelegraph.co.uk/news/13988210.1400-us-sailors-coming-ashore/

9 Sabbagh, Dan 2022 'UK armed forces introduce ban on use of sex workers abroad', *Guardian,* 20 July, www.theguardian.com/uk-news/2022/jul/19/uk-armed-forces-introduce-ban-on-use-of-sex-workers-abroad; Medeiros Passos, Anaís 2022 'The

use of violence by military personnel', in *Democracies at War Against Drugs*, Palgrave Macmillan, Cham, pp. 195–242.

10 Bourke, Joanna 2021 'Military sexual trauma: Gender, military cultures, and the medicalization of abuse in contemporary America', *Journal of War & Culture Studies*, vol. 15, no. 1, pp. 86–105.

11 Andreas 2004, p. 57.

12 Johnson, Helen 2021a 'The (im)proper meshing of the corporate media and the military-industrial complex', *Miscellany News*, 13 May, https://miscellanynews.org/2021/05/13/opinions/the-improper-meshing-of-the-corporate-media-and-the-military-industrial-complex/

13 Johnson, Helen 2021b 'The unprecedented consolidation of the modern media industry has severe consequences', *Miscellany News*, 29 April, https://miscellanynews.org/2021/04/29/opinions/the-unprecedented-consolidation-of-the-modern-media-industry-has-severe-consequences/

14 Johnson 2021a.

15 Johnson 2021b.

16 Tallam, Chad 2014 'Interpreting 9/11: The role of language and narrative in the construction of "American" identity', *Journal of Government and Politics*, vol. 5, no. 1, February, p. 1, http://dx.doi.org/10.18196/jgp.2014.0002.

17 Ibid.

18 Macdonald-Smith, Angela 2022 'Shell, Seven Group to build $3.6b Crux gas project', *Financial Review*, 30 May, www.afr.com/companies/energy/shell-seven-group-to-build-3-6b-crux-gas-project-20220530-p5apjt

19 Bacon, Wendy 2013 'Big Australian media reject climate science', *Conversation*, 1 November, https://theconversation.com/big-australian-media-reject-climate-science-19727

20 Arrieta-Kenna, Ruairi 2017 'Almost 90% of Americans don't know there's scientific consensus on global warming', *Vox*, 6 July, www.vox.com/science-and-health/2017/7/6/15924444/global-warming-consensus-survey

21 Burrowes, Tim 2009 '2UE fined $360,000 in John Laws cash for comments breach', *Mumbrella*, 17 July, https://mumbrella.com.au/2ue-fined-360000-in-john-laws-cash-for-comments-breach-7792

22 Robertson, James 2022 'ABC veterans decry political interference', *New Daily*, 13 February, www.thenewdaily.com.au/entertainment/tv/2022/02/14/abc-veterans-decry-political-interference

23 Amnesty International 2017 *Turkey: Jounalism is Not a Crime*, 1 February, www.amnesty.org/en/latest/campaigns/2017/02/free-turkey-media/

24 Richards, Jesse 2010 *The Secret Peace: Exposing the positive trend of World Events*, Book and Ladder Press, New York; Richards, Jesse 2018 'Giving thanks ... The secret peace continues', *Goodreads*, 3 December, www.goodreads.com/author_blog_posts/17655485-giving-thanks-the-secret-peace-continues; see also Martin, Brian 2024 *Better? Is the world going down the drain?* Irene Publishing, Sparsnäs, Sweden.

25 Lukin, Annabelle 2018 'War of words: Why journalists need to understand grammar to write accurately about violence', *The Conversation*, https://theconversation.com/war-of-words-why-journalists-need-to-understand-grammar-to-write-accurately-about-violence-96850

26 'When too much bad news is bad news' 2017 *Pulse News*, 3 October, https://blog.une.edu.au/pulsenews/2017/10/03/when-too-much-bad-news-is-bad-news/; see also Case, Antonia 2017, 'Media misery syndrome', *Womankind*, vol. 12, pp. 18–19.

27 Pilger, John 2010 *The War You Don't See* (video recording), Network; Lynch, Jake 2010 'Propaganda, war, peace and the media', in Richard Keeble, John Tulloch and Florian Zollmann (eds), *Peace Journalism, War and Conflict Resolution*, Peter Lang, London, pp. 69–86.
28 McIntyre, Iain 2009 *How to Make Trouble and Influence People,* Breakdown Press, Carlton.
29 Paasonen, Karl-Eric 1996 'Building the beast: Media construction of protest and protesters and the assignation of responsibility for violence', MA thesis, University of Queensland, pp. 6–64.
30 Hirst, Martin 2013 'Right to know: The "nation", the "people" and the Fourth Estate', *Conversation,*11 December, https://theconversation.com/right-to-know-the-nation-the-people-and-the-fourth-estate-21253
31 Kishi, Roudabeh, Stall, Hampton, Wolfson, Aaron and Jones, Sam 2021 'A year of racial justice protests: Key trends in demonstrations supporting the BLM movement', *Armed Conflict Location and Event Data Project*, 25 May, https://acleddata.com/2021/05/25/a-year-of-racial-justice-protests-key-trends-in-demonstrations-supporting-the-blm-movement/
32 Marsawa, Lubna, Hammad, Shatha and Abdellatif, Latifeh 2021 'Palestinians stage historic strike over Israeli abuses and Gaza bombing', *Middle East Eye*, 18 May, www.middleeasteye.net/news/israel-palestine-gaza-citizens-down-tools-protest-bombing-abuses
33 Flanagan, Kitty 2020 *Bridge Burning and Other Hobbies*, Allen and Unwin, Sydney.
34 Bower, Madeleine 2022 'What was Dylan Alcott doing on an all-woman panel for IWD?' *News.com.au*, 8 March; Stephens, Kim 2017 'Rape, revenge porn, fat-shaming: The all-women Q&A panel delve deep ahead of International Women's Day', *News.com.au*, 7 March.
35 Cited in De Michelis Silvia 2018 'Peace journalism in theory and practice', *E-International Relations*, 23 December, www.e-ir.info/2018/12/23/peace-journalism-in-theory-and-practice/
36 Yasuhiro, I. 2010 'Media's role in peace building: Departure from "Objectivity" to advocacy for peace', in C. Rinnert, O. Farouk and I. Yasuhiro (eds.), *Hiroshima and Peace*, Keisuisha, pp. 272–285.
37 Thier, Kathryn and Namkoong, Kang 2023 'Identifying major components of solutions-Oriented journalism: A review to guide future research', *Journalism Studies*, vol. 24, no. 12, pp. 1557–1574.
38 De Michelis 2018.
39 Heenan, Tom 2007 'Wilfred Graham Burchett (1911–1983)', *Australian Dictionary of Biography*, vol. 17, https://adb.anu.edu.au/biography/burchett-wilfred-graham-12265
40 Hughes, John 2011 'Oz-tak-Lihat (Australia doesn't see)', *Arena*, June, vol. 112, pp. 41–43.
41 Ibid.
42 Clark, Howard 2008 'Actions and solidarity campaign with South Africa', *War Resisters International*, 14 October, www.wri-irg.org
43 'Working to dismantle the Myanmar Military Cartel', 2023 *Justice for Myanmar,* www.justiceformyanmar.org/?78f7163a_page=1
44 Warne, Kennedy 2016 'Why wasn't I told?' *New Zealand Geographic*, vol. 142, www.nzgeo.com/stories/parihaka/
45 Cited in Warne 2016).
46 Ibid.

47 Ibid.
48 Richards 2010.
49 Richards 2018.
50 Ibid.
51 Glover, Richard 2018 *The Land Before Avocado,* ABC Books, Sydney, pp. 239–240.
52 Ibid.
53 Wilkinson, Richard and Pickett, Kate 2010 *The Spirit Level: Why Equality is Better for Everyone,* Penguin, London.
54 Hill, Symon 2021 'What if… armed forces were abolished?' *New Internationalist,* 7 October, https://newint.org/features/2021/08/09/what-if-armed-forces-abolished
55 Cited in Gillett, Nicholas 1965 *Men Against War,* Victor Gollancz, London, p. 65.
56 Hill 2021.
57 Gillett 1965.
58 Smith, Lyn 2010 *Voices Against War: A Century of Protest,* Mainstream, Edinburgh.
59 Acocella, Joan 2017 'Arundhati Roy returns to fiction, in fury', *New Yorker,* 29 May, www.newyorker.com/magazine/2017/06/05/arundhati-roy-returns-to-fiction-in-fury
60 Shute, Neville 1957 *On The Beach,* William Heinemann, London.
61 Paterson, Katherine 1990 'A midnight clear', in Ann Durell and Marilyn Sachs (eds.), *The Big Book for Peace,* Dutton Children's Books, New York, pp. 91–110.
62 Adee, Sally 2023 'Doom is booming', *New Scientist,* 11 November, p. 30.
63 Alderman, Naomi 2023 *The Future,* Simon and Schuster, New York.
64 Smith, Nicola K. 2021 'What is solarpunk and can it help save the planet?' *BBC News,* 3 August, www.bbc.com/news/business-57761297
65 Adee 2023.
66 Flood, Alison 2008 'Eoin Colfer to write sixth Hitchhiker's guide book', *Guardian,* 17 September, www.theguardian.com/books/2008/sep/17/douglasadams
67 Cited in Smith 2021.
68 Durell, Ann and Sachs, Marilyn 1990 *The Big Book for Peace,* Dutton Children's Books, New York.
69 Hammer, Everett 2020 'Angry optimism: Climate disaster and restoration in Kim Stanley Robinson's alternate futures,' in N. Ahuja, et al. (eds.), *Palgrave Handbook of Twentieth and Twenty-First Century Literature and Science,* Palgrave Macmillan, Cham, pp. 449–467.
70 Cited in Kinsella, John 2021 'Poetry that can teach us all', *Sydney Morning Herald (Spectrum),* 1–2 May, p. 16.
71 Fry, Declan 2021 'Dropbear by Evelyn Araluen review – A stunning scalpel wielded through Australian myths', *Guardian,* 26 March, www.theguardian.com/books/2021/mar/26/dropbear-by-evelyn-araluen-review-a-stunning-scalpel-wielded-through-australian-myths
72 Kinsella 2021, p. 16.
73 Ibid.

Chapter 7

DOMESTIC PEACE

There is little doubt that, despite a decline in direct violence reported by authors such as Pinker and Richards (referred to in previous chapters), there is still plenty around, with militarism widely accepted as justifiable and reinforced through violent films, computer games and even fairy tales, and order enforced by the threat of direct violence from the state (e.g. police and jails). In such a context, how do you live and parent nonviolently?

And does it make a difference? We may feel that only people 'in power' can make change and resolve the world's problems. But we already make a difference – through what we consume, the pollution we create, the businesses we support – the question is more: 'What kind of difference do we want to make?' And some of our behaviours have quite immediate effects, such as on our children. If we shout angrily at them, this has an obvious and immediate effect, whereas a childhood of gentle but firm parenting usually results in well-rounded adults.

Parenting Shapes the World

Robin Grille argues that democracy starts at home, and parenting changes the world:

> Psychohistorians have managed to trace a large number of significant world events – whose repercussions profoundly affect all our lives to this day – to their origins in prevailing childrearing customs.[1]

Grille shows how childhood experiences shape emotional makeup and beliefs, and how scars from repetitive hurts can affect behaviour much later:

> Much of what we take for granted as 'normal' social behaviours are in fact defensive vestiges, remnants from intergenerational mistreatment spanning thousands of years. Humanity has not completed its recovery from its traumatic past, and is still acting out this collective trauma in a thousand ways.[2]

Nonviolence author and activist Robert Burrowes holds a similar view: that fear, self-hatred and powerlessness embedded in individuals are the deep psychological imperatives that drive the violence in international systems, and all violence is an outcome of the visible and invisible violence inflicted by adults on children.[3] The manner in which these often-unconscious and deeply suppressed emotions are projected into the world is critical to understanding the many violent behavioural outcomes in our world. For example, 'when we do not let a child say what it wants (or ignore it when it does), the child develops communication and behavioural dysfunctionalities as it keeps trying to meet its own needs (which, as a basic survival strategy, it is genetically programmed to do)'.[4] If we want children to grow up to be nonviolent, truthful, compassionate, loving and courageous, they must be treated with and experience those positive traits.

Parenting is one of the most important tasks anyone can take on, yet there are no qualifications required or degrees offered in it. Making children's emotional well-being our top social priority brings benefits for all of humanity, and our child-rearing choices can be the most powerful agents for positive social change and planetary healing. Grille offers practical suggestions on how to move from authoritarian to authoritative parenting, where parents are firm when necessary, without being rigid disciplinarians or draconian, emotionally-distant martinets demanding obedience, as has often been the case in the past, especially with fathers. It's possible to promote children's emotional intelligence so they can grow to have the healthiest and most rewarding relationships with others, and fulfil their potential. Exploding the myth of perfect parents, however, Grille examines a range of traditional and non-traditional families, noting that child-rearing is a communal enterprise and providing a developmental map of the five stages of core emotional development in early childhood. He concludes that the continuing evolution of child-rearing may give us reason for hope.

The mother–infant/child relationship is an essential factor for whether a child becomes loving or violent.[5] Nurturing, breastfeeding (where possible), intimate safe touch and movement during the most sensitive stages of brain growth are important for healthy development. Children deprived of this nurturing are at risk on many levels, including lifelong patterns of depression, alienation, lack of impulse control, substance abuse and violence. Enormous amounts of primate research have proven that a failure in bonding causes the brain to develop abnormally, both anatomically and neuro-chemically. These effects can be observed as early as infancy in depressed infants and young children. Prescott's *The Origins of Love and Violence: Bonding and Brain Development*[6] is a useful resource if you want 'scientific proof' for the central thesis, although the reliance on primate research may be regarded as cruel, unethical and questionable.

Parenting Styles

Four main parenting styles are authoritarian, disengaged, permissive and supportive. Authoritarian parenting is characterised by structure, boundaries and discipline but does not encourage children to make their own decisions; consequently, they can lack self-worth. Disengaged parenting is when a parent shows care for their child's basic needs but neglects their deeper emotional needs, often resulting in anxious and insecure children. Permissive parenting involves an absence of structure, boundaries and discipline, which can lead to children lacking limits and social skills. For psychologist and parenting expert Jodie Benveniste, the best parenting style is a supportive one in which parents listen attentively to their children, set fair boundaries and encourage them not to be too concerned about making mistakes. Children raised under a supportive style generally have good social skills and are confident, emotionally mature and happy.[7]

To demonstrate the importance of parenting for peace, let's examine the impact that violent or abusive parenting within a culture of authoritarianism can have on children. While 'realist' theorists might believe that peace occurs at the highest levels according to who has the most power, this sort of micro-level analysis relating to psychology and emotional intelligence can shed light on a very different perspective of peacebuilding.

Joseph Stalin

Our first case study is Joseph Stalin, a brutal dictator who orchestrated the unforgivable murder and starvation of at least 20 million civilians between 1927 and 1953.[8] A conventional presumption is that he was inherently evil, the sort of person born with innate murderous tendencies (and who can only be resisted through violence). But let's look at his early life and test that hypothesis.

Both his parents had been born as serfs and were only emancipated in 1864. Stalin's two older brothers died very young, and Stalin was fortunate to survive smallpox, which he contracted when he was five and which scarred his face permanently.[9] His alcoholic father, Besarion (or Beso), was often involved in drunken brawls and would eventually be exiled from their hometown of Gori, Georgia, for attacking a policeman. Beso regularly beat and terrified his wife and son. Stalin claimed that he had once thrown a knife at Beso to prevent him from assaulting Stalin's mother, Keke. So he was brought up within an atmosphere of domestic violence, developed a great deal of fear and no doubt inner trauma, and grew to believe that violence was a valid – indeed necessary – solution to violent attacks. A childhood friend, Iremashvili, claimed that

> Undeserved and severe beatings made the boy as hard and heartless as the father was. Since all people in authority over others seemed to him to be like his father, there soon arose in him a vengeful feeling against all people standing above him. From childhood on, the realisation of his thoughts of revenge became the aim to which everything was subordinated.[10]

Beso's business eventually failed, and the family fell into poverty, was forced to leave their home and lived in an array of rented rooms over the next decade. Keke finally fled the abusive relationship, and with Joseph moved into the house of a family friend, a priest. A strict mother and devout Christian, Keke worked as a cleaner. Stalin's poverty, facial scarring and estranged father, along with local rumours that Beso was not Stalin's real father, cannot have helped his self-esteem. Even as a child, Stalin began to exhibit a number of disturbing idiosyncrasies. He and his friends formed a gang and often fought with other local children, a forerunner for his murderous activities later. He reputedly played with explosives and was cruel to animals, no doubt transferring his feelings of anger, sadness and hatred onto others. At 12, he was injured and hospitalised for months, sustaining a lifelong disability to his left arm.

His father subsequently kidnapped him and forced him to work as an apprentice cobbler in a factory, work which he reputedly found raw, harsh and dispiriting. After Stalin was rescued from this situation, Beso cut all contact with his wife and son, except for occasionally pestering Stalin for the money he earned singing in a choir. Stalin was further traumatized in 1892 when his school teachers took his class to witness some public hangings, an event which left a deep and lasting impression on him and provided further reinforcement for the idea that authority figures used violence to teach people lessons and resolve societal problems. Later, he joined a seminary, escaped into the imaginary world of Alexander Kazbegi's tales of heroic resistance and was repeatedly confined to a cell for his increasingly rebellious behaviour.[11]

This upbringing, devastating as it was for his psychic and physical well-being, was far from exceptional in that time and place, where society was accepting of authoritarian rule and a measure of violence within the home. Stalin's personality was therefore due to a complex blend of influences – including a dysfunctional family unit within a framework of patriarchal societal norms – that perpetuated violence in the home and, as a result produced violent individuals.

It's evident that Stalin's persona was shaped by poverty and disadvantage, a violent, demanding and dysfunctional father, and a strict, violent authoritarian society. In this light, it's easier to understand that Stalin was not born a psychopathic monster but was created as such by his upbringing, circumstances and the social milieu he experienced during his formative years. It's unsurprising that he would seek power to compensate for the psychic wounds, emotional turmoil and existential emptiness created by an early childhood filled with violence and abuse – at a time when his brain, body and personality were at crucial points of development. In fact, what is surprising is that Stalin developed an ambition to help others and to address poverty. He excelled at his studies, read widely and immersed himself in Marxism, rising to a position of unprecedented power as the leader of the USSR Empire. With a different upbringing, he may have become a valuable contributor to the world.

Adolf Hitler

Let's look at another person who also killed millions in the most atrocious ways – Adolf Hitler. Yet he was not *born* a monster but an innocent child. His ancestors were peasants, and his father Alois was born out of wedlock, a cause for great scandal in those days of the strict Christianity pervading Austria.[12] Hitler's mother Klara was Alois's second cousin and 20 years younger than Alois. She was his mistress and was pregnant at the time Alois's second wife died. A joint memoir by Hitler's half-brother, also called Alois, and half-sister, Angela, and the 2005 discovery in Germany of a journal written by Hitler's sister, Paula, offer remarkable insights into the dysfunctional nature of the Hitler family, reinforced by its rigid discipline, regimentation and frequent moves to new homes. One excerpt from the joint memoir describes the violence exercised by Hitler's father, and how Hitler's mother tried to protect her son from regular beatings:

> Fearing that the father could no longer control himself in his unbridled rage, she [Adolf's mother] decides to put an end to the beating. She goes up to the attic, covers Adolf who is lying on the floor, but cannot deflect the father's final blow. Without a sound she absorbs it.[13]

This violence intensified when Hitler's half-brother ran away from home at the age of 14, never to see his father again. Hitler then became the main brunt of his father's rages. Hitler's younger brother Edmund died of measles at the age of six; in fact, of his five direct siblings, only one lived past childhood.

Paula Hitler's journal reveals that Hitler echoed the violence and authoritarian nature of his father, claiming that her brother was a bully in his teens and would often beat her. Recounting the earliest memories of her childhood, when she was around 8 and Adolf was 15, Paula wrote: 'Once again I feel my brother's loose hand across my face'.[14] School reports described him as idle, wilful and disrespectful; he preferred war games and the adventure stories of Karl May.[15]

Historian Florian Beierl states that it's now possible to piece together a picture of 'a completely dysfunctional family that the public has never seen before. The terror of the Third Reich was cultivated in Hitler's own home'.[16] According to Swiss psychoanalyst Alice Miller, author of *For Your Own Good: Hidden Cruelty in Child-Rearing and the Roots of Violence*,[17] Hitler once told his secretary that during one of the beatings given to him by his father,

> he was able to stop crying, to feel nothing, and even to count the thirty-two blows he received. In this way, by totally denying his pain, his feelings of powerlessness, and his despair – in other words, by denying the truth – Hitler made himself into a master of violence and of contempt for human beings. The result was a very primitive person, incapable of any empathy for other people. He was mercilessly and constantly driven to new destructive acts by his latent feelings of hatred and revenge.[18]

Largely friendless in childhood, Hitler became increasingly reclusive, resentful and emotionally unstable in his teens, and suffered from chronic health issues. He never seems to have maintained a healthy, long-term romantic relationship. How much that impacted on his psychology is speculative, but it seems obvious that he was a deeply unhappy person on many levels.

Seeking a career in the visual arts, Hitler fought bitterly with his father, who wanted him to enter the Habsburg civil service. After his father's sudden death from a lung haemorrhage while Hitler was still only 13, and his mother's death from breast cancer soon afterwards, Hitler tried to pursue his dream to become an artist, but he failed to gain acceptance to the Vienna Academy of the Arts. He frittered away his inheritance, lived in homeless shelters, experienced poverty and survived by selling his watercolour scenes of Vienna. He departed for Munich in 1913, scarred by this period of poverty and hardship as a young man, and disillusioned by his failure to gain acceptance by the art establishment, leading to bitterness towards social elites in general. He was then forced into the military during World War I, enduring horrific conditions for months at a time, and it's hard to imagine anyone coming out of that without being mentally affected.

Combined with the attitudes towards violence and authority beaten into him from early childhood, it's little wonder that Hitler sought power and became a violent, authoritarian figure with few close relationships.

Alice Miller believes that most people repress their memories of childhood trauma and may be in such extreme denial about the way their parents mistreated them that they may actually, on a conscious level, *idealise* them rather than blame them.[19] This acts as a psychological defence mechanism, protecting the individual from the painful truth. Nevertheless, the unconscious rage and suppressed fantasies of revenge they feel against their parents constantly fizz beneath the surface, looking for an outlet. This outlet takes the form of displacement (the redirecting of one's rage onto innocent victims). According to Miller, Hitler's horrific actions can be traced back to this dysfunctional childhood; his heinous actions as an adult were driven by a psychotic and deranged lust for 'revenge on the world' for his childhood suffering.

Hitler's murderous impulses, however, might have amounted to little if others had not joined his pogroms. That so many people were drawn into his madness and obeyed his genocidal orders can partly be attributed to the fact that millions of Germans and other Europeans had experienced the same kind of upbringing he had, where order and obedience were prized above all, where violence was thought necessary, and undesirable feelings and real needs had to be suppressed as vigorously as possible. Many high-ranking Nazi officers had also suffered abusive childhoods, such as morphine-addicted Hermann Göring, whose mother had left him, aged six weeks, with a friend in Bavaria and did not see him again for three years.[20]

None of this excuses the horrendous, unforgivable atrocities perpetrated by these people, but we can begin to understand *why* they happened. These were not people who were necessarily born evil, but whose experiences as children facilitated that path. What also might have made a difference is a different set of opportunities and different sociopolitical and economic contexts. They might still have sought power, but without rigid patriarchal societies, materialistic economies and hierarchical political systems to exploit, this would have come to naught.

Parenting Has Improved

Authoritarian parenting was the norm in many societies in those days, so we are fortunate that attitudes towards parenting have changed and developed towards different, more compassionate, enlightened and empathetic styles that can help us transform those ancient cycles of violence passed on from generation to generation.

Nevertheless, there are still many disagreements on how we should parent, from letting children free-range to being 'helicopter parents' always hovering fearfully or interferingly around. Can we move from the vestiges of authoritarian parenting to supportive but authoritative parenting, which involves setting limits, being firm at times but also spending time discussing and debating issues?

Before we look at some aspects of parenting which can counter widespread cultural violence, let us examine some forms of that violence which impacts on children in their formative years, embedding cultural violence in their psyches so it creates unquestioned assumptions at an unconscious level.

Bringing Up Peaceful, Proactive Children Despite Cultures of Violence

As we've seen in previous chapters, despite some lessening of violence overall, there is still a great deal of structural and cultural violence permeating our societies,[i] such as screen violence. How should we bring up children within this violent milieu, so that they can develop healthily and become part of the solution rather than adding to the problems? Should they be allowed to watch violent films or M-rated films way before they're 15? How do we withstand the pressures that they are under when so many of their peers are allowed to watch such films, pressure which they then turn on their parents?

War Toys

And what if all their friends are given toy guns such as water pistols and have parties where they use these in mock battles? Is this just harmless play, or does it lead them to accept militarism from an early age, to accept that guns are an allowable part of society? Does it reinforce that guns have a great symbolic power as something that can easily resolve problems, can deal with the bad guys, the invaders or the 'Indians' who, for some strange, savage reason, are refusing to leave the cowboys alone?

As one *Creating Cultures of Peace* student noted:

> I have been teaching Prep (4-year-olds) and have been struck by how automatically the kids (boys in particular – in fact, almost always the boys) begin to play at violence, given any opportunity. The second they pick up a long stick, block, etc. it is a 'gun'. Everything seems to become a gun in a small boy's hand! They seem to want to 'shoot' each other for hours. I struggle to know how to deal with this. The main strategy I have

---

i One potential birthday gift for children is a giant, militaristic, wall-decorating k[illegible] emblazoned with a fighter jet, tank and helicopter and the words 'Happy birthday!' [illegible] is 'also great as a background for taking pictures at the party!'. Ironically, it warns th[illegible] the plastic wrapping can be dangerous.

> come up with has been redirecting the play, joining in with them with a different type of imaginative suggestion. The favourite has become 'torches' instead of 'guns' so lately the boys will run around with their sticks etc. 'looking for animals in the jungle'. Or sometimes the sticks can be 'shovels' and we are 'digging for treasure or dinosaur bones' etc. But it is hard! Because, like the kids with the horror films, these kids insist they love guns and playing army and everything.

One definitive study found that children who are allowed to play with toy guns are more likely to be violent in later life.[21] The findings included that parental attitudes to play-fighting and aggression are the most important factors in shaping a child's future behaviour, and that parents with attitudes that accept violence (such as using the 'if they hit you, hit them back' mantra) have more aggressive offspring. According to Professor Pamela Orphinas, of the University of Georgia,

> Parents have the opportunity to give clear and explicit messages to their children that fighting is not acceptable and show them some alternatives to solve conflicts. They can play an important role in preventing violence among adolescents.[22]

Sometimes, all you can hope for is that you will instil peaceful values in your children by modelling good practices yourself and maintaining clear, open, honest paths of communication. This includes talking through your decisions and rules and engaging in dialogue about issues of violence. Rather than making a big deal about guns and movie violence, a gentle talk about these topics, along with some clear guidelines and boundaries, and the possibilities of negotiated compromises, will probably have a greater long-term impact.

Although there is a danger that banning toy guns makes them more attractive and drives them underground, a counterargument is that such bans express adult disapproval of them. Many schools around the world have implemented zero-tolerance policies on guns, and in some cases, have suspended children for pointing their fingers in the shape of a gun and pretending to shoot another student.[23] Klaus Dodds, professor of Geopolitics at Royal Holloway, University of London, says

> We are a country addicted to war. We are a highly militarised society and I think children and the relationship to toys is one aspect of that broader debate about what Britain is and represents.[24]

Peace activists in Pakistan, where military tensions with India remain high, are campaigning hard against war toys, aiming to get imitation Kalashnikovs and Glocks off the streets because they help breed a culture of violence among children. Sana Ijaz, from Khyber Pakhtunkhwa Province, explains why they pose a threat in the restive north-western province: 'If we expose our children to these things from a tender age, it will not be difficult for them to fall into the hands of extremists when they are teenagers'.[25] Abubakar Siddique and colleagues write that NGOs, poets, singers and peace activists have been staging walks, petitioning the authorities and talking to parents and shopkeepers in the hope of minimising interest in the toy weapons that traders stock up on during Eid al-Fitr celebrations at the end of Ramadan.[26]

Another imaginative initiative is 'War Toys for Peace', which observes that a photographer has been on every battlefield since the Crimean War, yet none have been included in sets of toy soldiers mass-produced since the 1930s. They are working to add civilian photojournalist figures to those soldier collections sold around the world.

> Small as the change may appear, the presence of these figures radically alters the inherent play pattern of the classic toys – giving children more play options than *us versus them* – while also promoting ideas of press freedom and racial and gender equality.[27]

With several figures in development, each inspired by actual women and men who have dedicated their lives to documenting armed conflict, they hope to expand the programme into other product categories, including dolls, dollhouses, preschool toys and other non-military action figures. Their aim is to reach hundreds of thousands, and even millions, of children, better support their development and promote more peaceful ideals on a global scale.

Violence and Video Games

As children get older, they move on from mock gun battles to consuming more media and playing screen-based games, many of which have aggressive content. One meta-analysis by psychologists of video game research found that playing games with violent content increases aggressive behaviour and thoughts.[28] The analysis also showed that playing video games with hostile content creates a temporary decline in pro-social behaviours in both children and adults.

Another survey found that a typical day of media usage by 8- to 18-year-olds in America involved more than seven and a half hours overall, using a variety of media such as computers, video games, music and internet usage. Heavier consumers of media (more than 16 hours per day) were found to have low levels of personal contentment, as well as becoming easily bored and frustrated.[29]

An FBI investigation found that one of the characteristics of US school shooters is a fascination with violence-filled entertainment, most importantly video games such as 'Doom'.[30] Yet the US military hopes to use violent video games as teaching tools, claiming that they enable them to incorporate international conventions of warfare and human rights into their battlefield scenarios. Critics, however, respond that some of the most popular games allow players to commit violations of accepted international law, such as shooting wounded prisoners, torturing detainees or using prohibited chemical weapons – with no negative consequences.[31] Shooting enemies is the core element of many video games, and gun companies such as Barrett use video games to market their products to young people. Through secretive deals between game makers and gun manufacturers, they now include models of real-life guns in their games.[32]

Parents can help here by monitoring what games are allowed in the home, when they can be played and for how long. They can also model spending minimal – or at least moderate – time on their own phones and computers, and understanding and communicating how such devices and their platforms, services and apps are designed to be highly addictive through psychological strategies and sophisticated AI systems built on intrusive data gathering.[33]

Board Games and Violence

Even our board games can be examined for their relationship to violence or peace. 'Monopoly', for example, was originally devised by progressive writer Elizabeth Magie Phillips in 1904 at a time when games were marketed to parents to *teach* children as well as entertain them. First known as 'The Landlord's Game', Phillips created it to teach players about the dangers of wealth concentration and the destructive nature of monopolies and capitalism.[34] It was informed by the teachings of anti-monopolist Henry George, whose 1879 book, *Progress and Poverty*, widely read at the time, argued that governments had no right to tax labour (such taxes are a disincentive for productivity) but should only raise revenue from land taxes (such as council rates based on land value). George's followers insist that this is a fairer and simpler system, which makes land and home ownership more accessible and affordable, and which minimises bureaucracies.

Yet Monopoly is now generally played uncritically, almost as training for life under capitalism. Each player is alone and competing against everyone else, aiming to amass wealth and destroy others. With its emphasis on selfish accumulation, individualism rather than collegiality, and competition over cooperation, its values are the opposite of those required for positive peace, and it can thus be seen as encouraging structural and ecological violence (Figure 7.1). Although created by a woman, its primary symbol now is 'Mr

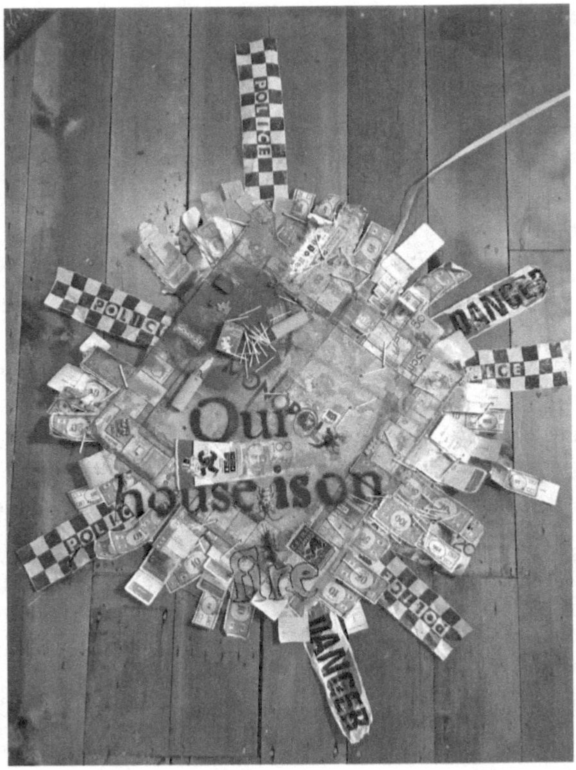

Figure 7.1 'Playing Monopoly While Our House Is on Fire', mixed media artwork by Francesca Nano-Branagan and Marty Branagan.

Monopoly', also known as 'Rich Uncle Pennybags', a man dressed as an early twentieth-century tycoon, which is now one of the most recognisable brand icons in the world, made more prominent by its association with fast food giant McDonalds.

Another game, 'Cluedo' (called 'Clue' in North America), has more obvious links to (direct) violence as each player has to guess who committed a murder, in what room and with what weapon. The weapon aspect is perhaps the most macabre, as the players regularly handle potential murder weapons – a lead pipe, a wrench, a rope, a pistol and so on. Of course, it is 'only a game', but imagining someone being bashed to death, as this game can enable, seems a further contribution to our society's desensitisation to and acceptance of violence.

Empathy Games

A more positive, emerging category of role-playing computer games is demonstrating how the genre can be used to discuss awkward and even painful subjects.

> Parents and lovers have replaced terrorists and aliens in a new generation of video games. The battlefield has given way to the bedroom. The goal is no longer world domination but paying child support.[35]

This booming genre of 'empathy games' asks players to inhabit their character's emotional worlds, dealing with themes such as poverty, homophobia and mental illness, or getting them to play citizen journalists documenting race riots. Using relatable scenarios that take participants on internal journeys rather than escapism, some empathy games incorporate moral decisions into futuristic settings, such as players acting as customs officers faced with difficult choices like whether to accept a bribe or let their family go hungry; keep their job or covertly admit deserving refugees.[36]

Cooperative and Nonviolent Activist Games

Artistic activities, such as making something together as a family or neighbourhood, can involve everyone equally, allowing them to add their own creativity to the project. Breaking the dependence on technology together helps relieve the addictive pressures that technologies can cause, and allows opportunities for group growth and harmony.

Numerous games which encourage cooperation rather than competition, and therefore have a calming instead of divisive effect on families, can be found in shops (including second-hand ones) or online, sometimes as free downloads.

There are even activist and nonviolent action games, such as 'A Force More Powerful' (www.aforcemorepowerful.org/game/), which follows the book and popular documentary series of the same name. 'Rise Up' is a crowd-funded board game produced by the TESA Collective, a worker cooperative that creates resources for social change as a counterpoint to games like 'Risk' that teach conquest and exploitation.[37] Rise Up is designed for activists, new and old, to practice building social movements, which can be as serious as ensuring a living wage or as silly as 'free pizza for everyone'. In an enjoyable way, participants learn the basics of movement-building, including its concepts, strategies and tactics. They can engage in a 'grassroots media campaign' or overcome obstacles like a 'rising wave of conservatism'. Because it's a collaborative game (like a cooperative version of Monopoly which the cooperative also makes), everyone wins or loses together. When you act (using ethically-made dice), you help your teammates. Even experienced campaign organisers can use the game to gain new perspectives on their work.

Sport: The Case for and Against

Sport has many benefits but can also encourage competitiveness, bullying, violence and sectarianism. Research shows that many elite athletes, such as David Beckham, Tiger Woods, Jelena Dokic and Andre Agassi, suffered parental abuse as children, and this abuse continues to occur in community sport.[38] This might include inordinate criticism, shouting, insults and humiliation, excessively training youths to extreme exhaustion or nausea, and ignoring a child following a losing sport performance. Controlling behaviour by parents is often portrayed as necessary for success as an athlete, but it can harm their confidence and self-esteem, cause anxiety, depression and dropping out of sport altogether. Evidence suggests that those elite athletes were successful *in spite of* the high-pressure home environment, not because of it.

While sports events can bring fans together in celebration and camaraderie, they often lead to spikes in violence against women and children.[39] This increase in violence is roughly the same whether the perpetrators' teams win or lose and is caused by 'a volatile mix of alcohol (and sometimes drugs), gambling, toxic masculinity, heightened emotions, tribalism and competition'.[40] The failure of sporting bodies and alcohol brands to discourage excessive drinking by fans is also at fault. As mentioned in Chapter 3, solutions include phasing out alcohol advertising in the media and restricting the type of outdoor ads and sponsorships seen at major sporting events.

Sport can also be used to let off steam in a safe way. It can lead to healthy exercise and encourage cooperation and teamwork within teams. It can be used to make peace in warring regions, as shown through the many resources available on the 'Peace and Sport' website (www.peace-sport.org). In Australia, there are high-level attempts to make children's sport less competitive and more fun, such as 'Let Kids Be Kids' by the 'Play By The Rules' organisation (www.playbytherules.net.au). Working collaboratively with groups like the 'Diversity and Inclusion in Sport Alliance', they explore how to reduce and deal with abuse from the sidelines and online, and how to reform intense parental behaviour and expectations. Parents and coaches should focus on letting children have fun, make friends, engage socially, get sunshine and fresh air, learn new skills, enjoy the moment and get the most out of the games they love.[41]

Discipline

Until the last few decades, discipline often involved corporal punishment, such as smacking. It is still acceptable in some places. One Singapore-based student observed that:

> [T]he element of culture has a huge impact upon the view of corporal punishment. Within Singapore any male under 50yrs may still receive a public canning and within the homes corporal punishment is still an

> acceptable form of discipline. Many proponents of corporal punishment within Singapore will argue that these tactics are contributing factors towards the structured and disciplined society that enjoys a minimal crime rate. It is not unusual to see parents disciplining children through corporal punishment approaches whilst in the street. It took some time to have our own children adjust to witnessing this, without expecting their father to 'save the child'.

However, child psychologist Michael Grose, founder of 'Parenting Ideas', suggests numerous reasons not to smack, including that smacking is ineffective in the long term, with the improvements in behaviour being only short-term. Smacking may lead to bullying and cause insecurities in children. Smacking may produce the opposite effect to that desired by the parents, in that the child may lose, rather than gain, respect for the adult who uses smacking.

Smacking has been found to negatively impact brain development and is associated with worse behavioural and emotional outcomes, according to child psychology writer Rinjani Soengkoeng. While it has long been thought effective for teaching respect and right behaviour, new research shows that it is unlikely to be effective as a form of discipline, as the connection between the unwanted behaviour and the punishment often is not clear. Additionally, children learn that they should do things because they might be punished if they don't, rather than because it's the right thing to do.[42]

Other problems with corporal punishment, write African peace scholars Beatrice Umubyeyi and Geoff Harris, include that children subjected to it are likely to accept it and use it when they become parents, thereby educating children to use violence and violating any commitment to nonviolence. However, many continue to use it in the home as they are unaware of any alternative methods of disciplining.[43]

Corporal punishment has been banned from many schools around the world after long campaigns by parenting experts. This has been a great step forward, but it also created a disciplinary vacuum for many teachers and parents brought up under corporal punishment regimes, with some abandoning discipline altogether and adopting permissive parenting styles. As noted above, this can prevent children from gaining a sense of boundaries and acceptable behaviour.

Arguably, better strategies to discipline children have been adopted, and this makes for better problem-solving in the long run, without the need to resort to violence. One concrete example of positive change is in classrooms, where a move encouraging greater collaboration amongst students is shown by circular desk arrangements. Verbal communication about issues is encouraged in dialogue between children, with little adult authority intervening. Parents can encourage positive behaviours by:

- Being clear about what is expected in different situations and sticking to these rules,
- Modelling acceptable behaviour,
- Explaining why behaviours are positive or negative, and
- Noticing and rewarding good behaviour.[44]

Hopefully, the world leaders of tomorrow will emerge from such systems, having been exposed to lots of challenges to develop skills in conflict transformation, without fear of suffering physical pain for punishments for which they may not understand the reason in the first place.

You Are the Adult in the Room

Parents tend to smack their children when they're experiencing high levels of negative emotion, which can be exacerbated by the stresses of modern living.[45] As adults, however, parents need to be responsible for managing their emotions and nurturing the parent–child relationship. They can regulate their own anger and stress by taking deep breaths or counting to 10, having a glass of water or even temporarily removing themselves from a situation to calm down before dealing with it. Buddhists call this acting from a 'cool heart', rather than reacting inappropriately or disproportionately while in emotional turmoil. Other strategies involve calling their partner or a friend for support, and investing in long-term strategies to minimise outbursts, such as daily yoga or regular exercise, which we discuss in the final chapter.[46]

Juggling parenting with work commitments can be difficult but can be aided by changing one's home and family arrangements to improve work–life balance, and negotiating family-friendly work arrangements such as working from home (which has remained high even after the COVID-19 pandemic has subsided). Working flexible or part-time hours, or sharing your job with another part-time employee may be other options. Changing work habits to support work–life balance can include leaving work behind at the end of the day by calling family members on the way home to take your mind off work and catch up on your family's day. Rituals or routines such as changing out of work clothes, taking a walk or doing a quick workout can mark the physical, mental and emotional shift from work to home, from worker to parent. Changing perspectives on work can occur by taking a moment in the workday to think about your children, and by taking them to social occasions at work.[47]

Sometimes poor behaviour can result from anxiety. This can be reduced by explaining to children how anxiety works and helping them recognise anxiety-inducing events so they can manage and minimise their feelings of anxiety. They can also be supported to develop the tools to regulate and push their anxious feelings to the background, such as through sufficient sleep, good nutrition and physical exercise, which is a great distraction and also releases feel-good endorphins that help young people feel better and more optimistic about the future.[48]

Communicating Well with Children

In Chapter 2, we looked at the importance of peaceful language and communication, and this is a vital aspect of parenting, as parents are the first language teachers and role models for children. Although most parents love their children, they may be unable to show this love, or unwilling to in case it 'spoils' them. They may rarely compliment the children, or only give back-handed compliments, so as not to 'give them a big head'. In many cultures, it is *de rigeur* to denigrate children as lazy or wilful or some other character flaw, and this is magnified when done in front of other people. Constantly calling them names does not help. All this might be regarded by the adults 'as a joke', but it can instil both self-doubt and resentment in the children, since their inner voice is shaped from birth by the parents' voices.

Breaking these ancient cycles of parental communication can be difficult but is important for peacebuilding. It can begin with small steps, such as criticising the behaviour, not the child, and sandwiching any criticism with some positive feedback.

The Alliance for Childhood[49] suggests the following for building close relationships with children:

- Take them for a walk;
- Supply them with art and writing materials so they can express their emotions and thoughts;
- Dedicate a room or area to peaceful reflection;
- Make time for creative play;
- Teach your children values;
- Set an example of peaceful behaviour;
- Teach your children about peaceful leaders like Emily Pankhurst, Mahatma Gandhi, Martin Luther King, Te Whiti and Elise Boulding.

Attempts to create wider peace through high-quality parenting can occur in an ad hoc way in small family units that hope to influence their immediate circles of family and friends. It can also occur in a more organised way, supported by major institutions. For example, family-based initiatives by organisations such as UNICEF illustrate that achieving peaceful families, even within societies immersed in armed conflict, is possible.[50] To safeguard the development of children and families affected by war, as well as promote resilient and peaceful cultures, UNICEF launched innovative early childhood development interventions in efforts to deter violence and lay a strong foundation for children to develop into proactive peace-advocating community members.

For instance, in Uganda, UNICEF has established early childhood education services in areas which have historically lacked social services. These services are aimed at responding to educational gaps and enabling children to have better cognitive and social development after years of violent conflict.[51] More than 424 centres were established across Uganda in the communities, benefiting more than 100,000 children aged from three to five. The initiative targeted marginalised families and played an important role in improving social cohesion and peace. By providing a platform for sharing peacebuilding messages to the families and the community, and by offering safety and security to children in the care centres, these initiatives promoted resilience and tolerance.[52]

Similar interventions were implemented in the Moyen-Cavallay and Tonkpi regions in Côte d'Ivoire. The interventions provide a platform to discuss conflict-related challenges affecting women, children, families and the community at large.[53] Mechanisms were also established to resolve conflicts within the families, thus rebuilding family – and eventually societal – cohesion, tolerance and cohabitation.

Parenting and Gender

One important question is that of the role of gender in child-rearing. I remember playing commandoes; cowboys and 'Indians'; soldiers; and ninjas, and doing lots of mock shooting, inspired by the movies I'd seen and comics I'd read. I'm pleased to say that my kids haven't followed down this path, apart from the odd aberration (such as an occasional desire to do paintball).

Is playing with guns something inherent to male biology, or is it more likely to be socialised into them in a continuation of a long tradition? Are boys parented differently, such as being given more latitude which excuses bad behaviour, and more readily forgiven noisy, unruly or violent behaviours under the ethos 'boys will be boys' or 'they're just being boys'?

Girls, on the other hand, are reined in earlier, are forbidden such behaviour or get moral pressure to behave in a 'lady-like' way rather than be a 'tomboy' While acknowledging some physical differences, can't boys learn not to be violent and competitive, through being set equal rules as those given to girls along with good advice and guidance? Should girls be given more latitude to be boisterous, climb trees, have rumbles and get dirty?

We should keep in mind here that the quietness and sedentary stillness we require in school classrooms is an aberration in human history, for most of which children have roamed freely, learning from their parents, siblings and peers rather than in large groups of similar ages and presided over by one teacher.

At the centre of the issue of whether boys and girls should be parented differently is the 'nature versus nurture' debate. Some differences between boys and girls can be observed, such as infant girls developing verbal skills faster than boys and being generally better at interpreting emotions, while boys have a better understanding of spatial relationships.[54]

Studies have also shown that boys and girls play differently in the playground. For example, girls tend to play in small groups and engage in activities which emphasise group support, such as skipping with ropes, while boys often play in larger groups and engage in activities which involve competition.[55] However, is this because our society impresses gender roles upon children from a young age, or is this because of biological differences between girls and boys? Many parents will parent their children according to gender roles, such as being less quick to comfort their sons when they hurt themselves, as well as being less likely to read their sons a bedtime story.[56]

Some research argues that this type of gendered parenting is the reason boys reach emotional milestones and verbal skills later than girls. Experts tend to agree that all children should be raised with the same values and expectations for behaviour, and in equally supportive and nurturing environments, regardless of gender.[57] Supporting gender diversity, intersex status and sexual diversity are also increasingly recognised as important for the well-being of young people.

Children and Environmental Peacebuilding

How we model behaviour towards our natural environment, and how we set up our homes and gardens can also be an element in creating a peaceful and nurturing atmosphere to raise children. If we build a tall fence as soon as we join a neighbourhood, and train a couple of large dogs to aggressively bark and leap at all passers-by, we are sending a message to our children and neighbours that we fear and dislike the world and need to protect ourselves vigorously from it, much like the border walls that separate the world's rich nations from the poor.[58]

On the other hand, town planners can mandate no front fences, as is the case in Canberra (low hedges are acceptable), a city devised under 'garden city' principles following the nature-friendly urban design by architects/town planners Marian and Walter Burley-Griffin, which maintained hills as public spaces with native vegetation. The first building regulations passed in 1924 for Canberra houses set a precedent that has been followed ever since. The lack of front fences (with a few exceptions, such as for embassies) builds community spirit and is generally liked and accepted by residents.[59]

Parents can model simplicity as a lifestyle choice, as advocated by eco-anarchist Ted Trainer as a solution to the global crisis of capitalism.[60] Trainer calls for de-growth, self-sufficient local economies, more cooperative and participatory ways such as commons, co-ops and working bees, and new values, replacing 'individualistic, competitive and acquisitive orientation to a world view focused on being content with frugal sufficiency and living within a supportive community in which all enjoy a high quality of life'.[61] This cannot be mandated from top-down but must be built from the bottom up, in 'prefigurative politics'.

Parents can also model environmentally-friendly behaviour, such as through composting food scraps, which can produce a valuable resource, reduce landfill by up to half and dramatically reduce the emission of methane, a potent greenhouse gas. They can minimise fast fashion, avoid aggressive tee-shirt logos and try to buy clothes in natural fibres rather than synthetic ones which shed micro-plastics. They can resist children's desires to buy knives or wear camouflage clothing or other military apparel (such as the US Army jacket I so desired as a child, or the army pants I wore hitch-hiking around Australia and at logging blockades). They can recycle; volunteer; encourage walking and cycling; bank and buy ethically; resist over-packaging; encourage healthy diets that are primarily plant-based; and seek out local organic products if they can afford them.[ii]

If they're fortunate enough to have a garden or balcony, they can transform them into a place of peace, beauty and sustainability (while reducing dependence on agribusiness and its high environmental footprint), as discussed in Chapter 5. Those who live in buildings with more gardens and plants are less aggressive, while visits to urban parks can encourage altruism.[62]

Pets have many benefits although (primarily) carnivores such as dogs have a high carbon footprint,[iii] bite 100 million people annually (mainly children and postal workers),[63] killing about 30,000 of these,[64] and they

---

ii Conventional agribusiness is heavily subsidised. Organic and ethical products currently tend to cost more, but the more the markets expand and get government, corporate and institutional support, the lower the prices should become.

iii Advocates note that having dogs results in a smaller footprint than having a child.

menace many more and cause countless noise pollution disputes. Dogs and cats are glamorised by advertising from the (meat-based) pet food industry but have a devastating impact on wildlife[65] unless in highly urbanised spaces or kept indoors (which rarely occurs); both are a luxury most of the world's people cannot afford. Instead, parents can facilitate interactions with animals by keeping, where possible, chickens, ducks or small pets, or making frequent visits to parks and wild spaces.

Regularly disconnecting families from technology and immersing them in nature, both tame and wild, can counter 'nature-deficit syndrome'; improve physical and emotional health; connect families; and provide a powerful therapy for depression, obesity, and attention deficit disorder. Similarly, environment-based education can improve school performances and develop skills in problem-solving, critical thinking, and decision-making.[66] Developing familiarity with and positive attitudes towards the natural world is crucial to its preservation and to countering ecological violence.[67]

*

This chapter has focused on parenting for peace, but many of the same principles and questions apply to how we interact with our siblings, peers, housemates, partners and friends in order to create peace in the family and beyond. The same ideals of clear communication, honesty, inner work, humility and holding strongly to ideals – while having flexibility and the ability to compromise – all equally apply. While better one-on-one interactions seem insignificant in the face of wars and the regional humanitarian crises they cause, learning effective nonviolent strategies for dealing with conflict from early childhood is imperative for achieving local and wider cultures of peace. The world is made up of billions of people profoundly impacted by their parenting. Among them are present and future world leaders and corporate CEOs, whose top-down actions can help cultivate world peace, especially if they are led there by large grassroots movements of mindful peacebuilders and charismatic movement leaders. The next chapter is on a subject closely related to this one – peace education.

Notes

1 Grille, Robin 2005 *Parenting for a Peaceful World,* Longueville Media, Alexandria, NSW.
2 Ibid.
3 Burrowes, Robert n.d. *Why Violence?* http://tinyurl.com/whyviolence
4 Burrowes, Robert 2012 'Why are human beings violent?' *Counter Currents*, 4 August, https://countercurrents.org/burrowes040812.htm

5 Prescott, James W. 2006 *The Origins of Love and Violence: Bonding and Brain Development* (CD-ROM), Byron Publications, Mullumbimby, NSW.
6 Ibid.
7 Beveniste, J. 2019 'What parenting style works best for children?', *South Australia Department for Education*, www.education.sa.gov.au/parenting-and-child-care/parenting/parenting-sa/parent-easy-guides/what-parenting-style-works-best-children-jodie-benveniste, para. 11–16).
8 Ghosh, Palash R. 2013 'How many people did Joseph Stalin kill?', *International Business Times*, 3 May, www.ibtimes.com/how-many-people-did-joseph-stalin-kill-1111789
9 Bullock, Alan 1993 *Hitler and Stalin: Parallel Lives*, Fontana Press, London, p. 3.
10 Cited in Bullock 1993, p. 4.
11 Bullock 1993, p. 5.
12 Ibid.
13 Cited in Diver, Krysia 2005 'Journal reveals Hitler's dysfunctional family', *Guardian*, 4 August, www.theguardian.com/world/2005/aug/04/research.secondworldwar
14 Ibid.
15 Bullock 1993, p. 6.
16 Cited in Diver 2005.
17 Miller, Alice 2002 *For Your Own Good: Hidden Cruelty in Child-Rearing and the Roots of Violence*, 3rd edition, Farrar, Straus and Giroux, New York.
18 Miller, Alice 1998 'Adolf Hitler: How could a monster succeed in blinding a nation?' *The Natural Child Project*, www.naturalchild.org/articles/alice_miller/adolf_hitler.html
19 Miller 1998, 2002.
20 Manvell, Roger and Fraenkel, Heinrich 2011 [1962] *Goering: The Rise and Fall of the Notorious Nazi Leader*, Skyhorse, London.
21 McVeigh, Tracy 1999 'Toy guns create violent adults', *Guardian*, 21 November, www.theguardian.com/uk/1999/nov/21/tracymcveigh.theobserver
22 Cited in McVeigh 1999.
23 Patton, Iain 2017 'The Glamorization of Toy Guns – Counter-productive Symbolism?' *Huffington Post*, 6 January, www.huffpost.com/entry/the-glamorization-of-toy-guns-counter-productive-symbolism_b_8860514
24 Cited in Patton 2017.
25 Siddique, Abubakar, Karimi, Zafar and Jan, Shabbir 2013 'Pakistani activists take aim at Toy Guns', *Radio Free Europe*, 5 August, www.rferl.org/a/pakistan-toy-guns-campaign/25066585.html
26 Ibid.
27 '"War Toys for Peace" Launches' 2020 *War Toys*, 27 November, https://wartoys.org/news/2020/11/war-toys-for-peace
28 Anderson, C. A. and Bushman, B. J. 2001 'Effects of violent video games on aggressive Behavior, aggressive cognition, aggressive affect, physiological arousal, and prosocial Behavior: A meta-analytic review of the scientific literature', *Psychological Science*, vol. 12, no. 5, pp. 353–359.
29 Rideout, V. J., Foehr, U. G. and Roberts, D. F. 2010 *Generation M2: Media in the Lives of 8-to 18-Year-Olds*, Henry J. Kaiser Family Foundation, pp. 1–78.
30 Thompson, Jack 2018 'The connection between school massacres and violent video games', *Washington Examiner*, 20 March, www.washingtonexaminer.com/opinion/op-eds/the-connection-between-school-massacres-and-violent-video-games

31 Soch, Jonathan 2015 'U.S. military hopes violent video games can serve as teaching tool', *Washington Times*, 19 April, www.washingtontimes.com/news/2015/apr/19/us-military-hopes-violent-video-games-can-serve-as/
32 Parkin, Simon 2019 'Shooters: How video games fund arms manufacturers', *Eurogamer*, 14 May, www.eurogamer.net/shooters-how-video-games-fund-arms-manufacturers
33 Wood, Charlie 2021 'How smartphones hijack the brain', *Brain Facts*, 8 January, www.brainfacts.org/neuroscience-in-society/tech-and-the-brain/2021/how-smartphones-hijack-the-brain-010821
34 Hoy, Benjamin 2019 'Monopoly was designed 100 years ago to teach the dangers of capitalism',*Conversation*, 15 March, https://theconversation.com/monopoly-was-designed-100-years-ago-to-teach-the-dangers-of-capitalism-112198
35 Begley, Patrick 2014 '"Empathy gaming" focuses on emotions and moral decisions', *Sydney Morning Herald*, 30 October, www.smh.com.au/technology/empathy-gaming-focuses-on-emotions-and-moral-decisions-20140904-10ch4z.html
36 Ibid.
37 Peters, Alele 2016 'This board game is designed for activists to practice building movements', *Fast Company*, 11 October, www.fastcoexist.com/3064323/this-board-game-is-designed-for-activists-to-practice-building-movements
38 Woessner, Mary, Parker, Alexandra and Pankowiak, Aurélie 2023 'What the David Beckham documentary tells us–and what it doesn't – about controlling parents in sport', *Conversation*, 18 October, https://theconversation.com/what-the-david-beckham-documentary-tells-us-and-what-it-doesnt-about-controlling-parents-in-sport-215437
39 Pescud, Melanie 2018 'Whether teams win or lose, sporting events lead to spikes in violence against women and children', *Guardian*, 13 July, https://theconversation.com/whether-teams-win-or-lose-sporting-events-lead-to-spikes-in-violence-against-women-and-children-99686
40 Ibid.
41 Woessner et al 2023.
42 Soengkoeng, Rinjani n.d. 'Is smacking children ever OK?' *Quirky Kids*, www.childpsychologist.com.au/resources/smacking-and-children
43 Umubyeyi, Beatrice and Harris, Geoff 2012 'Promoting nonviolent parenting among refugee mothers in Durban', *Social Work*, Issue 48, Number 4, pp. 456–465.
44 Soengkoeng n.d.
45 Regalado, M., Sareen, H., Inkelas, M., Wissow, L. S. and Halfon, N. 2004 'Parents' discipline of young children: Results from the National Survey of Early Childhood Health', *Pediatrics*, vol. 113, no. 6, pp. 1952–1958.
46 Soengkoeng n.d.
47 Raising Children Network 2021 'Work-life balance: Tips for you and your family', *Raising Children*, 27 July, https://raisingchildren.net.au/grown-ups/work-child-care/worklife-balance/work-life-balance
48 Grose, Michael 2019 'Michael Grose: Strategies to help your anxious child', *Parents*, 24 May, https://theparentswebsite.com.au/anxious-child/
49 Alliance for Childhood 2019 *Ten Steps for Peace Education*, http://allianceforchildhood.org/ten_steps
50 Ang, L and Oliver, S 2015 *A Systematic Policy Review of Early Childhood Development and Peacebuilding in Fourteen Conflict-affected and Post-conflict Countries*, UNICEF, UCL Institute of Education, University College, London, pp. 17–19.

51 Affolter, F. W. and Valente, A. A. 2020 'Learning for peace: Lessons learned from UNICEF's peacebuilding, education, and advocacy in conflict-affected context programmes', in *Children and Peace*, Springer, Cham, pp. 219–239.

52 Efevbera, Y., McCoy, D. C., Wuermli, A. J. and Betancourt, T. S. 2018 'Integrating early child development and violence prevention programs: A systematic review', *New Directions for Child and Adolescent Development*, vol. 159, pp. 27–54.

53 Ponguta, L. A., Donaldson, C., Affolter, F., Connolly, P., Dunne, L., Miller, S., Britto, P., Salah, R. and Leckman, J. 2018 'Early childhood development Programs, peacebuilding, and the sustainable development goals: Opportunities for interdisciplinary research and multisectoral partnerships', in *Developmental Science and Sustainable Development Goals for Children and Youth*, Springer, pp. 77–95.

54 Everyday Health 2019 *Parenting Boys vs. Girls: How Different Is It?*, www.everydayhealth.com/kids-health/parenting-boys-vs-girls-how-different-it/, para. 4.

55 Ibid., para.s. 5–6.

56 Ibid., para. 9.

57 Ibid,, para. 14.

58 Jacobs, Frank 2019 '"The West" is, in fact, the world's biggest gated community', *Big Think*, 12 October, https://bigthink.com/strange-maps/walled-world/

59 Saxberg, David 2016 'Why don't Canberra houses have front fences?', *ABC News*, 23 May, www.abc.net.au/news/specials/curious-canberra/2016-05-23/why-dont-canberra-houses-have-front-fences/7401744

60 Trainer, Ted 2017 'The solution to the global crisis of capitalism is simplicity itself', *Insurge Intelligence*, 21 July, https://ageoftransformation.org/the-solution-to-the-global-crisis-of-capitalism-is-simplicity-itself/

61 Ibid.

62 Baird, Julia 2020 *Phosphorescence: On Awe, Wonder and Things that Sustain You When the World Goes Dark*, Fourth Estate, Sydney.

63 'Dog bite attack statistics & bites by breed', 2023 The Law Offices of Samuel Fishman, www.lawofficesofsamuelfishman.com/dog-bite-statistics-by-breed/

64 'Deadliest animals worldwide by annual number of human deaths as of 2022', 2022 *Statista*,www.statista.com/statistics/448169/deadliest-creatures-in-the-world-by-number-of-human-deaths/

65 Doherty, Tim, Dickman, Chris, Nimmo, Dale and Ritchie, Euan 2016 'Invasive predators are eating the world's animals to extinction – and the worst is close to home', *The Conversation*, 20 September, https://theconversation.com/invasive-predators-are-eating-the-worlds-animals-to-extinction-and-the-worst-is-close-to-home-64741

66 Louv, Richard 2008 *Last Child in the Woods: Saving Our Children from Nature-Deficit Disorder*, Algonquin Books, New York.

67 Dobrin, Sidney I. and Kidd, Kenneth B. 2004 *Wild Things: Children's Culture and Ecocriticism*, Wayne State University Press, Detroit.

Chapter 8

PEACE EDUCATION

The last chapter raised the question of how an innocent baby can become a killer and even mass murderer. Here we ask what role education plays in whether people are violent or peaceful – whether they become a soldier remotely operating a lethal drone, a fervent terrorist plotting attacks or a dedicated peace advocate working for nonviolent change. Whether they are docile and apathetic, or empowered and assertive. Ignorant and easily led, or well-informed and independent. Passive consumers who acquiesce with violent systems, or active citizens who use nonviolent methods of conflict transformation. In short, how can our education systems (allied with our parenting) ensure more peaceful, engaged societies?

Peace education is understood as a significant, systematic mechanism for peacebuilding, and ultimately building cooperative systems that are a foundation for a united peace citizenship.[1] It has a long history, with Australian Aboriginal systems of education, leadership and organisation stretching back for millennia; these enabled Aboriginal nations such as the Nhunggabarra to thrive peacefully and minimise ecological violence through the development of intricate sustainability strategies over tens of thousands of years.[2]

It also occurs within a long Western philosophical tradition of education theory, beginning with Jean-Jacques Rousseau in the eighteenth century and including prominent educators such as Germany's Friedrich Froebel; Switzerland's Johann Pestalozzi; Bronson Alcott and John Dewey in the United States; and Italian Maria Montessori. This tradition argues that

> education is not just about the passive assimilation of facts and cultural traditions, but about challenging the mind to become active, competent, and thoughtfully critical in a complex world. This model of education supplanted an older one in which children sat still at desks all day and simply absorbed, and then regurgitated, the material that was brought their way. This idea of active learning, which usually includes a large commitment to critical thinking and argument, traces its roots back to Socrates.[3]

Military Influence on Universities

Education occurs within particular cultural milieus, many of which are influenced by militarism and the wealth and influence of the military-industrial-media-entertainment-finance-academia complex. Corporations from this complex have long sought inroads into universities to access the brightest minds and develop research partnerships. These partnerships also give them kudos and legitimise their activities. In turn, universities, facing declining governmental support in many countries, gain funding, infrastructure and equipment. Many US universities in particular are dependent on military funding and are thus less likely to support peace education, with its strong critiques of the complex.[4]

In 2016 the University of Melbourne, in the Australian state of Victoria, trumpeted the arrival of a new STELaRLab (Science, Technology, Engineering Leadership & Research Laboratory) in partnership with Lockheed Martin, the world's biggest and wealthiest arms corporation, and one of the most corrupt.[5] The collaboration was enabled by the Defence Science Institute, established in 2010 to facilitate the growth of defence science research networks between Victorian universities, government and defence industries. The university's Deputy Vice-Chancellor (Research), Professor James McCluskey, was keen to 'assist Lockheed Martin with their research goals'[6] which presumably include making weapons ever deadlier to humans. They want to 'work together to solve some of the world's most challenging problems'; it's unlikely that this includes reducing defence spending or addressing the global scourge of war. They also hope 'to have high impact'.[7] The Lockheed Martin bomb dropped by a Saudi-led airstrike on a schoolbus in Yemen in 2018, killing 10 adults and 44 children under the age of 15,[8] certainly achieved this goal.

Lockheed Martin has also been infiltrating schools such as Armidale Secondary College with what is mooted as a space-focused educational program, but which the *Australian Defence Magazine* reports as having an underlying motive of building a workforce to create 'next-generation, sovereign military satellite communication'.[9] They aim therefore not just to draw students into the sciences, but military science in particular. Further embedding militarism into the culture, they are complementing this programme by engaging 'an extensive Australian industry network'.[10] This financial influence is one factor in the rise of the physical sciences, often to the detriment of the arts, humanities and social sciences, as observed by Martha Nussbaum.[11]

In 2021 the AUKUS security deal was announced, in which the United Kingdom and United States will supposedly counter the rise of China by supplying Australia with nuclear and other submarines at a cost of

AUD$268,000,000,000 to $368,000,000,000 over the next 30 years.[12] Immediately, 'university after university has jostled to get a slice of the growing militarist pie [...] [and] the Western Australian state Labor government has announced $2.5 million for its public universities to develop short courses "to meet the defence industry's workforce needs,"' writes Deaglan Godwin[13] in Socialist Alternative's pro-revolution *Red Flag* magazine. Godwin argues that the University of Adelaide's dare to prospective students to 'make history' means helping to construct and maintain the newest weapons of mass destruction.

> None of this is so surprising. Although they dress themselves in the lofty language of Enlightenment liberalism, universities usually perform quite a mundane function for capitalism: they indoctrinate and train professionals, managers and bureaucrats. As huge research institutions, they help corporations and governments develop new technology to make greater profits or carry out the business of war more effectively.
>
> As Australian capitalism becomes more aggressive and militaristic, we can expect the universities to follow. Not just in rhetoric but in deed, with more teaching and research being concerned with 'national defence'. The task for students will be to reject this, and the drive to war that it serves.

Peace Education in Universities

Universities, however, are complex entities and, despite their limitations, they can be bastions of peace education, nonviolent activism, deep thought, wise research, international collaboration, intense debates, free speech and progressive politics. For example, it was academics at the University of Michigan, USA, who initiated large-scale opposition to the war in Vietnam when they held a 'teach-in' on 24 March 1967, attended by more than 3,000 people.[14]

Sometimes universities move away from militaristic impulses and towards the cultivation of peace. Ritsumeikan University in Kyoto, Japan, was complicit in the militarism and warmongering that led to Japan invading Manchuria in 1931 and attacking Pearl Harbour 10 years later. After the war, the university decided on a very different tack, dedicating itself instead to the pursuit of peace through tertiary education, with a 'core educational philosophy of "peace and democracy"'.[15] It is:

> committed to sincerely reflecting upon history and to building an institution where many cultures coexist in the spirit of international mutual understanding. Ritsumeikan will build relationships of

> trust, through research and education, as well as sports and cultural activities, and establish its roots in the local community, to create an academic institution open to international society. [W]hile respecting the principles of autonomy, democracy, transparency, non-violence and justice [...] [it will] search for solutions to the pressing issues facing humankind, [...] [and] foster learning and the development of individual talents in order to nurture just and ethical global citizens.[16]

An important aspect of putting this philosophy into practice is its housing of the Kyoto Museum for World Peace. Opened in 1992, it was the world's first comprehensive peace museum established by a university. Recently renovated and modernised, it reopened in September 2023, with guests including the Commissioner for Cultural Affairs, and the directors of the Hiroshima Peace Memorial Museum and the Okinawa Prefectural Peace Memorial Museum. The Kyoto museum's directors, such as Professor Kazuyo Yamane, are leading members of the International Network of Museums for Peace. It is supported by other institutions such as Hiroshima City University and its Hiroshima Peace Institute, whose theme for the 2022 Public Lecture Series was 'Enhancing Cultures of Peace', cultures which reject all forms of violence, spread trust, respect others and seek resolutions through dialogue.[17]

One important example of peace education is a cross-border mental health programme that brings Palestinian and Israeli students together, training postgraduate psychotherapy professionals in how to provide mental health support to war-traumatised children, with an emphasis on PTSD. It also offers workshops in cultural sensitivity, peacebuilding and conflict resolution. The initiative's aim is for the students to build relationships by training together, and apply that understanding and empathy in their communities and future careers. Programme co-leader Dr Esti Galili-Weisstub states that the students have learnt a lot about each other, and she believes that the fact that they want to continue the programme despite the recent upsurge in violence is 'a beacon of hope'.[18] For co-leader Dr Shafiq Masalha, an Arab Israeli clinical psychotherapist, the alliances being formed are 'a microcosm of the kind of understanding and collaboration they'd like to see at the political level'.[19]

Peace Studies

Universities around the world now recognize the importance of understanding what peace is and how to achieve it. Although some denigrate this as unimportant or airy-fairy, or too simple and obvious a field of studies, the question arises: If peace is so simple, why isn't there more of it? As one Peace Studies student at the University of New England noted:

> Working in science, the notion of peace studies is the source of much hilarity among my co-workers, but people are always shocked to learn what it is we talk & think about in the discipline. Unicorns and rainbows? Not so much. These are among the hardest questions in life and if only it was just abstract academic questions – the practical application of the study is so frustratingly difficult!

Peace Studies (Irenology) is a unique area that has been well-established in universities for many decades. It involves an interdisciplinary effort aimed at the prevention, de-escalation and solution of conflicts by peaceful means, thereby seeking 'victory' for all parties involved in the conflict. It is sometimes included in the broader field of peace and conflict studies, which values and interconnects individual and social relations with each other, while also focusing on the importance of understanding the role of structures in individual and social life. Its interdisciplinary nature allows the adoption of different perspectives from various academic disciplines and helps the development of conflict theory necessary to deconstruct conflicts to understand their root causes.[20]

Peace Studies is multi-disciplinary, multilevel and multicultural, both analytic and normative, and both theoretical and applied, with its own research tools and a specialised set of concepts. It has informal roots dating back to at least the nineteenth century and has officially been part of university studies since 1919 and a distinct academic discipline since the 1940s.

The Department of Peace Studies at Bradford University in the UK is one of the largest and oldest Peace Studies departments. Having started in 1973 with funding organised by local Quakers, including contributions from former prime minister Harold Wilson, novelist and playwright J.B. Priestley (one of the founders of the Campaign for Nuclear Disarmament), American violinist Yehudi Menuhin and British composer Benjamin Britten, it celebrated its 50th anniversary in 2023.[21] The previous year Peace Studies at the University of New England in Armidale, Australia, had celebrated its 40th anniversary with a conference, film festival and special edition of *Social Alternatives* journal: *A Sustainable Peace*.[i]

Peace Studies has numerous professional organisations such as the International Peace Research Association, which has biennial conferences, supported at government and/or university levels. Peace Studies also has a wide variety of dedicated journals such as the *International Journal of Peace*

i See www.une.edu.au/2022peaceconference and socialalternatives.com/issue/a-sustainable-peace/

Studies, *Journal of Peace Research*, *Peace and Conflict Review*, *Peace and Change*, *Journal of Peace Education*, *Journal of Peace-building and Development* and numerous online resources, such as through the War Resisters League.

There are more than 200 college and university Peace Studies programs in the United States alone, along with notable programmes at Australia's University of Sydney and University of Queensland, Otago University (New Zealand), the University of Hiroshima (Japan) and in Austria, Spain, Turkey, Germany and France. Such programmes and research agendas have now become common in institutions located in conflict, post-conflict and developing countries, such as the National Peace Council (Sri Lanka), Centre for Human Rights at the University of Sarajevo (Bosnia), Chulalongkorn University (Thailand), National University of Timor (Timor-Leste), University of Kabul in Afghanistan, Sir James Mancham International Centre for Peace Studies and Diplomacy (Seychelles), and Makerere University and Mbarara University in Uganda.

The phenomenal increase in the last few decades in the number of faculty, students and academic institutions with interests in the study of peace, conflict, justice and global security has led to new groups such as the Peace Studies Association.

Despite the growth in Peace Studies, many people, including journalists, remain unaware of its existence. In our discipline at UNE, we are rarely contacted for comment on issues of war and peace, and defence spending. Defence, war and military researchers often are, with think-tanks, sponsored by weapons manufacturers, regularly gaining pro-war front page coverage despite their lack of independence.[22] When I tell people I teach Peace Studies, I usually have to repeat the word 'peace' several times before they understand what I'm saying. Often, they are astounded that such a discipline exists. Yet everyone relies on or hopes for peace.

Not merely academic, the highly practical research of Peace Studies informs important real-world work, such as United Nations' peacebuilding missions. Many international organisations, agencies and international NGOs, including the United Nations, OSCE, EU, World Bank, International Crisis Group and International Alert, draw on Peace Studies research. Peace Studies is also a vital aspect of environmental sustainability and ecological peace, given that war, militarism and the military-industrial complex are major contributors to global warming and biodiversity decline.[23]

Peace Education in Schools

The 'Landscapes of Remembrance' article referenced in the Peace History chapter is also relevant here. The authors suggest 'various opportunities to engage outside the conventional classroom context in ways that get beyond uncritical acceptance of what may be given priority in official landscapes of remembrance, such as war memorials and war museums'.[24] They also argue that

> [h]ow we learn is just as important as what we learn. To seek to educate for peace in authoritarian or dogmatic ways is a contradiction in terms. Similarly, to claim to be 'preparing for peace by preparing for war', which is central to so much contemporary 'realist' thinking about peace and security, is to deny active hope that another world is possible. This is a crucial challenge for us as peace educators. In some small, yet potentially valuable ways, there are [...] various opportunities to invite dialogue on alternatives to violence through 'sites of conscience' as a learning medium.[25]

Classroom practices convey and reinforce strong, subtle and repeated social messages about what is and is not valued. Therefore, it is important for educators to understand and reduce their own biases and to develop practices which support positive peace, including through their narratives, words and body language, and the toys and games they encourage.

Whereas some well-intentioned peace education can be ineffectual and even counter-productive because of the unconscious biases of educators, institutions or funding bodies, 'critical peace education' asserts that

> all education efforts should involve a critique of the existing social order, and implores us to scrutinize all structures, including structures of education. This extends to educators and researchers alike, to also direct a lens at themselves to examine how structurally violent ways persist in what we do and how we produce knowledge.[26]

For peace education to be effective, particularly when considering intractable conflicts, it must be woven into the fabric of a community and the lives of its students.[27] Gender is an important aspect of peace education that aims for an egalitarian, non-sexist society (discussed in the next chapter).

The buildings and spaces in which we learn, educate, work and live are also important. Syrian architect Marwa Al-Sabouni teaches children in her war-torn regions not to move to more pleasant places but to improve their home environments: 'you should stay in your city for the sake of your own future and do something about it'.[28] Al-Sabouni works to educate the world about architecture's role in creating sustainable, peaceful cities.

Chapter 4 discussed the Christmas Truce of December 1914, when ordinary soldiers on opposing sides spontaneously declared a truce for the

Christmas period. They began to establish other agreements and even to fraternise, until the military authorities came down hard on these grass-roots declarations of peace, with the high commands on both sides issuing orders to prevent such an event from ever happening again. Memorials commemorating the Christmas Truce now stand at Frelinghien, France and in the National Memorial Arboretum in England. On the 100th anniversary, in 2014, the English and German national soccer teams staged a friendly match in England in remembrance of the soldiers' impromptu soccer games in 1914.[29] The Martin Luther King Peace Committee of Northumbria and Newcastle Universities produced resources to enable schools and churches to mark the centenary of the Christmas Truce. These included lesson plans, worksheets, hand-outs, PowerPoint slide shows and detailed plans for assemblies, carol services and Christmas productions. Their purpose was both to enable schoolteachers to help children learn about the remarkable events of December 1914 and to use the theme of Christmas to provide a counterpoint to the UK government's glorification of World War I as heroic. As the Peace Committee argues,

> These spontaneous acts of festive goodwill directly contradicted orders from high command, and offered an evocative and hopeful – albeit brief – recognition of shared humanity – and thereby [...] give a re-reading of the traditional Christmas message of 'peace on earth, and good will toward all people'.[30]

These education packs are a good example of peace education, of a conscious effort to counter the pro-military aspects of so much of the history that is taught in schools, something we examined in the History chapter. It's an effort to present a whole other side of human history to children, a history of rarely told stories of nonviolence, peacemaking and selfless social activism designed to make the world a better place.

Countering Misconceptions

Such education can counter the commonly held misconceptions that Jonathan Schell challenges in his 2003 book *The Unconquerable World*, mentioned in Chapter 2. The main one is the widespread belief that violence is necessary to overthrow a violent regime, which much historical evidence contradicts. The French Revolution, for example, was not achieved by the storming of the Bastille but more due to widespread cultural change and then defections by key Paris-based regiments. The overthrow of England's King James II in the Glorious Revolution of 1688 in England was determined mainly by a defection of parliamentarians and aristocrats rather than William of Orange's army. The American Revolution was primarily achieved through non-cooperation with the British, resistance to their judicial and taxation systems, and establishment of the Americans' own governing bodies. Fighting certainly occurred, but it was in defence of the revolution and its aim was to endure and outlast the British. The storming of the Winter Palace in the Russian Revolution, according to Schell, occurred after the revolution had already been won by a long propaganda campaign and through dialogues with the army. Theoretically, the Czarist regime was unassailable because of its huge army, but the soldiers were mainly of peasant origin and became sympathetic to communist ideals. They provided little resistance to the communist coup, with many switching to support it. These actions of persuasion and non-cooperation are important and effective nonviolent strategies and often operate in tandem with the 'constructive programme' of creating 'parallel institutions', or alternative bodies and processes, to replace repressive or outmoded ones.

These are just a few examples of case studies with which children could be presented, allowing them to explore alternative perspectives which don't privilege militarism but challenge it, and which show the importance of the nonviolent methods which Schell claims are the real causes of major social change.

Examples of Peace Education

We've looked at Bhutan previously (Chapter 4), with its alternative but increasingly praised model of Gross National Happiness (GNH). There, children are taught basic agricultural techniques and environmental protection as well as mainstream curricula. A new national waste management programme ensures that every piece of material used at school is recycled. The infusion of the GNH ideal into education has also meant daily meditation sessions for the children and teachers, and soothing traditional music instead of a loud buzzer or the clang of the school bell. As head teacher of a primary school in Thimphu, Choki Dukpa, says: 'An education doesn't just mean getting good grades, it means preparing them to be good people'.[31]

This is not an isolated case. All around the globe, NGOs and educators are introducing peace education into schools. For example, led by Dr Gohar Markosyan from the NGO Women for Development, Peace Education Centres have been established in 16 schools in the conflict zone of Armenia, according to the Global Campaign for Peace Education (www.peace-ed-campaign.org). More than 1,000 schoolchildren and hundreds of teachers were trained, and seminars were organised for more than 3,200 parents, with the aim of integrating and mainstreaming peace and conflict resolution education into school curricula, using a range of materials, games, drills and visual aids. Positive changes are being observed both in the pupils' behaviour and in their academic progress. Other benefits include increased:

- respect towards the history and cultures of various nations,
- understanding that each person is a bearer of peace,
- confidence, and
- ability to protect one's own rights and to understand one's own responsibilities.[32]

New Zealand is another country making progress towards positive peace through peace education, although primarily in the younger years to date:

> The curricular statements of New Zealand have made progress to educate students toward peace and non-violence and, in general, the early childhood curricular statement incorporates a greater amount of pro-peace content than the primary and secondary curriculum statement. Opportunities exist to strengthen peace education content in future New Zealand curricular statements.[33]

This is complemented by a plethora of other factors contributing to positive peace in New Zealand, including a Treaty, university places and scholarships for Maori students, reserved Maori seats in parliament, consulting with Maori on issues of public policy, and incorporating Maori values and culture into mainstream New Zealand culture and national identity. The latter includes singing the national anthem in Maori and English, celebrating biculturalism, Maori greeting ceremonies, performances of the Haka (albeit with aggressive connotations) at international sporting events, and teaching Maori language in all primary schools.[34]

In many societies, schools have the authority and legitimacy to conduct peace education in a formal and structured manner.[35] However, as we saw in Chapter 5, much of institutional education involves the glorification of war and thus the perpetuation of cultural violence. Peace education therefore requires 'setting new educational objectives, preparing new curricula, writing school textbooks, developing instructional materials, training teachers, and constructing a climate in the schools that is conducive to peace education'.[36] There are past instances of this occurring, such as in Victoria, Australia, after World War I, where the education minister required all textbooks to promote peace and global perspectives rather than exalt war.[37]

In an environment where young people learn the values, beliefs and actions of a society, peace education can provide tools to resolve conflict in a nonviolent manner.[38] It can also fundamentally change how heroes, bravery, identity and strength are depicted. Nonviolent campaigns, for example, involve strong leadership, moral courage and diplomacy; they develop character, skills and civil society institutions.[39] Learning about successful nonviolent struggles through textbooks, museums, memorials and public holidays would encourage nonviolence to be viewed as a brave and heroic pathway to conflict transformation and an alternative to the destructive path of violence.

Alternative School Systems

How we model behaviour towards our natural environment and how we set up our homes and gardens can also be elements in creating a peaceful and nurturing atmosphere to raise children. The international system of schooling known as Steiner Education began with Rudolph Steiner, who some regard as a visionary and others as a racist crackpot (and the system still contains problematic issues). Nevertheless, the system as it has evolved over the last century encompasses a holistic view of life which includes mainly using natural materials such as timber and mudbrick rather than synthetic ones in the classrooms, which are themselves designed to be harmonious and welcoming, often using curves rather than squares and sharp angles. Contrast this with many other schools which, partly because of funding issues, are utilitarian to the point of seemingly being designed along the lines of prisons! The Steiner schools' gardens and surrounds tend to be as natural as possible, with Armidale's version being heavily wooded with native species and plentiful native animals and birds. There is also a permaculture garden where children learn to grow food organically, and there are frequent long adventures into natural places, such as 10-day walks along beaches, bushwalks, canoeing trips and visits to farms.

To use a metaphor from nature, Steiner Education is not so much about gluing leaves of knowledge or information onto a tree's branches, but watering, feeding and mulching that tree within a safe, nurturing environment so that it thrives. It's about allowing children to have a childhood, without putting undue pressure on them, as some systems do, from before kindergarten, to achieve particular milestones and prepare for the high school exams and university. It also focuses on more than intellectual education, with practical skills, willpower, socialising skills and emotional intelligence being integral parts of the curricula. There are fewer exams than elsewhere, and it favours cooperation over competition.

This is an example of holistic education that, at its best, encourages a lifelong love of learning, and produces peaceful, empowered, highly principled and environmentally conscious people. There are other systems with similar aims, such as the internationally renowned Montessori teaching model. It is named after Maria Montessori whose priorities can be seen from her statement: 'Establishing lasting peace is the work of education; all politics can do is keep us out of war'.[40]

There is also a range of alternative Australian schools, such as the Byron Bay Community School which has been operating for more than 30 years, and an alternative bush school in Victoria called Candlebark School, founded and operated by innovative educator and author John Marsden, more famous as the author of the *Tomorrow When the War Began* series of books and subsequent film and TV series. Strongly influenced by Fitzroy Community School in Melbourne, Candlebark believes that children flourish by experiencing life at close quarters. It regards first-hand experiences as generally superior to second-hand experiences and tries to say 'Yes' as much as possible – yes to new ideas, yes to experiments, yes to innovations. If the school has a motto, it is 'Take care, take risks'. As anyone who has worked in public sector education, such as TAFE, knows, this is quite different from the risk-averse atmosphere and 'no can do' attitude that has taken over so many institutions, as the fear of litigation makes any risky practices more difficult to undergo and requires reams of paperwork.

Marsden later opened another school north of Melbourne for secondary students, using a new arts-focused curriculum. He states that

> Twenty, 30 or 40 years ago if you said to your mother or father you wanted to be a potter or a sculptor or bassist in a rock band they would have advised you to do a dentistry course instead. [...] But now people are considering [arts] as a serious career for their sons and daughters and there's nothing really out there that specialises in that kind of education.[41]

Some will have concerns that Marsden's *Tomorrow When the War Began* series taps into and reinforces Australia's old, race-based and largely unfounded fears of the so-called 'Yellow Peril'. They rehash an earlier plot by Mary Grant Bruce in her 1940 novel *Peter and Co*, and they display little understanding of nonviolence. Nevertheless, they demonstrate a good understanding of the teenage psyche, and it is worth considering Marsden's thoughts on careers in the arts:

> It took me a long time to reconcile that writing could be more than a hobby. Today the arts are an important part of the Australian economy and there has been a profound change in how children and their parents view the arts.[42]

Informal Peace Education

Within peace education, two primary models exist – a model that is indirect and does not directly challenge contextual elements within a specific conflict, and a direct education model which may specifically reference issues and themes involved within an intractable conflict.[43] Peace education also happens informally, outside formal institutions of learning. One exciting initiative is the Peace Boat (peaceboat.org), which travels the world working to promote peace, human rights and sustainability. Run by a Japan-based international NGO and guided by the UN Sustainable Development Goals, Yashiokadate Tatasuya writes that its global voyages (which take volunteers) offer a unique programme of activities based on experiential learning and intercultural communication.[44]

The 'Seeds of Peace' project (www.seedsofpeace.org) is an innovative programme designed to bring children from warring communities together to a neutral, non-threatening environment away from their home country so they can learn to understand each other better. It involves hundreds of Arab and Israeli teenagers travelling to a three-week international camp in Maine, USA, leaving behind the violence and hatred of their homelands to meet their 'enemies' face-to-face. Running since 1993, with a motto of 'We reject *what is*, when we know *what can be*', it is a

> remarkable attempt to plant the idea of peace in the hearts and minds of the next generation of Middle East leaders. [...] At times it's an emotionally wrenching process, but it can produce surprising friendships and an enduring commitment to building a future of peaceful coexistence.[45]

The camp provides young people with an opportunity to overcome their perceptions and pre-conceived fears of 'the other'. They must learn to live together and support one another through this process. By participating in everyday life and teamwork activities, the children learn about equality. Gradually, they realise that peace is a possibility and there are no excuses for violence. Acceptance of their differences allows them to form friendships and bond without fear. Through this experience the children become ambassadors for peace when they return to their own country.

Education with simpler aims (but still relating to community peace and well-being) occurs in Australia's *BackTrack* organisation (backtrack.org.au), which deals with at-risk youth, many of whom are Aboriginal. It aims to keep children alive, out of jail and chasing their hopes and dreams, helping them develop healthy foundations for positive life pathways.

Another example of left-field peace education that uses the arts can be seen in the work of Yo-Yo Ma and his Silk Road Ensemble, about which there is an excellent documentary called 'The Music of Strangers'. One of the world's most renowned classical musicians and a UN peace ambassador, Yo-Yo Ma has travelled the world, performing in front of audiences ranging from presidents to schoolchildren. His musical encounters led him to believe in music's power to diminish ideological differences: 'We always focus on what unites rather than what divides'.[46] He invited musicians from around the world to join him in an experiment in intercultural engagement. The Silk Road Project serves as a useful prototype for international cooperation. The musicians must develop a shared vocabulary to compose and perform together – a complicated endeavour since different musical cultures have unique forms of notation. For example, Sandeep Das, who plays an Indian hand drum called the tabla, does not use a notation system at all, which compelled the ensemble to find new ways to collaborate. To resolve disagreements ranging from which pieces of music to perform to how the project should evolve over the next decade, they established a rotating leadership council to set the organisation's artistic direction.

Their concerts provide rare opportunities to bring people together in places like Syria and Turkey. Performing in far-flung corners of the globe, they are uniquely positioned to take in the diversity of ideologies that people uphold as truth. On a daily basis, they also see how music breaks boundaries. In the midst of political discord, the musicians within the Silk Road Project see an opportunity to foster other kinds of cross-cultural encounters. 'Political power is unbelievably strong', says Ma. 'But cultural power is a different kind of strength'.[47]

Another such artistic educator is Doreen Rao, a member of the Zen Peacemakers Order and the Artistic Director and Conductor of the New Millennium Festival Concerts, an innovative peacemaking initiative with concert series in New York, Toronto and London.[48] Having studied the educational and social benefits of demilitarised nations exemplified by small countries such as Costa Rica, Panama and Iceland (although the latter now has joined NATO as a result of Russia's invasion of Ukraine), Dr Rao visited Costa Rica with a delegation of musicians, Zen artists and filmmakers to promote the peace initiatives of A World Without Armies. The delegation offered a benefit performance of traditional Japanese music, painting and poetry that included the premiere film screening of 'Hope' by Catherine Margerin. Celebrating the 60th anniversary of the United Nations and hosted by the Costa Rica's unique UN-mandated University for Peace, the televised performance was attended by key government officials, peace scholars, graduate students and social agencies and led to Dr Rao's plan to organise and conduct an international world peace choir to study and travel in countries without armies. A pioneer of exciting and energising performance-based music education,[49] she has since travelled to many countries to promote tolerance and understanding through the shared joy of choral music, and established the New Millennium Festival, an educationally-oriented choral festival for children and youth choirs dedicated to the performance of new music and to peace education.

Another project aimed to mark the 60th anniversary of the atomic bombings in Hiroshima and Nagasaki and to remember the people who died during and after the bombings. Dr Rao travelled with a delegation of spiritual leaders, scholars, physicians and artists to distribute 270,000 Jizo images to the children, families and survivors – one Jizo for every man, woman and child who died as a result of the atomic bombs. Peace performances, art panels, banners, origami, ceramic statues and quilts with Jizo images also marked this remembrance.

Informal peace education also occurs in one-on-one interactions. One *Creating Cultures of Peace* student expounded on her peace pilgrimage to Palestine/Israel:

> My hosts here open their home to foreigners, talk courageously and honestly about what it is like to live in Palestine, take their guests on tours all around the West Bank and cook magnificent Palestinian food. This is their mission, their form of nonviolent action. I have been fascinated to see how venerated Yasar Arafat is and how Saddam Hussain was considered a friend of Palestine. It has been such a privilege and challenge to spend time with this family and to listen to their lives including their despair, rage and hate. Tomorrow I return to the relative safety of Israel. To my utter amazement I have loved my time in Israel and have found the Israelis I have encountered warm, friendly and welcoming. Not what I was expecting. I do love the way travel always challenges my preconceptions.

*

In conclusion, there are seedlings of peace education throughout the world, flourishing in some places, struggling elsewhere. Peace education could occur in a much more focused, high-profile and strategically resourced way in primary and secondary schools, as well as universities. This chapter has hopefully shown that there is a wide range of possibilities for peace education, from peace studies in universities to alternative school systems to informal education through music and the arts, a topic we explore further in Chapter 10.

Notes

1 Johnson, D. and Johnson, R. 2005 'Essential components of peace education', *Theory into Practice,* vol. 44, no. 4, p. 283.

2 Sveiby, Karl- Erik and Skuthorpe, Tex 2006 *Treading Lightly: The Hidden Wisdom of the World's Oldest People,* Allen and Unwin, Crows Nest.

3 Nussbaum, Martha C. 2010 *Not For Profit: Why Democracy Needs the Humanities,* Princeton University Press, Princeton, p. 18.
4 Giroux, Henry A. 2007 *The University in Chains: Confronting the Military-Industrial-Academic Complex,* Paradigm, Boulder, pp. 13–101.
5 Swanson, David 2022 'Protests around globe target world's biggest weapons company lockheed Martin', *Scoop,* 30 April, www.scoop.co.nz/stories/WO2204/S00254/protests-around-globe-target-worlds-biggest-weapons-company-lockheed-martin.htm
6 University of Melbourne 2016 *University Welcomes Lockheed Martin to Melbourne,* 2 August, www.unimelb.edu.au/newsroom/news/2016/august/university-welcomes-lockheed-martin-to-melbourne
7 Ibid.
8 Whalen, Andrew 2019 'How one protester made sure lockheed Martin never forgets its role in deadly Yemen school bus Bombing', *Newsweek,* 7 May, www.newsweek.com/lockheed-martin-yemen-school-bus-bomb-war-resolution-death-toll-saudi-arabia-1418598
9 'Lockheed Martin and STEM punks launch education program' 2022, *Australian Defence Magazine,* 24 October, www.australiandefence.com.au/defence/cyber-space/lockheed-martin-and-stem-punks-launch-education-program
10 Ibid.
11 Nussbaum, 2010.
12 Hitch, Georgia 2023 'What is AUKUS and when are we getting nuclear submarines?' *ABC News,* 20 March, https://www.abc.net.au/news/2023-03-14/what-is-aukus-submarine-deal-details-announced/102091510
13 Godwin, Deaglan 2023 'Australian Universities join the drive to war', *Red Flag,* 15 May, https://redflag.org.au/article/australian-universities-join-drive-war?fbclid=IwAR2Vd3pdv72s11KVrYbn5n2E4zbgXdMSKjHVRe4TXkBzByDWF7yCHU4nLxI
14 Innes, Brian 2002 *Snapshots of the 60s,* Brown Reference Group, London, p. 135.
15 Ritsumeikan University 2006 The Ritsumeikan Charter, https://en.ritsumei.ac.jp/profile/charter/
16 Ibid.
17 Hiroshima Peace Institute 2023 *Hiroshima Research News,* vol. 26, no. 1.
18 Moran, Padraig 2023 'Mental health program that brings Palestinian and Israeli students together "a beacon of hope"', *CBC,* 19 October, www.cbc.ca/radio/thecurrent/israel-gaza-children-trauma-1.7001588
19 Ibid.
20 Askerov, Ali 2020 'An interdisciplinary academic field- Peace and conflict studies', *Researchgate,* February, www.researchgate.net/publication/339416022_An_Interdisciplinary_Academic_Field-_Peace_and_Conflict_Studies, p. 1.
21 Hammond, Grace 2023 'University of Bradford Peace Studies department celebrates 50 years of impacting world affairs', *Yorkshire Post,* 4 May, www.yorkshirepost.co.uk/arts-and-culture/film-and-tv/university-of-bradford-peace-studies-department-celebrates-50-years-of-impacting-world-affairs-4126757
22 See Chapter 6 and Kampmark, Binoy 2023 'Media peddling "Red Alert" rubbish slammed', *Independent Australia,* 12 March, https://independentaustralia.net/business/business-display/media-peddling-red-alert-rubbish-slammed,17310
23 Branagan, Marty 2013 *Global Warming, Militarism and Nonviolence: The Art of Active Resistance,* Palgrave Macmillan, Basingstoke, pp. 1–36.

24 Herborn, Peter J. and Hutchinson, Francis P. 2014 'Landscapes of remembrance and sites of conscience: Exploring ways of learning beyond militarising 'maps' of the future', *Journal of Peace Education*, vol. 11, no. 2, p. 145.
25 Herborn and Hutchinson 2014, p. 146.
26 Arnøy, Joakim 2023 'Non-formal Peace Education Founded on European Youth Work: A practitioner's critical reflection', *Peace and Change*, vol. 48, pp. 281–297.
27 Johnson and Johnson 2005, p. 280.
28 Coslovich, Gabriella 2018 'Marwa Al-Sabouni on the battle to rebuild Homs', *Sydney Morning Herald,* 25 August, www.smh.com.au/world/middle-east/marwa-al-sabouni-on-the-battle-to-rebuild-homs-20180821-p4zysz.html, p. 27.
29 Baime, A. J. and Janssen, Volker 2022 'WWI's Christmas Truce: When fighting paused for the holiday', *History*, 4 October, www.history.com/news/christmas-truce-1914-world-war-i-soldier-accounts
30 Cited in Chambers, John 2015 'Western front 1914 – Christmas Truce – 1914', *Belfast Child*, 24 December https://belfastchildis.com/2015/12/24/western-front-1941-christmas-truce-christmas-1914/
31 Cited in Kelly, Annie 2012 'Gross national happiness in Bhutan: The big idea from a tiny state that could change the world', *Guardian*, 2 December, www.theguardian.com/world/2012/dec/01/bhutan-wealth-happiness-counts
32 Markosyan, Gohar 2016 'The importance of peace education in ending violence and conflict (Armenia)', *Global Campaign for Peace Education*, 24 February, www.peace-ed-campaign.org/importance-peace-education-ending-violence-conflict/
33 Standish, Katerina 2015 'Looking for peace in National Curriculum: The PECA Project in New Zealand', *Journal of Peace Education*, vol. 13, no. 1, p. 8.
34 Liu, J. H. and Sibley, C. G. 2006 'Differential effects of societal anchoring and attitude certainty in determining support or opposition to (bi)cultural diversity in New Zealand', *Papers on Social Representations,* vol. 15, no. 1, p. 9.
35 Bar-Tal, Daniel, Rosen, Yigal and Nets-Zehngut, Rafi 2010 'Peace education in societies involved in intractable Conflicts', in Gavriel Salomon and Edward Cairns (eds.), *Handbook on Peace Education*, Psychology Press, New York, p. 24.
36 Ibid.
37 Donaldson, Carina and Lake, Marilyn 2010 'Whatever happened to the anti-war movement?' in Marilyn Lake and Henry Reynolds with Mark McKenna and Joy Damousi (eds.), *What's Wrong with ANZAC? The Militarisation of Australian History*, p. 73.
38 Bar-Tal, Rosen and Nets-Zehngut 2010, p. 22; Mayton, D. M. 2009 'Cultural and societal perspectives of nonviolence', in *Nonviolence and Peace Psychology: Intrapersonal, Interpersonal, Societal, and World Peace,* Springer, New York, NY, p. 157.
39 Bartkowski, Maciej J. 2012 *Recovering Nonviolent History,* Lynne Rienner, Boulder, p. 340.
40 Guetta, S. 2013 'From peace education to culture of peace: Context and issues', *Studi Sulla Formazione,* vol. 16, no. 1, p. 167, https://doi.org/10.13128/Studi_Formaz-13492
41 Rawlinson, Clare 2015 'Author John Marsden to open new arts-focused secondary school', *ABC News,* 30 January, https://www.abc.net.au/news/2015-01-30/john-marsden-to-open-new-arts-secondary-school/6055674
42 Kennedy, Barry 2015 'Author John Marsden has bought Macedon Grammar, will transform into specialist art school', *Herald Sun,* 30 January, www.heraldsun.com.au/leader/north/author-john-marsden-has-bought-macedon-grammar-will-transform-into-specialist-art-school/news-story/bb0d48e7db4526946f4c21ea7fa71795

43 Bar-Tal, Rosen and Nets-Zehngut 2010, p. 27.

44 Tatasuya, Yashiokadate 2009 'The floating peace village: An experiment in nonviolence', in Lynda-Ann Blanchard and Leah Chan (eds.), *Ending War, Building Peace,* Sydney University Press, Sydney, pp. 151–162.

45 Wallach, John 2000 *The Enemy Has a Face: The Seeds of Peace Experience*, United States Institute of Peace Press, Washington, pp. 15–35.

46 Smith, Ryan P. 2016 'Yo-Yo Ma's silk road ensemble celebrates our differences through song', *Smithsonian Magazine*, 19 May, www.smithsonianmag.com/arts-culture/yo-yo-mas-silk-road-ensemble-celebrates-our-differences-through-song-180959155/

47 Segran, Elizabeth 2013 'A Yo-Yo Ma project brings together musicians from warring nations', *Atlantic*, 10 October, www.theatlantic.com/international/archive/2013/10/a-yo-yo-ma-project-brings-together-musicians-from-warring-nations/280458/

48 'Doreen Rao' n.d. *Hal Leonard*, www.halleonard.com/biography/194/doreen-rao

49 Hower, Eileen M. n.d. *A Vision for Choral Music Education: The Imagination and Influence of Master Teacher and Conductor Doreen Rao*, The Pennsylvania State University, State College.

Chapter 9

GENDER, SEXUALITY AND PEACE

War Resisters International defines gender as 'a social construction of ideas that assign certain roles, attitudes, images and behaviour to us depending on the sex we were assigned to at birth and the gender identity that we and society identify us with'.

What does gender have to do with peace?

> With a gender lens, we can understand how violence and (gender) power relations are mutually constituted in all spheres of social life, and how the different forms of violence are gendered. This gives us an important insight into our work for peace and justice.[2]

The relationships between gender, sexuality, violence and peace are complex. They're sometimes obvious, such as in war or domestic violence casualty numbers, but often hidden, embedded deeply and even unconsciously in language, conventions, behaviours, thought processes and all the policies and institutions that arise from these. Women have long struggled to emerge from the gendered restrictions and oppressions of patriarchal societies.

In Japan, for example, while most women dress more conservatively than in the West, and it's rare to see them in shorts, tights or skimpy tops, a great deal of the culture is highly sexualised, such as manga comic books and graphic novels, video games and related advertising (Figure 9.1). That said, there are some strong female characters in the enchanting Studio Ghibli anime films such as *My Neighbour Totoro* (1988), *Spirited Away* (2001), *Howl's Moving Castle* (2004) and *Ponyo* (2008).

Tokyo has 'maid cafés' where (mainly) men are waited on by servile young women dressed as maids[3] (see Figure 9.2), although their costumes are not as revealing as in the US chain 'Hooters'.[4] One Japanese pop group, AKB48, consisting of 48 young women sometimes dressed as schoolgirls and who are not allowed to date, is another symptom of the patriarchal infantilising of women that occurs in many countries.

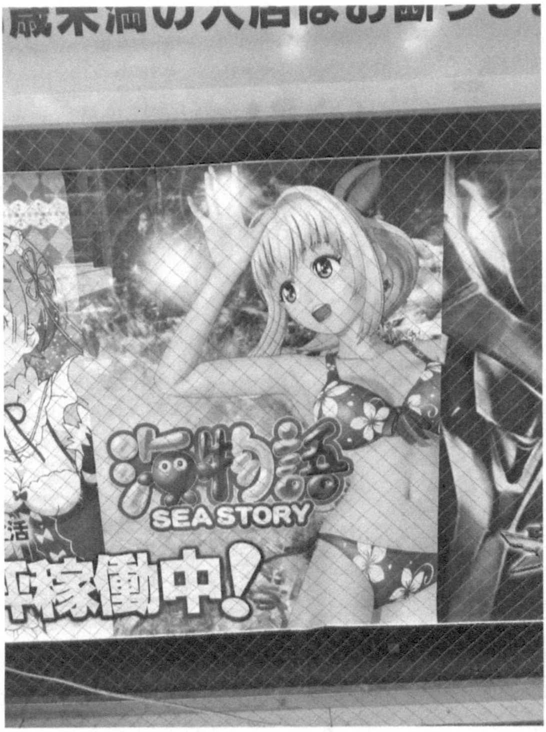

Figure 9.1 Sexualised manga billboard in Tokyo.

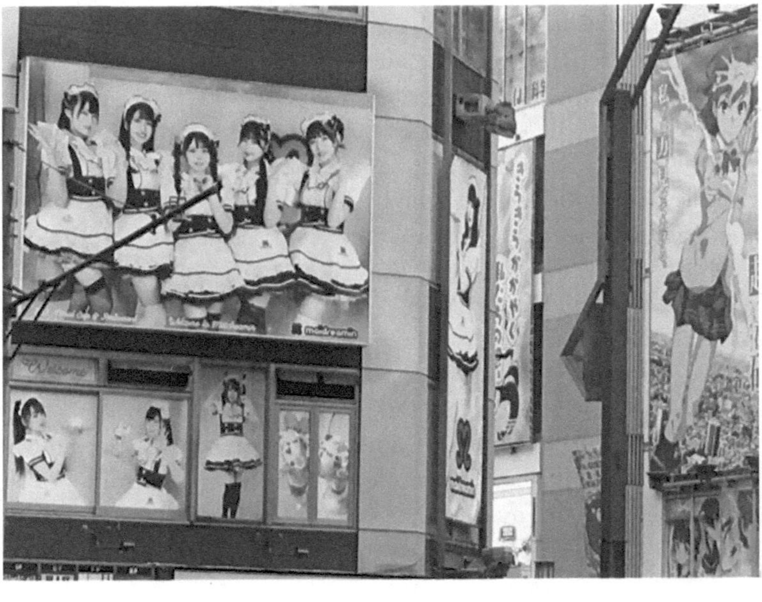

Figure 9.2 'Maid cafés' billboard in Tokyo, Japan.

Whether complicit or as an ironic response, one Japanese women's fashion trend is to dress like dolls. There is an entrenched division of labour, and sexism is rife in politics, business and the home, partly for cultural reasons. 'Japan is a country where people find it difficult to speak out regardless of your age or gender,' says Momoko Nojo, 23, who organised a petition to force out former Tokyo Olympics boss Yoshiro Mori over sexist remarks, with his eventual replacement being Seiko Hashimoto, a much younger, female, former Olympics minister.[5] Generational change is occurring, but it's very slow.

Women have long been at the forefront of peace activism, partly because they suffer the most from war, which increasingly deliberately targets women, children and other civilians.[6] Women led peace initiatives prior to and during World War I, such as in 1914 when a group of 101 British suffragists created 'The Open Christmas Letter', a public message for peace, addressed 'To the Women of Germany and Austria' prior to the first Christmas of the year.[7] Their German and Austrian counterparts responded warmly, expressing agreement and solidarity. In the contemporary era, actor Jane Fonda has led a lifetime of protest, beginning with anti-war activism in the 1960s, followed by support for Native American causes, and is still regularly arrested in her 80s for climate activism.[8]

Women have played essential roles in countless peacemaking, peacebuilding and nonviolent struggles, with their actions often being pivotal points in campaigns, such as the 1950s Women's Strike for Peace, which helped end McCarthyism, and Rosa Parkes' civil disobedience, which ignited the US civil rights movement.

The original 'tree huggers' were the women of Chipko in India, who protected a forest with their bodies. Kenya's National Council of Women was led by Wangari Maathai into tree-planting and eventually the Green Belt movement. This not only planted millions of trees, reduced ecological violence and created carbon sinks, wind-breaks, firewood for cooking and biodiversity refuges, but it also created strong networks and empowered the women to initiate national anti-corruption campaigns. Although Maathai was assaulted and jailed, she became a government minister and a Nobel Peace Prize-winning international spokesperson for 'cancel the debt' campaigns, thereby also challenging structural violence.

Union activists Anna Walentynowicz and Alina Pienkowska were key actors in Poland's *Solidarnosc* (Solidarity) movement, the first effective mass resistance in the USSR. The protest camp for peace by the women of UK's Greenham Common was an essential part of removing cruise missiles and the US Air Force personnel from there. Women led peacemaking in Bougainville[9] and Aung San Suu Kyi led the Burmese struggle for human rights and democratisation, but after gaining power was criticised for her inaction over massacres of Rohingya people by military forces.[10]

In Northern Ireland, Mairead Corrigan Maguire and Betty Williams co-founded the Women for Peace movement (later The Community for Peace People) which grew rapidly despite the fraught and frightening environment. They are among the few women recognised for their actions, being jointly awarded the Nobel Peace Prize in 1976 for their efforts to end the conflict and promote human rights. Their work was aided by Marjorie 'Mo' Mowlam, then UK secretary of state for Northern Ireland, who added momentum to the process, restored ceasefires, cut through conventions, made difficult decisions and oversaw the negotiations which led to the 1998 Good Friday Agreement.[11]

In a keynote address to a 'Cultures of Peace' conference in Boston, cultural peace pioneer Elise Boulding described the many women's groups, particularly in Africa and in places in Asia like Sri Lanka, which are:

> coming together to hold up their own traditional peacemaking practices. They are going into the village councils and saying, we know how to deal with this. And they are successfully disarming guerrillas and militias and armed people in civil wars. They are [...] engaging in a process of [...] disarmament and in starting another process of consultation based on tradition. You're not going to read about these groups in the New York Times or the Boston Globe, but they are happening. These efforts need to be honored. The women's program in the International Fellowship of Reconciliation and the International Peace Bureau are doing some very important work. One of the important projects in the Culture of Peace is [...] going into areas like Nicaragua, like Mozambique, working with former soldiers and guerrillas, people who have been killing and torturing each other, and developing a reconciling project, listening to each other and learning to respect the difference instead of trying to obliterate it. [...] [T]he more Culture of Peace projects we have like this, the better off we will be.[12]

Women also engage substantially in what Amy Piedalue terms 'slow nonviolence' – 'ideas and actions focused on long-term, incremental (but substantial) change, which resist both the visible and invisible effects of structural violence'.[13] She gives the example of Muslim communities in India and the United States, working in grassroots women's organisations that

> negotiate and theorize tangled webs of marginalization and their violent effects [...] responding to the slow violence of dispossession, operationalizing the everyday as a site of politics, and constructing more equitable relationships. This slow nonviolence varies across place and community, but demonstrates a purposeful effort to contest violence as

> organizers encounter it, as a complex, everyday, layered, diffuse, *slow*, and yet material reality.[14]

Maciej Bartkowski, challenging the patriarchal nature of much writing on resistance, points out that the roles of women in nonviolent action have often been ignored or dismissed, and 'the predominantly masculinist views and writings of the forebears of strategic nonviolent resistance are now seen as having suppressed alternative discourses, including the recognition of women's agency'.[15]

Women and World War II Nonviolent Resistance

Let's look in more depth at two case studies, commencing with women's involvement in unarmed (and sometimes armed)[i] resistance in World War II, something largely overlooked afterwards by society and historians in a glaring example of historiographical gender imbalance. Women were major players in the Resistance to Nazi occupation using a wide variety of non-violent tactics, including symbolic actions, overt non-cooperation and covert tactics. The latter were more widespread, as would generally be expected in resistance to a ruthless authoritarian regime with pervasive policing and surveillance networks. Four types of covert tactics in particular were employed, including smuggling and hiding people; and sabotage, which some argue is nonviolent and necessary in extreme circumstances.[16] Other tactics included gathering and communicating intelligence, and using underground media to support and foment resistance as well as undermine Nazi morale and war efforts. In terms of effectiveness, the most easily quantifiable tactic was smuggling and hiding people, with thousands of people rescued from certain death in concentration camps.

Women were vitally involved from the very start of resistance, often playing leading roles. Resistance member Germaine Tillion recalls that in the France of 1940 '[t]here were no men left. It was women who started the resistance. Women didn't have the vote, they didn't have bank accounts, they didn't have jobs. Yet we women were capable of resisting'.[17] With one and a half million French male soldiers in prisons, women stepped into the resistance void. They took on many roles new to them, fulfilling them more than competently until men returned and the usual patriarchal structures reasserted themselves: 'the debacle of defeat brought about a partial and temporary redistribution of

---

i Some engaged in sabotage (regarded by some as nonviolent, especially in exceptional circumstances); others occasionally engaged in armed combat, with one example being Nancy Wake, who distributed weapons and led combat.

roles, before deeply rooted social conventions gained the upper hand once more'.[18] This is a recurring phenomenon within social movements, as noted by Selina Gallo-Cruz:

> the power to mobilize and effect change is located in sometimes unexpected and unseen dimensions of a social system, which women activists have used with great success, but which continues to pose limitations post-conflict.[19]

Leading activists included Nancy Wake, an anti-communist Australian married to a Frenchman; Frenchwoman Ruth Kneppel, codenamed Malou; and upper-class Pole Christine Granville (born Krystyna Skarbek). Their effectiveness was extraordinary. Granville, for example, made the first contact between the French resistance and Italian partisans in preparation for D-Day; she facilitated the defection, with no loss of lives, of an entire German garrison on a strategic mountain pass; and she audaciously freed Resistance leaders from prison. She was of 'inestimable value' to the overthrow of Nazism.[20]

Others such as left-wing Parisian art historian Agnès Humbert and Belgian-born Parisian Suzanne Spaak showed great ability to swiftly build broad networks of resistance, complemented by women who published newspapers and smuggled people and information. Their successes question traditional narratives that armed men and violence are more effective against ruthless opponents than unarmed women using nonviolent methods.[21]

As Blanc notes, 'women are all too often relegated to a position of secondary importance'.[22] The lack of visibility of women in World War II aided their effectiveness as covert resisters but was one reason, post-war, for gaining less recognition than men: of 1,036 resistance heroes honoured by de Gaulle with the Order of Liberation, only six were women.[23]

There is some progress towards belatedly recognising these women's contributions, mainly led by women historians such as Margaret Rossiter (*Women in the Resistance*), Clare Mulley (*The Spy Who Loved: The Secrets and Lives of Christine Granville*), Anne Nelson (*Codename Suzette* and *Red Orchestra*) and Michele Huppert (*Malou: French Resistance Fighter*), as well as memoires by Resistance members such as Agnès Humbert (*Resistance*). Such histories are doubly important because, as well as enduring exclusion from public platforms post-war, women often downplayed their roles and shunned publicity.

Agnès Humbert, for example, consistently underrated her contribution with a self-deprecating approach that 'betrays the deeply-ingrained attitudes towards the place of women in a society dominated by men'.[24] Describing herself as merely the group's typist, she was in fact 'a prominent figure constantly at the forefront of events',[25] who helped the opposition to grow and diversify.

being an essential element of the development of French resistance from 'small autonomous entities' to a crystallised, cohesive, effective organisation.[26]

These histories demonstrate how 'women can step out of the construct of conventional femininity to defy all the stereotypes, if only they are given the chance'.[27] Despite their humility and lack of recognition,

> [W]omen were an outstanding presence throughout the movement. Fulfilling a wealth of different roles, responsible at the highest levels, setting up and often running their own groups, these women played an active part at every level and in every field.[28]

As Sophie Poldermans notes, 'women are often depicted as the main victims [of war], while it is often precisely women who resist under such circumstances and show genuine leadership'.[29]

Women Nonviolently Resisting Ecological Violence

In our second example, let's look at how Australian women have engaged in a wide variety of forms of action against ecological violence, including nonviolent protest-oriented activism such as the successful blockade of a proposed dam on the wild Franklin River[30] and anti-uranium campaigns at Roxby Downs and Jabiluka[31] – the latter being successful. They have led national organisations such as The Wilderness Society and blockades of old-growth logging in the northeast forests of New South Wales (NSW), with more than a million hectares of forests preserved and a doubling of the area's national park estate.[32] Movement strategists Annie Kia and sisters Boudicca and Carmel Flint (the latter being the first person to 'lock on' at an anti-coal protest in Australia) led an extraordinary campaign at Bentley near Lismore in northern NSW, involving most of the community (including two female mayors who climbed protest tripods) which successfully halted the extraction of unconventional gas in the region.[33] Georgina Wood continues to lead Lock the Gate, a contemporary climate movement, after many years. In all of these movements, women have played essential leadership, strategising and creative roles.

While it is important to avoid essentialist attitudes that confine women to particular roles, it should be noted that women have often played peacemaking roles in these movements,[34] bravely confronting groups of aggressive male opponents, helping to make nonviolent actions more effective, peaceful, safe and therefore attractive to a diversity of people. These are the types of cooperative actions which Germaine Greer advocates, 'far from people's ideas of state structure and viable social structure, very subtle forms of interrelation which do not follow a hierarchical pattern which is fundamentally patriarchal. [...] [I]t's women who are going to have to break the spiral of power and find the trick of cooperation'.[35]

Many have moved between different but related roles as their life circumstances change or particular needs or issues arise. Many shifted from confrontational, difficult but necessary activism to more sustainable, constructive, alternative-building actions as permaculture practitioners, Earthcare teachers, landcare advocates, environmental lawyers, councillors and park rangers. This strengthening of new, parallel processes is part of the solutions-oriented 'constructive programme' of nonviolence. Common to all these women is that they rarely were well remunerated for their work, or gained widespread recognition in the media or history books.

Few gained prominent political positions, partly out of fundamental disagreement with the dualistic, oppositional culture of politics and its co-option by vested interests. In a recent development, however, in 2022 a number of women 'teal' independents, motivated largely by federal climate inaction, were elected to federal parliament with new Greens members in a seismic shift in the Australian political landscape which hastened moves towards renewable energy and loosened the duopoly of the two-party system.[ii36,]

Women and Peace Movements

These eco-activists have been complemented by women leading peace movements, such as Gem Romuld, director of the Nobel Peace Prize-winning International Campaign to Abolish Nuclear Weapons, which achieved the incredible success of getting nuclear weapons declared illegal by the majority of the international community, through the Treaty on the Prohibition of Nuclear Weapons, adopted in 2017 and entering into force on 22 January 2021. She was ably supported by older women, such as Sue Wareham OAM, president of the Medical Association for Prevention of War, and Australian foreign minister Penny Wong, who overruled her department and insisted on sending an observer to the first meeting of countries that support the Treaty,[37] although her party has yet to honour its pre-election promise to sign onto the Treaty.

---

ii The duopoly is attempting to reassert control, but their campaign has faced a cultural challenge through 'How to Rig Elections', one in a series of Juice Media's satirical 'Honest Government Ads', starring two women, Ellen Burbidge and Zoë Amanda Wilson.

It is clear, therefore, that women's involvement in building positive peace has been both long-term and effective, with Marie O'Reilly[38] observing that women's inclusion helps prevent conflict, create peace and sustain security after war ends. This does not, however, translate to high-level involvement in international forums:

> In the field of international development, decades of evidence of women's positive impact on socioeconomic outcomes has changed the way governments, donors, and aid organizations do their work. The same cannot be said for the field of peace and security, where women have been thoroughly and consistently excluded. Despite a crescendo of calls for women's participation in decision-making surrounding peace and security over the last two decades, change has been slow to follow. For example, women made up just two percent of mediators and nine percent of negotiators in official peace talks between 1992 and 2011. And just two percent of funding dedicated to peace and security goes to gender equality or women's empowerment.[39]

Militarisation of Women

Rather, there has been a conscious effort to militarise women, according to feminist author Cynthia Enloe, because this is 'crucial for the militarisation of governments and of international relations. The militarisation of women has been necessary for the militarisation of men'.[40] She argues that 'to omit gender from any explanation of how militarisation occurs, is not only to risk a flawed political analysis; it is to risk, too, a perpetually unsuccessful campaign to roll back that militarisation'.[41] Zillah Eisenstein similarly argues in 'Resexing Militarism for the Globe' that instead of liberation, women's entry into the military should be understood as the newest stage of militarising global capitalism:

> Women in the military may make the military look more democratic as though women now have the same choices as men [...] (but) this is because there is less democracy, if democracy means choice and opportunity [...] [T]his stage of patriarchy often requires women to join the army in order to find a paying job or a way to get an education.[42]

This echoes an earlier observation by Sybil Oldfield that '[w]omen are not essentially anti-militarist, but militarism is essentially anti-feminist [...] The validation of violence has to be called in question by the physically weaker sex'.[43] As feminist linguist Dale Spender astutely observed,

> Feminism has fought no wars. It has killed no opponents. It has set up no concentration camps, starved no enemies, practiced no cruelties. Its battles have been for education, for the vote, for better working conditions, for safety in the streets, for child care, for social welfare, for rape crisis centres, women's refuges, reforms in the law. If someone says, 'Oh, I'm not a feminist', I ask, 'Why? What's your problem?'.[44]

Feminist Histories

As noted above, women are now writing histories which reverse the historiographical gender imbalance, and feminist researchers are showing that 'the empirical evidence is overwhelming: where women's inclusion is prioritized, peace is more likely – particularly when women are in a position to influence decision-making'.[45] This is because:

> Women promote dialogue and build trust. They consistently bridge divides and build coalitions for peace. They bring different perspectives to bear on what peace and security mean and how they can be realized, contributing to a more holistic understanding of peace that addresses long-term needs as well as short-term security. Whether preventing conflict, contributing to peace processes, or rebuilding their societies after war, women take an inclusive approach.[46]

Women are also taking charge of telling feminist history through film. Melinda Houston[47] describes (albeit in militaristic language) how '[a] new front has opened in the history wars – a battle we're all pretty happy to see fought'. She describes three recent shows, including *Impeachment,* a 2021 series about Monica Lewinsky and 'systematic white, male power that consumes and discards anything in its path [...] a story that can only emerge when you let women control the narrative'.[48] Others are *Janet Jackson* (2022) and *Pam and Tommy* (2022), about Janet Jackson and Pamela Anderson respectively, which are not so much rewriting history as 'casting a corrective light on the women involved in man-made scandals'.[49]

Seismic Cultural Shifts

Sometimes cultures can change very quickly. The 1960s and 1970s anti-war movements in France, Italy, New Zealand, Australia, the United Kingdom, the United States and elsewhere led to (or at least were part of) a dramatic cultural movement which questioned not just the Vietnam War (or American War, as the Vietnamese call it) but all militarism and wars. The radicalised participants – many of them students – engaged in a holistic questioning of many aspects of society.[50] As well as environmental problems, with the birth of Greenpeace being an example of the recognition of the interconnectedness of the environment and peace, major targets were patriarchy and gender, with a strong questioning of traditional modes of masculinity.

Patriarchy, while often benefiting men, also restricts them to narrow social roles and pushes them towards risk-taking hyper-masculinities.[51] Clementine Ford argues that 'the status quo might revere men as a class, but it destroys them as individuals. And it teaches them to destroy others in return'.[52] Tony Webb goes further, claiming that '[m]en are [...] the primary victims of violence',[53] although this seems to ignore a great deal of the direct, structural and cultural violence which women and non-binary people face. Increasingly, activists are explicit that there is an epidemic of *male violence*, not helped by high levels of misogynistic social media, and 'strong sexual violence' and 'content that may distress' in movies. Countering this requires re-examination of our conceptions of masculinity, as well as concerted efforts by all levels of society to make our language and ways of interacting more likely to engender peace.[54] To some extent, this is occurring despite retrograde currents.

In those turbulent times, inspired by the advice of the former Beatle, John Lennon, in a good example of the power and influence of a famous cultural figure, men and boys everywhere began to grow their hair long for peace. When criticised by parents, teachers, headmasters and other authority figures, some would point out that Jesus was usually depicted with long hair and that he was an advocate of peace (in some parts of the gospels, though not in all, such as the statement that 'I have not come to bring peace, but a sword').[55]

This global generation of long-haired males was often accused of 'looking like girls' or of being homosexual, although usually in stronger, derogatory terms. This criticism and ostracism were not new. Men had traditionally been the ones to go to war. If they refused to go, or even if they *couldn't* go, they would be presented with white feathers by some women and labelled as cowards and shirkers.

Nevertheless, there have always been conscientious objectors to military service, originally led by religious groups such as the Quakers, the Bruderhof and the Jehovah's Witnesses, or in India, the Jains. More recently, due to the enormous pressure that built up in the Vietnam era because of so many draft dodgers and resisters, there is now, in many countries, a recognition that an individual can have valid secular moral resistance to war. However, there is often a demand that some form of service towards society be performed instead.

Men's Groups and Feminism

Men's groups sprang up – sometimes as a reaction to women's activism, or fear or resentment of the changes, but also by men genuinely seeking to examine and transform themselves and their roles in society. As Tom Meagher writes,

> violent men are socialised by the ingrained sexism and entrenched masculinity that permeates everything from our daily interactions all the way up to our highest institutions. [...] Even the term 'violence against women' sounds like a standalone force of nature, with no subject, whereas 'men's violence against women' is used far less frequently.[56]

In the 1970s, a 'men's liberation' movement (not to be confused with the more recent, reactionary 'men's rights' movement) sprang up. This loose network of men in Britain, the United States and elsewhere sought to respond positively to second-wave feminism and to free men (and the females around them) from narrow definitions of masculinity that left little space for emotions other than anger.[57] These shifts have been amplified by the rise of the #MeToo movement, the Harvey Weinstein scandal and many similar exposés, and 'the ubiquity of sexism and sexual abuse is finally becoming part of the mainstream conversation about patriarchal culture as a result'.[58]

Women too began to question their assigned gender roles in a major wave of feminism. This built on earlier movements such as the suffragette movement, which had gained women the vote in many – but not all – countries through concerted mass use of nonviolence (along with some instances of violence, which may have helped or may have set back the movement). In this later wave, many women went further by cutting their hair, wearing clothes traditionally associated with men, such as overalls, singlets and boots, and burning their bras in strong symbolic acts. They also demanded rights such as equal pay and equal access to jobs monopolised by men, including management positions and jobs in blue-collar industries. Women also demanded that men partake more equally in parenting and household chores.

This era saw the beginning of 'positive discrimination' and affirmative action to ensure gender equality, including gender quotas in parliaments, government departments and private businesses, and women's safe spaces, such as women-only carriages in Japanese trains (Figure 9.3).

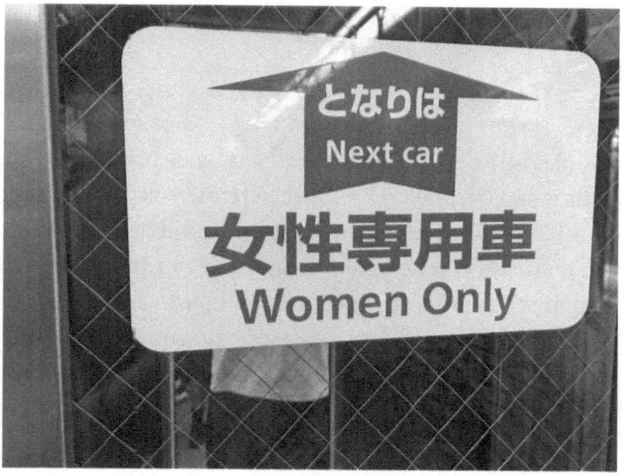

Figure 9.3 Women-only carriage in Japanese train.

LGBTQIA+[iii] Issues

Around the same time, there was an explosion of lesbians and gay men 'coming out' and demanding equal treatment by society and under the law, a movement that is ongoing in the marriage equality struggle (with Australia finally catching up to countries such as Ireland). Related to this is the continuing struggle for recognition of queer, bisexual, transgender, intersex, asexual/agender and questioning people.

Although homosexuality is still criminalised in some countries, elsewhere there has been definite progress. The Sydney Gay and Lesbian Mardi Gras began in 1978 as a celebratory protest commemorating the Stonewall riots in 1969 in New York City, and calling for an end to police harassment and discrimination against homosexuals in employment and housing, and the repeal of all anti-homosexual laws. Organised by the Gay Solidarity Group, it was planned as a street festival, but permission was revoked and 53 participants were arrested, many of whom lost their jobs following the publication of their names by the *Sydney Morning Herald*. Nevertheless, another Mardi Gras parade was held the following year and every year after that, and it is now the largest Pride event in Oceania, and a major income-generating tourist drawcard, with its hundreds of thousands of participants including police officers

iii Lesbian, Gay, Bisexual, Transsexual, Queer/Questioning, Intersex, Asexual/Agender plus unspecified categories.

(sometimes controversially), firefighters, and emergency services and defence personnel.

In 2023, the Australian prime minister marched for the first time, and rainbow signage in the state government's buses, bus stops, trains, ferries and light rail announced 'Ride with Pride', echoed by fashion items, shop displays, banners, murals and a Stan movie platform. Inner-city streets were closed for a festival, and a Customs House photographic exhibition covered Aboriginal and LGBTQIA+ history. The celebration received prominent radio, television and newspaper coverage. An activist element remained, however, with stickers evident such as: 'Queer liberation not rainbow capitalism', and widespread relief with the resolution of murder cold cases and announcement of an inquiry into others.[59]

Women and Artistic Activism

All of the activism above had a strong cultural element involving, at its most obvious, hairstyles, clothes and fashion, but also linking with sexual and political economics, the environment, peace activism and peacebuilding.[60] There was also an explosion in artistic activism, with 'happenings' and 'outrageous' performances such as ones involving nudity, like the musical Aquarius, that challenged prudish laws and censorship.[61] Women were strongly involved in these artistic actions, such as when the Guerrilla Girls (www.guerrillagirls.com) protested inside art museums about the fact that so few women artists are featured whereas the walls are filled with nude women painted by men, thereby contributing to a social narrative that constructs women as passive objects for the delectation of men.

Arts curators and institutions are now proactively countering this through exhibitions that highlight forgotten or under-recognised women artists. Recent examples include the 2023 exhibitions 'Women and Abstraction' at the National Museum of Modern Art in Tokyo (www.momat.go.jp) and 'The Women of Surrealism' at Le Musée de Montmartre in Paris (museedemontmartre.fr). The latter notes that many women played decisive roles in the surrealist movement, but their works were neglected by museums and undervalued by the art market, with the gallery director Fanny de Lépinau stating that 'This exhibition underlines my absolute determination to present works by artists who have often been overlooked in the history of art.'

Similar challenges to patriarchy continue to occur across the entire cultural milieu, such as with Iranian women removing their hijabs in public, Australian national radio broadcaster ABC Classic having all women presenters on International Women's Day in 2023, and with gender-neutral language developing around the world, led by (primarily young) LGBTQIA+

activists as well as early childhood teachers, despite some resistance. For example, critics of the changes in English to 'they' rather than 'she' or 'he' argue that 'they' as both singular and plural can be confusing and complicate a sentence's syntax, but Miriam Berger[62] responds that 'Shakespeare and Jane Austen, among many other famed English writers, didn't think so. They used singular "they" and "their"'.

A translation of Homer's *The Odyssey* by Emily Wilson[63] removes the sexism of previous translations by men due to their (perhaps unconscious) biases. This book, although filled with plenty of horrendous violence – such as the hanging of a group of slave women simply for being associated with (or perhaps the rape victims of) the wrong men – ends with a call to peace.

Artistic challenges to patriarchy and war include the international Femen movement of topless women protesters, although Kira Cochrane[64] wonders whether the activists' breasts are obscuring the message. *Ms Magazine*, created by Gloria Steinem during the Women's Liberation Movement, uses images, words and creativity to shed light on violence and inequality against women, and *A Mighty Girl* (www.amightygirl.com) is an enormous online collection of books, music and toys that are geared towards the empowerment and positive portrayals of girls.

'Lysistrata: Make Love, Not War' is a humorous account by Erin Sanders[65] of an ancient Greek play by Aristophanes, written in about 411 BCE, about women's peacemaking using a sex strike in Athens and Sparta to bring an end to the Peloponnesian War. This tactic (among many) was more recently revived in 2006 by Colombian women opposed to gang violence[66] and in Liberia to bring about peace in the 1999–2003 Second Liberian Civil War, although peace activist Leymah Gbowee concludes that it was problematic and 'had little or no practical effect, but it was extremely valuable in getting us media attention'.[67]

Since 2006, the #MeToo movement (https://metoomvmt.org/) begun by African American activist and rape survivor Tarana Burke has led to a high-profile cultural shift. Tracey Nicolls[68] argues that its global manifestations are potentially a powerful peacebuilding initiative. Using feminist theory in conversation with Peace Studies and improvisation theory, she observes that, in this era, rape culture is best understood as a form of structural violence. Controversially, she claims that a female counterpart to the concept of 'toxic masculinity' is 'complicit femininity', and there is a need to move beyond consent to conceptualise a robust 'respectful mutuality'.[69] With cultural attitudes and behaviours able to be shifted through the introduction of disrupting narratives, the movement enables peacebuilding opportunities to shape cultural reconstruction and use the improvisatory resources of 'culture-jamming' as a mechanism to dismantle rape culture.

#MeToo and Social Media

Social media has proved useful in building social movements such as #MeToo (but has also led to retrograde steps).[70] The digital arena's ability to amplify personal narratives on a global scale catalysed the #MeToo movement's rapid ascension.[71] Highlighting the crucial role of online platforms in contemporary social movements, this digital mobilisation facilitated a collective reckoning with the pervasive issues of sexual misconduct.[72]

This extends beyond just raising awareness. Rather, it has fostered a societal shift in recognising and combating sexual misconduct, marking a significant moment in the ongoing discourse on gender and power dynamics. Leveraging the collective power of widely shared narratives, #MeToo has sparked significant discussions across numerous sectors, encouraging institutions to reassess their policies and practices regarding sexual misconduct.[73] The movement has been augmented by astute leadership, which has employed a blend of personal testimony and strategic activism to challenge entrenched norms and practices, and navigated a delicate balance between amplifying individual stories and advocating for systemic change. An inclusive approach has been crucial in fostering a diverse and unified movement.[74]

Nevertheless, appalling rates of domestic and family violence continue in both wealthy nations such as Australia and less developed countries such as India. It's increasingly recognised that men need to become more involved in anti-violence campaigns.[75]

Men and Culture Change

Some men are challenging patriarchal language and narratives, such as Michael Sell in *Approaching the Qur'an: The Early Revelations*, who makes a point of addressing the relationship the Qur'an and women share, highlighting the gender neutrality of its text. He notes that: 'the Quran is misunderstood due to the "loss of the Qur'anic gender-dynamic translations", strengthening beliefs that the Quran is concentrated on 'male-centered language'.[76] Further emphasised by Sell is that from a linguistic perspective, the Qur'an does not promote a 'he' over a 'she', that God is neither identified as feminine nor masculine, and to believe so is against Islamic theology.

There is also optimistic new research that suggests that men's behaviour change programmes in Australia have been effective, leading to behaviour change in the short and longer term, with violence reduced in all areas rather than shifting from one form to another, such as from physical violence to financial abuse.[77] The report found that the programmes did not stop all men from being violent or stop all the violence of the men who made changes. Although some partners of the men were positive, former partners who had left the perpetrator were negative, saying the programme had not protected them or came too late to matter to them. However, David Smythe, chairman of Violence Free Families who conducted the research with the Department of Social Work at Melbourne's Monash University, believes that the programmes are 'one of the most useful and cost-effective tools currently available [...] [and] showed the men were making substantial reform and maintaining it, though often with some difficulty'.[78]

Government support for such programmes is important. But is it compromised by the narrative 'cognitive dissonance' of governments on the one hand supporting violence prevention and on the other hand spending far more on lethal weapons and large, permanent forces trained to kill people they've never met?

Conclusion

Some people question whether we should discuss gender at all, believing that this contributes to ongoing stereotyping. Others are adamant, however, that we must explore it, albeit sensitively. For Carolyn Stephenson,[79] gender equality is both an important human rights goal for women and a necessary framework for looking at the whole conceptualisation of cultural peace.

Despite the complexities and challenges of unravelling gendered violence and extricating societies from patriarchal and militaristic modes, there are some signs of progress, of evolution towards more equal, free and peaceful societies. Although frustratingly slow and subtle at times, this difficult work can add momentum to global shifts in consciousness, behaviour and institutions, particularly if it's aided by artistic activism, discussed in the next chapter. It must occur at all levels, from group dynamics and inner work (see Chapter 11) to United Nations commissions and conventions, and the Spotlight Initiative, a global, multi-year initiative that, like activist group Women in Black, focuses on eliminating all forms of violence against women and girls.

> Working with gender awareness to change both ourselves, and the (power) dynamics within our organisations, is an important personal and organisational transformation that in itself acts to diminish structural violence in our societies.[80]

Notes

1 War Resisters International 2014 *Handbook for Nonviolent Campaigns,* War Resisters International, London, p. 23.

2 Ibid.

3 Juric, Alana 2022 'Maid Café secrets Spilled by a former maid: The good, the bad and the ugly moments of a Japanese maid café job', *Tokyo Weekender*, 28 December, www.tokyoweekender.com/art_and_culture/entertainment-art_and_culture/maid-cafe-secrets-spilled-former-maid/

4 Nestel, M. L. and Rogers, Jon 2021 'Hooters girls' fury over "X-rated" uniform change prompts backflip', *News.com.au*, 19 October.

5 Oi, Mariko 2021 Why Japan can't shake sexism', *BBC* 9th April, www.bbc.com/worklife/article/20210405-why-japan-cant-shake-sexism

6 See, for example, Hackworth, Jerusha Laleh 2020 *Female Empowerment and Education in Post-War Sierra Leone*, PhD thesis, University of New England, Australia.

7 Oldfield, Sybil 2003 *International Woman Suffrage: November 1914 – September 1916*, Taylor & Francis, New York, p. 46.

8 Osmanski, Stephanie 2023 'Jane Fonda's history of social and environmental activism', *Green Matters*, 13 January, www.greenmatters.com/p/jane-fonda-activism

9 Howley, Pat 2002 *Breaking Spears and Mending Hearts*, Zed Books; Federation Press London; Annandale, N.S.W, pp. 163 – 174.

10 Keane, Fergal 2017 'The Rohingya crisis: Why won't Aung San Suu Kyi Act?' *BBC News*, www.bbc.com/news/world-asia-41187517

11 'Political tributes to Mo Mowlam' 2005, *BBC News*, 19 August, http://news.bbc.co.uk/1/hi/northern_ireland/4165230.stm

12 Boulding, Elise 1999 'Elise Boulding keynote', *Ikeda Centre*, www.ikedacenter.org/resources/elise-boulding-peace-cultures-and-living-difference

13 Piedalue, Amy D. 2019 'Slow nonviolence: Muslim women resisting the everyday violence of dispossession and marginalisation', *Politics and Space*, vol. 40, no. 2, pp. 373–390.

14 Ibid.

15 Bartkowski, Maciej 2013 *Recovering Nonviolent History: Civil Resistance in Liberation Struggles,* Lynne Rienner Publishers, Boulder, pp. 341–343.

16 Hastings, T. 2020 'Property damage, violence, nonviolent action, and strategy', *Minds of the Movement* (blog). ICNC, June 2, 2020, https://www.nonviolent-conflict.org/blog_post/property-damage-violence-nonviolent-action-and-strategy/

17 Cited in Agnès Humbert 2008 [1946] *Résistance: Memoirs of Occupied France* (trans. B. Mellor) Bloomsbury, London, p. 309.

18 Blanc, J. 2008 'Afterword' in Humbert [1946] 2008, p. 294.

19 Gallo-Cruz, Selina 2016 'More powerful forces? Women, nonviolence and mobilisation', *Sociology Compass*, Vo'.10, no. 9, pp. 823–835.

20 Mulley, Clare 2012 *The Spy Who Loved: The Secrets and Lives of Christine Granville*, Macmillan, London, p. 253.

21 Branagan, Marty 2022a 'Women and nonviolent resistance to WWII Nazism', *Social Alternatives*, vol. 41, no. 3, October, pp. 68–75; Branagan, Marty 2022b 'Women and nonviolent resistance to Nazism in WWII: Media, sabotage, smuggling and hiding people', *Social Alternatives*, vol. 41, no. 4; Branagan, Marty 2023 'Spying, sabotage, subversion, people-smuggling: The brave women who resisted the Nazis through nonviolence', *Conversation*, 25th April, https://theconversation.com/spying-sabotage-subversion-people-smuggling-the-brave-women-who-resisted-the-nazis-through-non-violence-199863

22 Blanc 2008, p. 291.

23 Huppert, M. 2021 *Malou: French Resistance Fighter*, Real Film and Publishing, Melbourne, p. 62.

24 Blanc 2008, p. 292.
25 Ibid.
26 Blanc 2008, pp. 284–286.
27 Purnell, S. 2020 *A Woman of No Importance: The Untold Story of Virginia Hall, WW2's Most Dangerous Spy*, Virago Press, London, p. 6.
28 Blanc 2008, p. 293.
29 Poldermans, Sophie 2019 *Seducing and Killing Nazis: Hannie, Truus and Freddie: Dutch Resistance Heroines of WWII*, Sophie's Women of War Press, USA, p.xxiii).
30 Branagan, Marty 2020 'The Franklin River Campaign: A case study in creative nonviolent wilderness conservation', in Robyn Bartel, Marty Branagan, Stephen Harris, and Fiona Utley (eds.), *Rethinking Wilderness and the Wild: Conservation, Conflict and Co-existence*, Routledge, London.
31 Branagan 2023; Branagan, Marty 2014, 'Australian opposition to uranium mining: A history of nonviolence development', *International Journal of Rural Law and Policy*, No. 1, http://epress.lib.uts.edu.au/journals/index.php/ijrlp/issue/view/303
32 Hawley, Janet 2003 'Tree Amigos', *Sydney Morning Herald*, 28 June, pp. 18–23.
33 Ricketts, Aidan 2021 *Complexity Theory and Social Movement Praxis: Emergence, Adaptability and Unpredictability*, PhD thesis, University of New England, Armidale.
34 Branagan Marty 2021 'Women in environmental nonviolent action', in K Standish, H Devere, A Suazo and R Rafferty (eds) *The Palgrave Handbook of Positive Peace*, Palgrave Macmillan, Singapore.
35 Greer, Germaine 1970 Untitled track one in Sinead O'Connor, 1994, *Universal Mother*, Ensign Records, London.
36 Rimmer, Susan Harris 2022 'Is this the end of the two-partysystem in Australia? The Greens, teals and others shock the major parties', *Conversation*, 22 May, https://theconversation.com/is-this-the-end-of-the-two-party-system-in-australia-the-greens-teals-and-others-shock-the-major-parties-182672
37 Hurst, Daniel 2023 'Penny Wong overruled department by sending observer to anti-nuclear treaty meeting', *Guardian*, 8 February, www.theguardian.com/world/2023/feb/07/penny-wong-overruled-department-by-sending-observer-to-anti-nuclear-treaty-meeting?CMP=oth_b-aplnews_d-3
38 O'Reilly, Marie 2016 'Inclusive security and peaceful societies: Exploring the evidence', Inclusive Security (Prism), March, www.inclusivesecurity.org/publication/inclusive-security-and-peaceful-societies-exploring-the-evidence/
39 Ibid. See also Yidana, Godwin 2024 *Women and the Myanmar Peace Process: A Black Pro-feminist Analysis*, PhD thesis, UNE, Australia.
40 Enloe, Cynthia 2000 *Maneuvers: The International Politics of Militarizing Women's Lives*, University of California Press, Berkeley, p. 3.
41 Cited in War Resisters International 2014, p. 22.
42 Eisenstein, Zillah 2008 'Resexing militarism for the globe', in R. L. Riley, C. T. Mohanty and M. B. Pratt (eds.), *Feminism and War: Confronting US Imperialism*, Zed Books, London, p. 30.
43 Oldfield, Sybil 1989 *Women against the Iron Fist: Alternatives to Militarism 1900–1989*, Basil Blackwell, Oxford, p. 29.
44 Cited in Cleal, Olivia 2023 'Australian "feminist's feminist" Dr Dale Spender AM dies age 80', *Women's Agenda*, 27 November, https://womensagenda.com.au/latest/australian-feminists-feminist-dr-dale-spender-am-dies-age-80/
45 O'Reilly 2016.
46 Ibid.

47 Houston, Melinda 2022 'At last, TV sets the record straight on these Salacious scandals', *Sydney Morning Herald,* 23 February, www.smh.com.au/culture/tv-and-radio/tv-is-casting-a-fresh-light-on-the-women-involved-in-men-s-scandals-20220221-p59y7p.html?ref=rss

48 Ibid.

49 Ibid.

50 Marwick, Arthur 1998 *The Sixties,* Oxford University Press, Oxford.

51 Plummer, David and Geofroy, Stephen 2010 'When bad is cool: Violence and crime as rites of passage to manhood', *Caribbean Review of Gender Studies*, no. 4, pp. 1–17.

52 Ford, Clementine 2018 'Macho "pranks" and the devastating cost of male emotional repression', *Guardian*, 2 October, www.theguardian.com/world/2018/oct/02/macho-pranks-and-the-devastating-cost-of-male-emotional-repression

53 Webb, Tony 2017 'Men, masculinities and violence', *New Community*, vol. 14, no. 3, Iss. 55, pp. 24–33.

54 O'Dea, James 2012 *Cultivating Peace: Becoming a 21st Century Peace Ambassador,* Shift Books, San Rafael.

55 Matthew 10:34.

56 Meagher, Tom 2014 'The danger of the monster myth', *The Drum*, 22 April, www.abc.net.au/news/2014-04-18/meagher-the-danger-of-the-monster-myth/5399108

57 Vaughan, James 2018 'Men's liberation: What today's #MeToo sceptics can learn from their 1970s brothers', *Conversation*, 2 March, https://theconversation.com/mens-liberation-what-todays-metoo-sceptics-can-learn-from-their-1970s-brothers-92530

58 Ibid.

59 'NSW inquiry to investigate 40 years of unsolved Sydney Gay hate deaths' 2022, *ABC News*, 16 April, www.abc.net.au/news/2022-04-16/nsw-inquiry-into-sydney-gay-hate-deaths/1009951508

60 Marwick 1998.

61 Phipps, Jennifer 1997 *I Had a Dream: Australian Art in the 1960s*, National Gallery of Victoria, Melbourne; Desmond, Michael and Dixon, Christine 1995, 1968, National Gallery of Australia, Canberra.

62 Berger, Miriam 2019 'A guide to how gender-neutral language is developing around the world', *Washington Post*, 15 December, www.washingtonpost.com/world/2019/12/15/guide-how-gender-neutral-language-is-developing-around-world/

63 Wilson, Emily 2018 *The Odyssey* (translation), Norton, London.

64 Cochrane, Kira 2013 'Rise of the naked female warriors', *Guardian,* 21 March, www.theguardian.com/world/2013/mar/20/naked-female-warrior-femen-topless-protesters

65 Sanders, Erin Ladd 2010 'Lysistrata: Make love, not war', *In the Name of Peace*, Murdoch Books, Sydney, pp. 19 – 31.

66 Shain, Samantha 2012 'Colombian women use sex strike to demand gangster disarmament (Huelga de Piernas Cruzadas)', *Global Nonviolent Action Database,* 28 October, https://nvdatabase.swarthmore.edu/content/colombian-women-use-sex-strike-demand-gangster-disarmament-huelga-de-piernas-cruzadas-2006

67 Cited in Morales, Helen 2013 'Aristophanes' Lysistrata, the liberian "sex strike", and the politics of reception', *Greece & Rome*, vol. 60, no. 2, pp. 281–295.

68 Nicolls, T. 2020 *Dismantling Rape Culture: The Peacebuilding Power of "Me Too"*, Routledge, London.

69 Ibid.

70 Branagan 2013, pp. 143–175.
71 Sancho, G. R. 2021 'Activism and affective labor for digital direct action: The Mexican #MeToo campaign', *Social Movement Studies*, vol. 22, no. 2, pp. 145–162.
72 Shukla, S., Singh, P. and Malik, G. 2020 "#MeToo movement: Influence of social media engagement on intention to control sexual harassment against women', *Journal of Content, Community & Communication*, vol. 12, no. 6, pp. 1257–1269.
73 Field-Springer, K, Draut, H., Babrow, F. and Sandman, M 2021 '(Re)claiming stories in the #MeToo Movement: Righting epistemic wrongs of physical, mental, and emotional harms of sexual violence', *Health Communication*, vol. 37, no. 8, pp. 982–991.
74 Trott, V. 2020 'Networked feminism: Counterpublics and the intersectional issues of #MeToo', *Feminist Media Studies*, vol. 21, no. 7, pp. 1125–1142.
75 Roberts, Georgia 2024 'Attorney-General Mark Dreyfus says men need to "Step Up" in domestic violence crisis', *ABC News*, 19 April, www.abc.net.au/news/2024-04-19/dreyfus-says-men-need-to-step-up-in-domestic-violence-crisis/103743900; Kale, Sirin 2021 '"The time for men to step up is right now!": What all men can do to help end violence against women', *Guardian*, 17 March, www.theguardian.com/society/2021/mar/17/the-time-for-men-to-step-up-is-right-now-what-all-men-can-do-to-help-end-violence-against-women
76 Sell, Michael 1999 *Approaching the Qur'an: The Early Revelations*, White Cloud, Ashland, p. 202.
77 Perkins, Miki and Social Affairs 2017 'Can violent men change? The signs are positive, research finds', *Age*, 30 April, www.theage.com.au/national/victoria/can-violent-men-change-the-signs-are-positive-research-finds-20170430-gvvu66.html
78 Ibid.
79 Stephenson, Carolyn M. 2009 'Gender equality and a culture of peace', in Joseph de Rivera (ed), *Handbook on Building Cultures of Peace*, Springer, New York, pp. 123–138.
80 War Resisters International 2014, p. 23.

Chapter 10

ARTISTIC ACTIVISM

Artistic activism is a dynamic practice combining the creative power of the arts to move us emotionally and intellectually, with the audacity and strategic planning of activism necessary to bring about social change and measurable shifts in power. It creates art that is a form of political or social currency, actively addressing power structures rather than merely representing or describing them.

Why do we need artistic activism? Isn't art a bit of an indulgence when there are so many serious issues that require addressing?

Despite the horrors of ongoing conflicts and wars in the Middle East, Ukraine and Africa, there has been some excellent news of late in the world of peacemaking and peacebuilding. After a long campaign involving many diverse people and methods – including artistic activism – nuclear weapons have been declared illegal by the international community.[1]

This is a major breakthrough, as the international community by and large has recognised officially that the use of these weapons constitutes a grave crime against humanity. This is not the end of the campaign, however, but the beginning, as the nuclear-armed nations – the United States, United Kingdom, France, China, Russia, Israel, India, Pakistan and North Korea, supported by their allies such as Australia – continue to oppose the move. Can the arts, humour and creativity play a role in such a serious and important campaign?

Out of step with world opinion, there are now opportunities to put pressure on those countries to comply with the will of the majority of the world, as well as to comply with the international laws and UN agreements which already indicated that such weapons were legally problematic. Now there is a definitive international agreement which will give the majority of the world's countries the leverage to ramp up nuclear disarmament. This will allow sanctions and boycotts, as well as diplomatic pressure and divestment campaigns, such as those emerging from 2024 campus peace/justice protests globally.

However, there needs to be a lot more work in changing worldviews about nuclear weapons at all levels, and in building community groundswells of support for action, because there have been similar previous agreements which haven't yet had much traction, such as the Kellogg–Briand Pact. This was an agreement to outlaw wars of aggression, signed on 27 August 1928, by 15 countries, including Australia, and eventually by most of the established nations on Earth.[2] Nevertheless, the world is now more interconnected, and opinion polls indicate a strong will for nuclear disarmament. The time is ripe for adding new dimensions to the campaign.

Cultural Change by 'Mayors for Peace'

One way to strengthen and diversify the campaign is by using the arts. An organisation which is doing just that is Mayors for Peace, which originated in June 1982 at the Second UN Special Session on Disarmament, when Hiroshima's then-mayor, Takeshi Araki, called for cities around the world to unite and transcend national borders to work for the abolition of nuclear weapons. The cities of Hiroshima and Nagasaki then established the 'World Conference of Mayors for Peace through Inter-city Solidarity'. Now simply called Mayors for Peace, it is a growing global network with over 8,200 'cities for peace'.

In addition to open letters, appeals, petitions, webinars, summits and conferences, numerous cultural activities take place such as atomic bomb poster exhibitions, children's art competitions such as 'Peaceful Towns' in Germany, distributing seedlings from atomic bomb survivor trees, and pottery workshops for school children in Evora, Portugal, which use the region's traditional craft to create ceramics on the theme of peace.

There is a Mayors for Peace Flag Day across Germany every year on 8 July, while November is 'Culture of Peace Month' in Hiroshima, with activities including online testimonies by *hibakusha* (atomic bomb survivors) to school students in Cervia, Italy. Manchester, UK, has a Young People's Peace Trail with opportunities to learn about the city's history and peace through visiting war-related memorial sites. Santos in Brazil held a Peace Run involving professional athletes and children running together through the city, carrying a torch as a symbol of peace. Sardasht in Iran held a 'Little Narrators' workshop to help children communicate the history of their city, including bombs and chemical attacks, to the world.[3]

At the other end of the spectrum are artists who perform in the middle of war zones, such as cellist Vedran Smailovic, known as the Cellist of Sarajevo. After 22 people were killed when a bakery in Sarajevo was shelled by Serbs, Smailovic, dressed in formal concert attire, braved shelling and sniper attacks to play Albinoni's Adagio in G Minor over 22 days, one day for every person killed there.[4] Nearby, the Kamerni Theatre defied the siege of Sarajevo by offering over 800 theatre and music performances as well as prayer vigils.[5]

Cultural Streams of Peacebuilding

There is a long history of cultural peacebuilding[6] and its most assertive form, artistic activism. Although the evening news can often be dispiriting, it's worth remembering that all over the world, creative people are working for a better world. This occurs in every medium imaginable, from cartoons to rap, theatre to sculpture, sometimes with unexpected effects. Puppetry, for example, is often dismissed as 'childish' and overlooked as a politically charged medium, but groups such as The Bread and Puppet Theatre, founded in New York City, aid socially engaged groups during protests in multiple ways, such as evoking solidarity, creating accessible messages and allowing for acts of violence to be met with acts of creation. They can disguise the crucial conversations of our times behind smiles and laughs and be vehicles to express controversial ideas with less risk to the protesters.[7]

Australian Aboriginal artists such as Fiona Foley and Tracey Moffat, actors such as Leah Purcell, Rachael Maza and Aaron Pederson, and musicians such as Christine Anu and Tiddas have articulated rights, cleverly interrogated how Aboriginal people are viewed, and exposed direct, structural and cultural violence.

Classical Peace

In the realm of classical music, Offenbach was a pioneer of satirical opera, creating large-scale works which lampooned contemporary mores and political figures such as Napoleon III, while Vaughan Williams wrote a plea for peace in 1936: 'Dona nobis pacem' ('Grant us peace'), a call to learn from the carnage of World War I and avoid war.

Benjamin Britten's lifelong pacifism was central to much of his work.[8] Britten composed a *Pacifist March* for the 1930s Peace Pledge Union, a group whose admirers included influential writers Aldous Huxley (whose *Brave New World* is still popular) and Bertrand Russell (who influenced Paul McCartney and the Beatles' turn towards peace music). Britten was tried as a conscientious objector and, as public service, gave two concerts in 1945 with the violinist Yehudi Menuhin at the newly liberated Belsen concentration camp. This experience would influence later works like his 1962 *War Requiem,* which used the war poetry written by shell-shocked World War I soldier Wilfred Owen, who was killed days before the Armistice.[9] Others following in his footsteps include Philip Glass and his mesmeric, minimalist opera 'Satyagraha' (Sanskrit for 'truth force' or nonviolent action based on truthful assertiveness and dialogue), a moving account of Mahatma Gandhi's formative experiences in South Africa.

Both classical and pop musicians have performed concerts in solidarity with Ukraine, with 10,000 people attending a 2022 concert in Berlin, where the crowd held banners with slogans opposing the Russian invasion. Held near the Brandenburg Gate, a symbol of a divided Germany during the Cold War, many performers wore shades of blue and yellow, the colours of the Ukrainian flag. Jamala, a Ukrainian singer who won the 2016 Eurovision Song Contest with her song '1944', told the audience via video link that 'music is a peaceful force' and that 'if all the musicians united it would be the strongest peace army in the world'.[10]

Russian and Hong Kong Activism

At the same time, anti-war Russians, faced with laws that criminalise truthful war reporting and peace protests (for which 15,000 people were arrested in 2022), have turned to subtle and subversive tools for political expression such as graffiti, street art and coded posters advertising protest actions or with QR codes that direct a viewer to a particular website.[11]

This echoes actions in Hong Kong where pro-democracy notes have covered walkways, tunnels, shop windows, street signs and billboards 'like a swarm released onto the wild, to pollinate and colonise the city'.[12] Black-clad teams were deployed to paper footpaths with posters at jogging speed, sometimes for kilometres at a time. Their assembly line efficiency involved one group spraying glue, another placing the posters in a checkerboard pattern and a final crew using long umbrellas to tamp them into place. Pedestrian walkways and underpasses became irreverent 'impromptu galleries of dissent', with images of Chinese president Xi Jinping placed on the ground, forcing commuters to walk on his face.[13] All this is supported by the quieter work of full-time artist/activists such as Chinese-born Ai Weiwei, who uses photography, sculpture and installation to explore social and political issues, calling attention to human rights violations on an epic scale and expanding the definition of art to include new forms of social engagement.

The 1960s (and Onwards) Counter-culture

Sometimes there are mass outbursts of counter-cultural activity, such as in the anti-war movements of the 1960s and 1970s, as people sought dramatic ways to express their outrage at war without resorting to violence.[14] Music has long been used in the role of implementing social change by creating choruses and anthems for movements that bring people together and build a strong common ground. In the 1960s and 1970s, Joan Baez and Bob Dylan wrote and played stirring anthems for the times, such as 'We Shall Overcome', 'The Times They Are a Changing' and 'Masters of War', while the Beatles used their immense popularity to move from simple love songs into powerful statements about peace, such as John Lennon's 'Imagine' and 'Give Peace a Chance'. (On the Amsterdam Peace Museum website, you can find a video of former US president Bill Clinton being talked into singing this with a young woman.) 'Respect' (1967) by Aretha Franklin (written by American soul singer Otis Redding) is a soulful cry for respect to be accorded to women, reaffirmed later, in tandem with British pop duo The Eurythmics, by 'Sisters Are Doing It for Themselves' (1985).

Other musicians of the 1960s who performed protest music include Bob Seger, Pete Seeger, The Doors, Creedence Clearwater Revival, Barry McGuire with his 'Eve of Destruction' and Donovan's 'Universal Soldier'. One of the most memorable events of protest music in this era was when renowned guitarist Jimi Hendrix performed his version of 'Star-Spangled Banner' at the legendary Woodstock festival in 1969 in the United States, turning it into the screams of bombs falling on Vietnam and Cambodia.

Billie Holiday's 'Strange Fruit' captured the ugly essence of lynchings and the opposition to the Civil Rights movement. 'We Shall Not Be Moved', later covered by Mavis Staples, expressed determination, while Sam Cooke's song 'A Change is Gonna Come' captured both the struggle, adversity and the hope for change that Martin Luther King Jr and the song-driven Civil Rights movement brought. *A Change is Gonna Come* is also the title of a riveting book about civil rights music, complemented by an inspirational 2009 documentary called *Soundtrack for a Revolution*.

James Brown could be both flamboyantly assertive and pacific, with songs such as 'Say It Loud – I'm Black and I'm Proud' (1968) affirming his outspoken pride in his identity, while he was one of the few people capable of calming cities such as Boston in the angry aftermath of Martin Luther King Jr's assassination.

Jamaican American Harry Belafonte is a good example of someone who used both his work and his fame as platforms for advocacy and activism. He broke barriers by starring in anti-racist feature films such as *The World, The Flesh and the Devil* (1959) and releasing hit songs such as 'Dayo-O (The Banana Boat Song)' (1954). He financially backed the civil rights movement, bailed out Martin Luther King Jr from prison in Alabama and helped promote the 1963 March on Washington.[15] His refusal to tour in the US South added momentum to the end of segregation (as did the Beatles' refusal to play to racially segregated audiences on their 1964 tour).[16] In 1985, Belafonte instigated the United States for Africa fundraiser to relieve famine in Ethiopia. He praised peace initiatives by the Soviet Union. He opposed apartheid in

South Africa, the US blockade of Cuba, the invasion of Grenada and US military actions in Iraq, and was an ambassador for UNICEF.[17]

Can Rock and Punk Promote Peace?

Rock music has often had an orientation towards social criticism, such as the anti-war songs of Irish groups like The Cranberries, U2 and Sinead O'Connor which have all been part of moving Northern Ireland towards peace. The UK ska band The Specials sang against racism, and the Rolling Stones put out songs like 'Undercover of the Night', about violent repression in Nicaragua. However, they disappointed many activists by breaking a boycott that many musicians have had against playing in Israel, similar to the cultural and sporting boycotts that were such an important element of ending apartheid in South Africa. In Australia, Redgum, Goanna and Midnight Oil have been prominent protest bands, with the latter's 'Maralinga' and 'The Power and the Passion' inspiring civil disobedience in central Australia. Bob Marley led the reggae genre with his poignant songs against hatred, racism and war, while African protest music has been led by the Beninese superstar Angelique Kidjo and Nigeria's Afro-beat legends Fela Kuti and his son Femi Kuti.

Another type of resistance music is a genre that emerged after rock – punk. You may wonder at its inclusion here, particularly if you consider cultural peace to consist of things like meditation music or choral songs. A counter-argument, however, is that any music that aims to counter direct, structural or cultural violence is validly part of a culture of peace, and that such music can be loud, joyous, sexy, celebratory, assertive and even raucous rather than just quiet, chaste or humble. Some people may hate it, but you can't please everybody. Examples in this genre include the many anti-war and protest songs of The Clash, Crass, the Dead Kennedys, the Saints and Pussy Riot, while Insurge's 'Lock On' is an exuberant song which celebrates and encourages nonviolent civil disobedience.

Assertive Artistic Activism

The arts in general have often been a part of social movements for a better world and have supported a variety of protests that are assertive rather than aggressive, upfront and forthright rather than meek and mild.

For example, the central South Korean village of Seongju – once a quiet Buddhist pilgrimage site – has begun to protest against the US imposition of a missile defence system there. These protests are contrary to the usual polite mores of Korean culture and have had many cultural aspects, such as banners, candlelight protests, stickers and badges circulated around the country, local officials shaving their heads, people playing guitar, and dances and songs that are unexpectedly joyful.[18]

The artworks of Australian painter and film-maker George Gittoes are assertive critiques of war. His work is often highly confronting, depicting the horrible consequences of war in a personalised way, by working directly from images of the victims, often children. You do not get a feeling of peacefulness in front of one of his pictures involving graphic violence. Do Gittoes' pictures add to the violence of the world or are they important statements – reflections and expositions – that should be more common? Could the disquiet one feels on viewing a Gittoes work then translate into action against war? Could it prick the conscience of someone who profits from war, such as through their investments in arms companies?[i]

Resistance Music in South Africa and Timor Leste

South Africa's Apartheid was one of the most brutal and securitised systems of racial segregation that the world has ever known. Yet its successful overthrow was aided by numerous nonviolent tactics, including global boycotts of trade with the regime, and 'liberation music' which both fuelled and united the movement. Throughout every phase of the struggle, music was a communal act of expression that shed light on the injustices of apartheid, drew people together and fortified them even as they walked defiantly to the gallows. 'Nkosi Sikelel'I Afrika', which was adopted as the African National Congress's official anthem, was both a soothing prayer and an emblem of hope and unity. Some songs were mournful, while others were upbeat and energetic, with powerful chants that built in intensity and volume as hundreds and sometimes thousands of participants joined in. International performances by exiled musicians of songs such as 'Meadowlands', about forced removals, allowed international audiences a window into South Africa and exposed the oppression suffered by the majority of citizens. Music both strengthened existing communities and united members of communities that were in supposed opposition to one another. After apartheid, a national anthem was composed with elements of both African and British hymns and was thus a communal expression that not only symbolises unity but enacts it.[19]

Protest music also played a part in Timor Leste's liberation from Indonesia's brutal occupation. With most musical instruments taken by Indonesian military forces, in 1999 a group of exiled musicians formed the 'Dili Allstars', recorded an

i It's surprising how many and what sort of companies are connected to the war industry. They like war, or at least acquiesce to it, because it is profitable. Divesting from such companies is an important way of reducing support for war and building an economic culture of peace.

album in Melbourne of independence songs, and smuggled 500 cassettes into the tightly controlled country. One track in particular, 'Libertade', was played widely on Timorese buses and taxis and became the resistance movement's anthem.

Other Genres

To move on to other genres, rap and hip hop have often got a bad rap – so to speak – as being sexist and celebratory of violence. This is sometimes true, but the similar sexism and violence of some country-and-western music often go unchallenged. There has often been significant social commentary in the lyrics of groups such as Public Enemy and NWA with their call to empower African Americans and resist oppression, while Australian groups like the Hilltop Hoods, Bliss 'n' Eso and A.B. Original have consistently presented strong anti-racist arguments.

A.B. Original continues a long tradition of excellent Australian Aboriginal bands, from No Fixed Address, the Warumpi Band and Dan Sultan to Yothu Yindi and its call for a treaty, or the all-girl group Tiddas with lyrics that challenged racism and environmental damage. Kev Carmody, throughout his career, has argued for equity and land rights in songs like 'From Little Things Big Things Grow' (written with Paul Kelly) and given alternative perspectives on uranium mining and nuclear weapons, such as in the classic song 'Thou Shalt Not Steal'. These Aboriginal artists have been supported by musicians like Peter Garrett, Missy Higgins and John Butler.

Another musician who has utilised music to institute nonviolent social change is feminist icon Ani DiFranco. Her lyrics always have a strongly political background, and her songs have raised awareness and challenged many social issues. These include 'Trickle Down' which focuses on racism and gentrification, 'To the Teeth' which calls for gun control, 'In or Out' which questions traditional sexuality labels, 'Play God' which has become a cry for reproductive rights and 'Fuel', a powerful song about how violence is often caused by entrenched injustice. DiFranco has performed at benefit concerts, donated songs to charity albums and been involved in numerous progressive causes and protests, like Bob Geldof and Bono before her with their Live Aid concerts.

Other issues brought to light through songs in the 2000s by artists such as Eminem, Green Day, the Flaming Lips and Bright Eyes include international wars, terrorism, misinformation about weapons of mass destruction, and economic unease. Since 2010, activist music has protested school shootings and other violence through songs like Kendrick Lamar's 'Alright' about police shooting unarmed African Americans, Beyoncé's 'Freedom' about systematic racism, and the late Prince's 'Baltimore' about police brutality.

Many politically charged songs were released following Donald Trump's 2017 election, matching a climate that inspired more than three million women to take to the streets. These songs include Gorillaz's 'Hallelujah Money' and Fiona Apple's 'Tiny Hands'.

Dance

Dance is closely associated with music and serves as a fun, inclusive and creative way of protesting, drawing crowds and attention to campaigns. Examples include song and dance at the 2017 Oscars protesting Donald Trump, and LGBTQIA+ activists holding a dance party outside Trump's house to oppose his controversial actions supporting fossil fuels. Mallika Sarabhai uses dance as a protest vehicle, while 'flash mobs' organised via social media are prominent in many modern movements. Dance can also form a joyful part of a blockade, and usually gets more latitude from police, thereby prolonging the blockade.

Poetry

Chapter 6 examined some examples of written poetry. Spoken poetry posted on public forums also takes on issues in a creative way. One such poet is Holly McNish, who posts on the very public space of YouTube on issues including refugees, women's rights, sexism and war. Earlier poets include Wilfred Owen, mentioned above, Australian Aboriginal Kath Walker, who later reverted to the name Oodgeroo Noonuccal (with her poem 'No More Boomerang' later covered by Aboriginal band Coloured Stone), New England's environmentalist and land rights advocate Judith Wright and the great Chilean poet-diplomat Pablo Neruda.

Activist Film, Photography and Theatre

Right across the spectrum of cultural and artistic activity, you will find examples of strong, clever, witty, subtle, challenging creations. There are many great films, such as *Ten Canoes* and Australian Aboriginal-directed ones by Rachel Perkins and Ivan Sen, with screenplays by people like Louis Nowra. There's the emotive photography of Tracey Moffat. There are incisive, sometimes strident documentaries by John Pilger, David Bradbury or Michael Moore. A documentary *The Art of Un-War* (2022) celebrates Polish American conceptual artist Krzysztof Wodiczko, who has dedicated his life and art to denouncing militarism and war. His powerful public art interventions disrupt the valorisation of state-sanctioned aggression and challenge our complacency towards war, xenophobia and displacement.

An Indian UN peacekeeping contingent in Somalia used film to build cooperation with the locals, in a gentle approach to peacekeeping. They initiated many social contacts by showing Indian movies, as well as holding joint musical performances and establishing an orphanage and hospital. These efforts received local praise and were seen as a 'good start in restoring peace'.[20]

Theatre has a long history as an arena for dissent and freedom of expression, from the ancient Greek play Lysistrata mentioned in the previous chapter, to resistance plays in colonised Indo-China, to the enduring social comment of Shakespeare with his critiques of authority and human nature. There are the left-leaning plays of Bertolt Brecht and the French 'situationists', the absurdist and existentialist plays of Samuel Beckett, Eugène Ionesco and Jean Genet, and the inspired lunacy, surrealist chaos and anti-establishment humour of Monty Python.

Oases of Freedom of Expression

In Türkiye, it's surprising to find that, despite heavily-armed troops and tanks in the streets, the jailing of journalists and the suppression of academics, the modern art museum in Istanbul is a rare oasis of freedom of expression, showing, for example, photos of the banned protest movement.

Other examples of pro-peace visual arts (see Figures 10.1, 10.2, 10.3 and 10.4) range from the Yirrkala Aboriginal bark petition for land rights

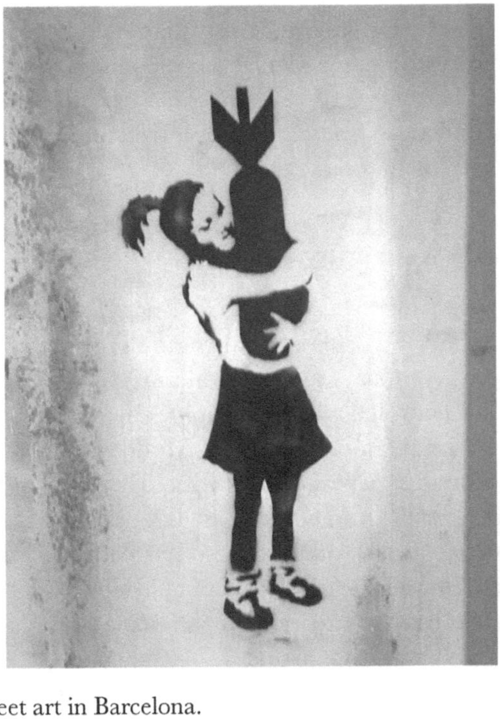

Figure 10.1 Street art in Barcelona.

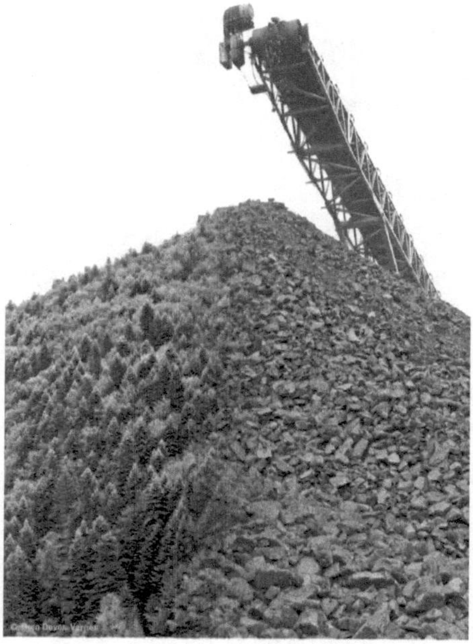

Figure 10.2 'Forest to Coal', by teenaged artist Theo Devos-Vernes.

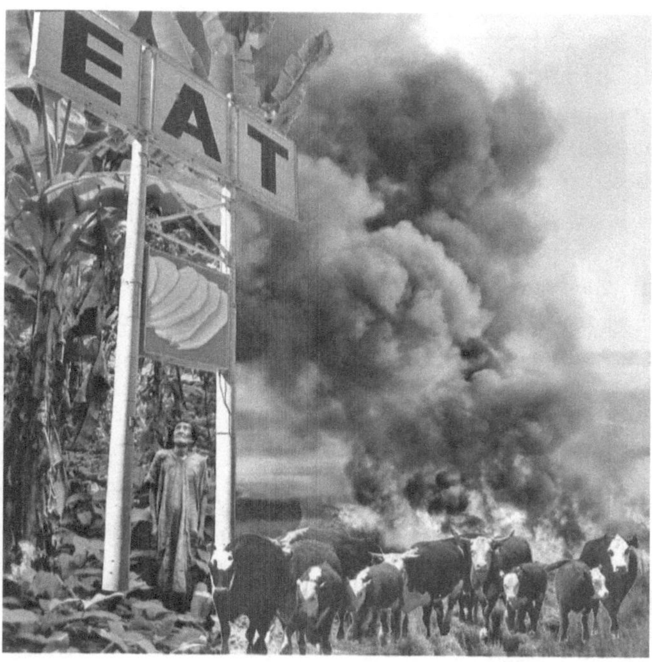

Figure 10.3 'Eat the Amazon', by UNE Peace Studies student Rachael Spink.

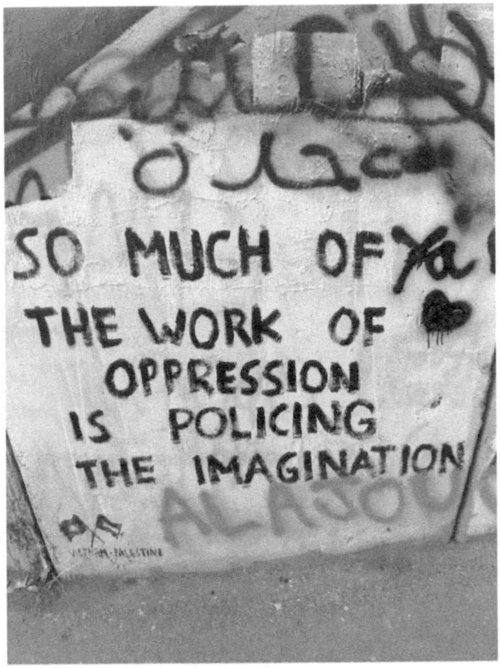

Figure 10.4 Graffiti on 'security wall' in Palestine/Israel. Photo attribution: Elspeth Liberty.

to Picasso's painting Guernica and his powerful Peace Dove symbol. One extraordinarily bold 'dissent event'[21] by Australia's satirical Chaser team included a 'motorcade' which infiltrated a heavily securitised 2007 Commonwealth Heads of Government Meeting involving George W. Bush, with one of the Chaser group dressed as Osama bin Laden. Thanks to clever camera work, the prank was later watched by millions.[22]

So, while there are always cultural and other forms of violence on the planet, there is, at the same time, a constant stream of counter-narratives posited by artists of all varieties. It's probably impossible to quantify their effects on the world, but we can say that, at the very least, this stream provides a good starting point for social change. It impacts on both the artists and those who view their work. It creates conversations. It gets people to question their ideas, assumptions, beliefs and worldviews. It creates zeitgeists and contributes to changing the tides of public opinion on which our social, political and economic systems rest. This stream or undercurrent, if better understood, supported and resourced, could turn into a river and then an unstoppable flood of peaceful and positive social change.

From Fear to Engagement

Let's now look more closely at the motivations of artistic activists – or artivists – in their own words. At a time of runaway global warming and ongoing armed conflicts, when so many people seem paralysed by despair, one advantage of artistic or creative activism is in moving people beyond fear and towards engagement. Filmmaker Alex Kelly, who has worked for Naomi Klein's New York-based climate-change non-profit organisation This Changes Everything, calls for fear to be replaced by:

> work that triggers conversations, that makes us think about other possibilities – ideas beyond capitalism, beyond closing our borders, towards a more inclusive, more just, wiser and more creative world. A world that we can all see ourselves in and that we are excited to engage to fight [sic] for.[23]

Despite tens of thousands of scientists researching and communicating climate issues,[24] there is still inadequate awareness and action, partly because trillion-dollar fossil fuel corporations have cleverly muddied the rising waters, but also because the communication of scientists and environmentalists has not been dynamic enough or pitched appropriately. Scientific reports are often difficult for non-scientists to digest. Public relations expert Bob Pickard[25] has listed 20 key problems with climate communication, including 'story fatigue' and bland, stale, repetitious, confusing or unengaging stories.

Elizabeth Boulton cites some innovative activities such as ARTCOP21, a gigantic global climate art festival, but calls for tens of thousands more, arguing that

> If a new human civilisation is to emerge that can live within its ecological limits, artists and communicators must have a prominent place, alongside the great scientific and technological innovators of our times. Humanity will never be able to defeat a threat it cannot perceive.[26]

One way to develop awareness of climate change is through multimedia performance (Figure 10.5). An example is *Re-Growth?* - a collaborative project by Ros Bandt (soundscape) and Jutta Pryor (visuals), commissioned and performed by musician and academic Alana Blackburn, which aims to reach people in a creative and respectful way. Using storytelling, imagery, sound and metaphor, it responds to past tragedies as a springboard to a better future for regional communities, with the impetus for the work derived from the unprecedented drought and bushfires of 2019/2020 and the devastating impact they had on the Anaiwan (New England) area of Australia.

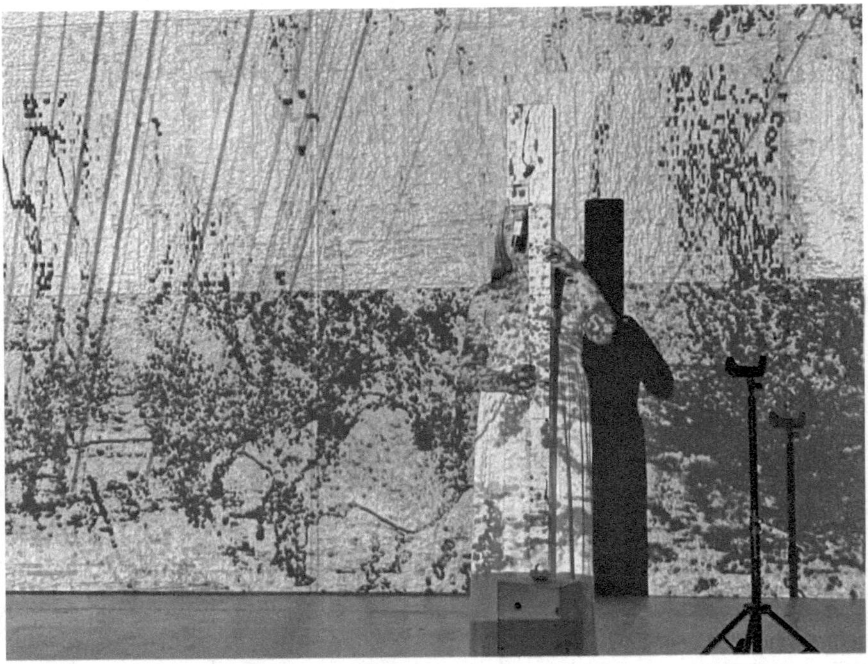

Figure 10.5 Alana Blackburn performing 'Earthsong' during a performance of *Regrowth?* Photo attribution: Ros Bandt.

Articulating why the arts are suited to shape and frame narratives around environmental issues, Dr Blackburn says:

> I wanted to find another way of reaching out to local and national communities in a way that the news couldn't. Scientific researchers have been calling on interdisciplinary action to engage the public, in particular, the creative arts to evoke emotional responses to climate change.[27]

Communicating the probabilities and dangers is only one aspect. Just as important is engaging people, suggesting solutions and influencing behaviour. Countering militarism, war, inequity and global warming requires major changes to our societies and cultures. Housing is a Human Right (www.housingisahumanright.org) is an arts-informed activist organisation that has had large-scale impact on mortgage buy-backs after the 2008 global financial crisis. It believes that fundamental structural change in the Western world is not an impossibility, and art is the way to achieve it. It uses informative videos posted on platforms like YouTube to show how homelessness in places such as Los Angeles can be quickly solved by simply granting people access to the thousands of units and offices left vacant by landlords, local authorities and developers.

Deep Changes

These large structural changes need to be preceded by cultural movements which, in turn, are led by changes in people's worldviews. Elizabeth Boulton calls for climate communication to 'engage with people's "deep frames" – beliefs formed over a lifetime, which are mostly subconscious':

> [C]limate communication needs to engage people at a philosophical, sensory and feeling level. People need to be able to feel and touch the new climate reality; to explore unfamiliar emotional terrain and be helped to conceive their existence differently. How is this to be done? The world must turn to its artists: storytellers, film-makers, musicians, painters and multi-media wizards, to name a few.[28]

Alex Kelly disputes the view that artistic activism is peripheral to the struggle. She believes it is an integral aspect of communication and education:

> Some people think of art in activism as the cake decorators that just come in and make everything look good, [but] other people have deep understanding of what is a cultural strategy. And it's not just about the art as objects or as banners, or as pieces that decorate the cake, but about this really deep embodiment of ideas in a poetic way, which can transfer ideas more deeply than just straight information.[29]

Making It Personal

One of the artists helping people to 'feel and touch the new climate reality' is Zaria Forman. Her search for a larger purpose for her work, one that would consciously speak to a sociopolitical issue, was crystallised after a visit to Greenland where she was confronted with the environmental, social and emotional impacts of a warming world. Her response was a set of hyper-realistic drawings of beaches and cracked and severed icebergs which are both stunning and devastating. Her aim was to give 'people a chance to experience remote landscapes at the forefront of climate change. […] to transport viewers to that place in time'.[30] 'It's impossible', she says, 'not to fall in love with these places once you witness them, and when you love something, you want to protect it'.[31]

The art of Hanifa Abdul Hameed is also deeply personal, speaking to topics such as gun violence, abortion, racism and sexism: 'All of the artwork I create is influenced by either experiences I've faced, or a friend has. It reflects what's happening around the world, and in my life.' Hameed's goal is to promote awareness and representation, and to communicate some of the social and political experiences of South Asian women and other women of colour.[32]

Increasing Empathy

Musician Billy Bragg believes that music can increase empathy. He hopes, for example, that the title track of his 2021 album *The Million Things That Never Happened* can help heal divisions and unite us after all the loss and trauma of the COVID-19 pandemic.[33] He backs this cultural work with more obvious activism, such as raising money for frontline health workers and live music venues.

The Panorama Project, a regional Arts North West (New South Wales) community art project during the pandemic, helped people cope with the isolation and upheaval many felt, on top of the problems caused by extreme weather events. Project coordinator Michèle Jedlicka wrote to the participants that:

> your [...] books have been viewed by hundreds of hands in libraries in large and tiny towns along the way. Your talents, insights and visions capturing the extraordinary times of 2020 definitely hit a chord with so many people. Your work made a difference to so many people, and I know first-hand, from the people who told me as the project travelled, that they felt connected to others because many things they read or saw reflected their own feelings and landscapes, and it helped people to not feel so alone.[34]

For award-winning playwright Richard Jordan, climate-themed theatre explores the politics of perception and inter-generational violence at the heart of the unfolding climate crisis (Figure 10.6). It is not about communicating a particular viewpoint, but asking questions, breaking down fixed positions, and encouraging compassion and understanding:

> I don't view theatre as a vehicle for 'spreading awareness', but rather to help us question and consider our already strong feelings and positions on an issue, and how we relate to the positions of others. Sometimes art and science are pitted against each other, but we are of course two sides of the same coin: searching for truth into the experience of being alive.

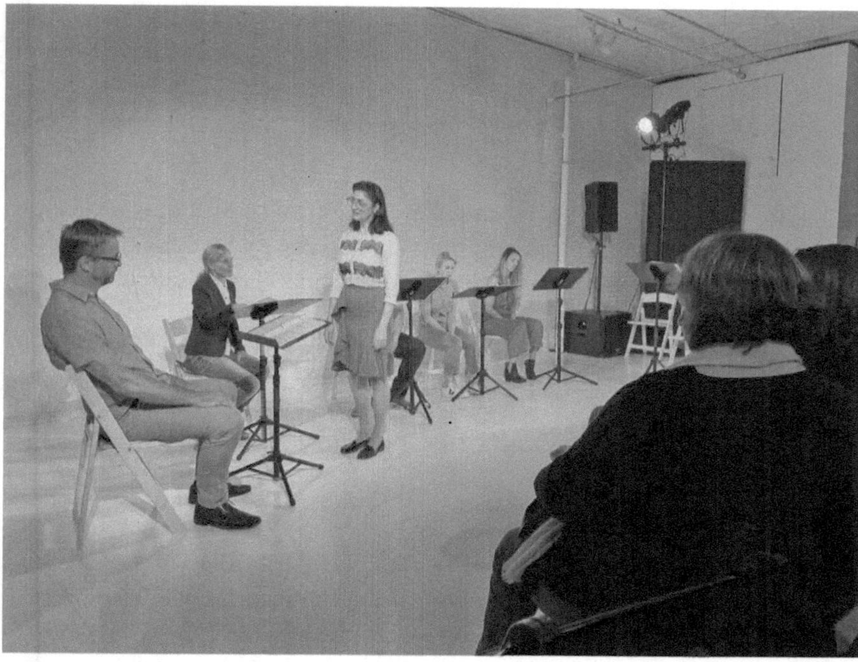

Figure 10.6 New York City reading of Richard Jordan's play *The Tiniest Thing*. Photo attribution: Richard Jordan.

> We need each other. All of us. And great theatre can help to remind us of that.[35]

A diversity of approaches is essential if a wide range of people are to become engaged. Zaria Forman says that 'Psychology has proven that we take action and make decisions based on our emotions more than anything else. [Art] taps into our emotions in a way that statistics and news stories may not [...] But we need the numbers, the statistics, the news, and the art. We need all the tools in the toolbox'.[36]

Getting People Laughing

Humour is one of the most effective ways of engaging the emotions, communicating and posing questions. As Kathy Lette notes, 'Laughter straps a big shock absorber to your brain. [...] If you can laugh at something, it takes the sting out of it. [...] [I]f you can disarm with charm, you're more likely to get your message across'.[37]

Douglas Adams' immensely popular *Hitchhikers Guide to the Galaxy* has strong anti-war themes throughout its humorous five-part 'trilogy' (with an additional volume by Eoin Colfer and a fan-fiction edition by this author).[38] Adams lampooned the futility and waste of war preparations in one passage in which

> mighty ships tore across the empty wastes of space and finally dived screaming on to the first planet they came across – which happened to be the Earth – where due to a terrible miscalculation of scale the entire battle fleet was accidentally swallowed by a small dog.[39]

Adams satirised how battleships are named: 'the G.S.S. *Daring,* the G.S.S. *Audacity* and the G.S.S. *Suicidal Insanity*'. In the following passage, he sent up the way wars are often justified by governments using clever, sophistic arguments:

> Sometimes, after some of the worst of these outrages, the Dwellers in the Forest would send a messenger to either the leader of the Princes of the Plains or the leader of the Tribesmen of the Cold Hillsides and demand to know the reason for this intolerable behaviour. And the leader, whichever one it was, would take the messenger aside and explain the Reason to him, slowly and carefully and with great attention to the considerable detail involved.
>
> And the terrible thing was, it was a very good one. It was very clear, very rational, and tough. The messenger would hang his head and feel sad and foolish that he had not realized what a tough and complex place the real world was, and what difficulties and paradoxes had to be embraced if one was to live in it.
>
> 'Now do you understand?' the leader would say.
>
> The messenger would nod dumbly.
>
> 'And you see these battles have to take place?'
>
> Another dumb nod.
>
> 'And why they have to take place in the forest, and why it is in everybody's best interest, the Forest Dwellers included, that they should?'
>
> 'Er [...]'
>
> 'In the long run.'
>
> 'Er, yes.'
>
> And the messenger did understand the Reason, and he returned to his people in the Forest. But as he approached them, as he walked through the Forest and amongst the trees, he found that all he could

remember of the Reason was how terribly clear the argument had seemed. What it actually was he couldn't remember at all.
And this, of course, was a great comfort when next the Tribesmen and the Princes came hacking and burning their way through the Forest, killing every Forest Dweller in their way.[40]

Finding Common Ground

In earlier chapters, we discussed the Christmas truces of 1914, which were greatly facilitated by music. This music grew in intensity, initially as rivalry but increasingly with a sense of common ground:

> [I]n peaceful sectors, it was not uncommon for units to sing in the evenings, sometimes deliberately with an eye towards entertaining or gently taunting their opposite numbers. This shaded gently into more festive activity; in early December, E.H.W. Hulse of the Scots Guards wrote that he was planning to organise a concert party for Christmas Day, which would 'give the enemy every conceivable form of song in harmony' in response to frequent choruses of Deutschland Über Alles.[41]

Music can break down barriers and encourage liminal atmospheres where dramatic changes can occur to people's behaviours and worldviews, such as laying down weapons and realising that the strangers you have been firing at have many things in common with you.

Clothing Critiques in Beauty

Military intelligence officer and Peace Studies PhD student Cass Brooker combines her propaganda expertise with art skills to encase critiques and questions in beauty, with the aim being to spur climate action. In one image (Figure 10.7), a robotic bee with the Doomsday Clock on its back and a nuclear-powered brain is 'juxtaposed against a bunch of seemingly beautiful blooms – but which are actually introduced exotic species not native to Australia'.[42] She asks:

> In light of recent pollinator deaths and invasive species thriving in damaged ecosystems, does our future resilience and sustainability require innovation in providing technological solutions, such as robotic pollinators? The background music and texturally imperfect artwork itself speaks to the contribution that creativity provides to critical thinking and innovation.[43]

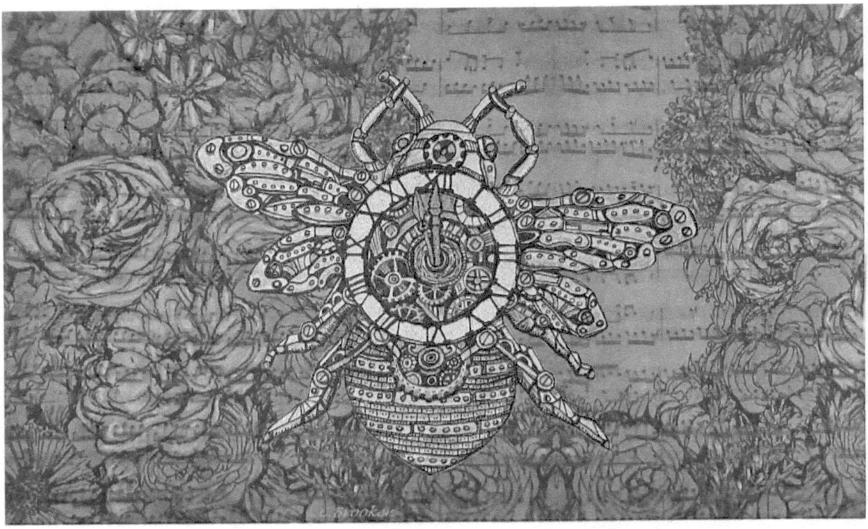

Figure 10.7 'Robo-Bee' (2023) by Cass Brooker.

ICTs and Creative Activism: Unpredictable and Unprecedented

Information and communication technologies (ICTs) have led to rapid changes in societies. Some are alarming, such as bizarre conspiracy theories, promoted on the internet, which can cause death, such as through inciting people to violence[44] or persuading people against being vaccinated.[45] At the same time, ICTs have allowed creative activism to grow in unpredictable and unprecedented ways, through DIY and maker-cultures, new virtual landscapes and embodiments, and multi-sensory digital communities. This could be a doorway towards more inclusive, more just, wiser and more creative societies, provided that we combine real-world action with the power of digital networking:

> The choice is ours: will we get mired in online fear-mongering, bullying and life-threatening trolling, or rise to creative online/ offline worlds we can yet only imagine?[46]

Creative Partnerships

Sometimes a small creative action can grow unexpectedly through collaboration. Artivist Allana Beltran lived for months at a time on suspended platforms 40–50 metres above the ground in the Weld Valley, Tasmania, in 2006, as part of a blockade community intent on stopping the entry of heavy logging machinery into the valley. After being repeatedly ejected from the site by police, she staged an elaborate piece of low-tech performance art early one morning in 2007 to obstruct both roads into the logging site. Wearing wings of white cockatoo feathers, a long white curtain around her waist, and her face painted white, she precariously suspended herself 10 metres above the ground, strapped to a giant tripod. Despite some of the 60 police shouting at her through megaphones, Allana remained in position for 10 hours, listening to Tibetan monk music through headphones.

Her then-partner, Ben Morrow, hung from a bridge over the Weld River to block the other entry point. The performance protest led to arrests and ongoing stresses, with Allana pursued for $10,000 in costs and Ben sued by the state logging agency and Tasmania Police (although both legal actions failed).

This bold visual spectacle may have passed largely unnoticed if not for a photograph of Allana taken by Matthew Newton, who has decades of experience in visual journalism from the frontlines of forest activism. His *Weld Angel* image brought the struggle to protect Tasmania's Southern Forests to global attention, appearing in numerous television broadcasts internationally and in major newspapers and magazines such as *Le Figaro* and *Vanity Fair Italia*. His 'haunting image became a potent symbol of the anti-logging movement' that publicised the absurdity of the ensuing court cases and helped save parts of the Weld Valley forest, which are now included in the Tasmanian Wilderness World Heritage Area.[47]

This demonstrates the power of high-quality photography combined with theatrical activism, and it inspired numerous copycat angels in protests around the country. World-class photography by Olegas Truchanas and Peter Dombrovskis's iconic image *Rock Island Bend, Franklin River,* had earlier been pivotal in saving the wild south-west of Tasmania from damming and logging.[48]

Irish-born and Brooklyn-based graphic designer Deva Pardue is the founder of 'For All Womankind', a design initiative for 'fempowerment'. In 2016, she created a 'Femme Fists' image to raise money for reproductive rights and provided a free download, which went viral after Barbadian singer Rihanna posted it. Although Pardue was delighted when people began making their own versions of the image, even getting it tattooed, she was infuriated when corporations such as the Walmart-owned clothing brand ModCloth began using it without her permission.[49]

Nonviolent Direct Action and the Arts

At the most activist end of the spectrum, the arts, humour and creativity can be immensely useful for nonviolent direct action. As discussed above, they can help movements communicate to external audiences as well as within their groups. Other benefits include the following:

- During the preparations and training for a major campaign, singing together and playing games can help break the ice, introduce people to each other, build trust and solidarity and create well-bonded groups.
- At the start of actions, music and performance can arouse, motivate and encourage civil disobedience (which requires courage). Rousing songs can fortify people in the middle of action or console them when in custody.
- Music can also be used to calm situations and prevent or end violence. It was frequently used for this purpose in the US civil rights movement and in Australia's successful campaign to preserve Tasmania's Franklin River.
- The arts can make actions more diverse, colourful, memorable and engaging.
- They can also make them welcoming and fun rather than frightening, and can help draw in people and grow the movement. As a woman comedian said in a huge Sydney rally at the peak of 1980s anti-war activism, 'Disarm today. Dat arm tomorrow!'
- As with dance, the ability of performance to distract or cloak serious obstructive action in humour makes it more effective in shutting down a place or operation, and minimising arrests and their ensuing costs.
- The arts also provide more options and opportunities for activism, and more ways of expressing emotion, thereby helping to prevent burnout, a phenomenon which loses too many activists.[50]

Nonviolence advocates have long suggested that, contrary to popular belief, countries and groups can use nonviolent means – 'social defence' – to defend themselves just as effectively (and more cheaply and sustainably) as with military force, provided they involve clever strategies and well-trained mass movements.[51] There are many historical precedents, such as India gaining independence from British rule, Danish resistance to Nazi occupation, and Czech and Baltic countries resisting Russian occupation. There are also incipient movements such as Nonviolent Peaceforce and Peace Brigades International. As with protest movements, social defence can be enhanced by mesmerising music, striking visual arts, riveting theatre, breathtaking performance, wild costumes and – above all – humour, provided the situation is appropriate for it. Easy, no. Achievable, yes.

Nonviolent direct action (NVDA), in turn, creates cultural change, as seen in the four-decades-long tradition of forest blockading to prevent logging in north-east New South Wales, which led to a regional movement of social and cultural renewal, pride in a symbiotic 'feral' sub-culture deeply influenced by elements of the forests it sought to preserve, community development, job training,[52] informal education[53] and enduring respect for activists. Many relationships began at blockades, and many children ensued. In that region, NVDA is hip and sexy. Can new generations of creatives make it hipper and sexier?

Celebrating Nonviolence Past; Imagining Peaceful Futures

As journalist, novelist and philanthropist Sophie Kerr once wrote: 'If peace [...] only had the music and pageantry of war, there'd be no more wars.'[54] Imagining is the first step towards realising a vision, so an alternate future which we could imagine would involve diverting some of the immense resources that governments use to celebrate their military forces culturally – the formation flyovers; marching bands; smart uniforms; badges, ribbons and ceremonies for bravery; war memorials and war movies – to instead celebrate peace and improve nonviolence, to commemorate those who have engaged in courageous nonviolent actions within dictatorships or conflict zones, or the hard work of dedicated, persistent peacebuilding over long periods.

Conclusion

Peacebuilding and social movements are enhanced and augmented in multiple, often complementary and synergistic ways by the arts (and inner work, as we'll discover in the next chapter). Charlotte Ashwanden, a dance meditation teacher who has squatted and lived in intentional communities, applying 'human permaculture' as a complement to peace practices, notes the power and courage of artistic activism:

> We may not consider the power of a song, a painting, or a dance, until we see it moving the two supposed enemies to tears and watch their transformation. Even in communities of sustained violence, artists are still creating – like the story of the cello player who set up in the [...] 'Bread Massacre Square' of Sarajevo – so that the music could help to heal his fellow citizens.[55]

Notes

1 Sabbagh, Dan 2021 'Global Nuclear Weapons Ban begins – without the world's nuclear powers', *Guardian*, 22 January, www.theguardian.com/world/2021/jan/21/global-nuclear-weapons-ban-begins-without-the-worlds-nuclear-powers

2 Nelson, Richard 2018 'The Kellogg-Briand pact: world treaty to outlaw war – archive, 1928', *Guardian*, 15 June, www.theguardian.com/world/from-the-archive-blog/2018/jun/14/kellogg-briand-pact-outlaw-war-paris-1928
3 *Mayors for Peace* n.d. Mayors for Peace Secretariat, Hiroshima.
4 Cahill, G. 2003 'Focus on Europe', *Strings*, vol. 18, no. 4, Nov/Dec 2003, p. 8.
5 Kollontai, P. 2010 'Healing the heart in Bosnia-Herzegovina: Art, children and peacemaking', *International Journal of Children's Spirituality*, vol. 15, no. 3, p. 210.
6 See Lederach, J.P, 2005 *The Moral Imagination: The Art and Soul of Building Peace*, Oxford University Press, Oxford.
7 Plummer, Sarah 2021 'Puppets in protest', *HowlRound Theatre Commons*, 6 April, https://howlround.com/puppets-protest
8 Jaffé, Daniel 2014 'Benjamin Britten: Peace and conflict', *Classical Music*, 3 March, www.classical-music.com/reviews/benjamin-britten-peace-and-conflict-2
9 Tuppen, Sandra 2013 'War and peace in Britten', *British Library*, 9 July, https://blogs.bl.uk/music/2013/07/war-and-peace-in-britten.html
10 Reuters 2022 'Berlin concert draws 10,000 in solidarity with Ukraine', *Reuters*, 21 March, www.reuters.com/world/europe/berlin-anti-war-concert-draws-20000-brandenburg-gate-2022-03-20/
11 Wood, Colleen and Lerner, Alexis 2022 'Facing severe repression, Russians are turning to antiwar graffiti', *Waging Nonviolence*, 21 March, https://wagingnonviolence.org/2022/03/facing-severe-repression-russians-turn-to-antiwar-graffiti/
12 Lim, Louisa 2022 *Indelible City: Dispossession and Defiance in Hong Kong*, Text Publishing, Melbourne, p. 15.
13 Lim 2022, p. 16.
14 Kirkby, Ryan J. 2015 'Dramatic protests, creative communities: VVAW and the expressive politics of the sixties counterculture', *Peace and Change*, vol. 40, no. 1, January, pp. 33–62.
15 Phillips, Bronwyn 2022 'King of Calypso', *Australian Women's Weekly*, iss.8, p. 99.
16 Womack, Kenneth 2020 'The Beatles in Jacksonville, 1964: Inside the Fab Four's historic stand against segregation', *Salon*, 27 June, https://www.salon.com/2020/06/27/the-beatles-in-jacksonville-1964-inside-the-fab-fours-historic-stand-against-segregation/
17 Phillips 2022, p. 99.
18 Letman, Jon 2017 'Postcard from Seongju's Anti-THAAD Protest', *Diplomat*, 29 June, https://thediplomat.com/2017/06/postcard-from-seongjus-anti-thaad-protest/
19 Vershbow, Michaela E. 2010 'The sounds of resistance: The role of music in South Africa's anti-apartheid movement', *Inquiries*, vol. 2, no. 6, pp. 1–2.
20 Krishnasamy, K. 2015 'Civil community-peacekeeper relations in UN peacebuilding: The case of South Asian peacekeepers', *Asian Journal of Peacebuilding*, vol. 3, no. 2, pp. 189–213.
21 Scalmer, Sean 2002 *Dissent Events: Protest, the Media and the Political Gimmick in Australia*, UNSW Press, Sydney.
22 Valentish, Jenny and Zhou, Naaman 2020 'How the chaser invaded Apec: "A small video tape was secreted behind his scrotum"', *Guardian*, 20 January, www.theguardian.com/tv-and-radio/2020/jan/20/how-the-chaser-invaded-apec-a-small-camera-was-secreted-behind-his-scrotum
23 Harris, Daniel X. 2015 'Art, activism and our creative future', *Conversation*, 20 August, https://theconversation.com/art-activism-and-our-creative-future-46185

24 Boulton, Liz 2016 'It's time for a new age of enlightenment: Why climate change needs 60,000 artists to tell its story',*Conversation*, 8 June, https://theconversation.com/its-time-for-a-new-age-of-enlightenment-why-climate-change-needs-60-000-artists-to-tell-its-story-58774

25 Pickard, Bob 2013 'The climate change PR disaster: Why is global warming so poorly communicated? International Public Relations Association, www.ipra.org/news/itle/the-climate-change-pr-disaster-why-is-global-warming-so-poorly-communicated/

26 Boulton 2016.

27 Johnston, Jacob 2022 'Re-growth through performance – The unique sound and visual work that is addressing environmental issues', *University of New England*, 12 January, https://blog.une.edu.au/hasse/2022/01/12/re-growth-through-performance-the-unique-sound-and-visual-work-that-is-addressing-environmental-issues/

28 Boulton 2016.

29 Cited in Harris 2015.

30 Cited in Singh-Kurtz, Sangeeta 2022 'Creating for change: Art as activism', *Marie Claire*, 19 January, www.marieclaire.com/culture/art-as-activism/

31 Ibid.

32 Ibid.

33 September, p. 19.

34 Jedlicka, Michèle (Arts North West) 2021 email to Panorama Project participants, 29 September.

35 Johnston, Jacob 2021 'The Tiniest Thing' in The Big Apple – Dr Richard Jordan's award-winning play receives reading at theatre festival in NYC', *University of New England*, 14 December, https://blog.une.edu.au/hasse/2021/12/14/the-tiniest-thing-in-the-big-apple-dr-richard-jordans-award-winning-play-receives-reading-at-theatre-festival-in-nyc/

36 Cited in Singh-Kurtz 2022.

37 Cited in Murray, Therese 2022 'How to Lette it loose', *The Senior*, 2 May, p. 35.

38 Branagan, Marty 2018 *Locked On! The Seventh and Most Illegal in the Hitchhiker's Guide Trilogy*, Irene Publishing, Sparsnäs, https://irenepublishing.com/?product=locked-on

39 Adams, Douglas 1995 [1979] *The Hitchhikers Guide to the Galaxy*, William Heinemann, London, p. 135.

40 Adams 1995 [1979], pp. 456–457.

41 'The Christmas Truce' n.d *World War One*, www.worldwar-1.co.uk/the-christmas-truce/

42 Brooker, Cass 2023 *'Story of Entry'*, Research Pathways Conference 2023 UNE Artwork Competition.

43 Ibid.

44 Badham, Van 2021 *QAnon and On: A Short and Shocking History of Internet Conspiracy Cults*, Hardie Grant, Melbourne and London.

45 Newitz, Annalee 2021 'Should social media come with a health warning?' *New Scientist*, 7 August, p. 24.

46 Harris 2015; see also Branagan, Marty 2013 *Global Warming, Militarism and Nonviolence: The Art of Active Resistance*, Palgrave Macmillan, Basingstoke, pp. 143–175.

47 Catley Nicky 2023 'Tasmania's Weld Angel: A forest saviour', *Australian Geographic*, 22 May, www.australiangeographic.com.au/photography/2023/05/weld-angel-the-forest-saviour/

48 Tasmanian Museum and Gallery 2016 'The power of change', permanent exhibition, Hobart.
49 Singh-Kurtz 2022.
50 For more detail, see Branagan 2013, pp. 176–216.
51 Johansen, Jørgen and Martin, Brian 2019 *Social Defence*, Irene Publishing, Sweden.
52 Bible, Vanessa and Howard, Tanya 2020 'Wilderness, civil disobedience, and community: Breaching the divide in the age of extinction', in Robyn Bartel, Marty Branagan, Fiona Utley and Stephen Harris (eds.), *Rethinking Wilderness and the Wild*, Routledge, London; Ricketts, Aidan 2003 'Om Gaia dudes: The North East Forest alliance's old-growth forest campaigns', in Helen Wilson (ed.), *Belonging in the Rainbow Region*, Southern Cross University Press, Lismore, p. 141.
53 Branagan, Martin and Boughton, Bob 2003 'How do you learn how to change the world? Learning and teaching in Australian Protest Movements', *Australian Journal of Adult Learning*, vol. 43, no. 3 (November), pp. 346–360.
54 Cited in Larson, Jeanne and Micheels-Cyrus, Madge (comps) 1986 *Seeds of Peace*, New Society Publishers, Philadelphia, p. 221.
55 Ashwanden, Charlotte 2017 'Permaculture and community part 1: Permaculture as a tool for peace', *Permaculture News*, 2 November, www.permaculturenews.org/2017/11/02/permaculture-community-part-1-permaculture-tool-peace/#google_vignette

Chapter 11

PEACE WITHIN

Spirituality and culture have long been intertwined, as evidenced by the ancient rock art of Australian Aboriginal people, much of which has deep significance and spiritual meaning for them.[1] Related to spirituality are concepts such as religious beliefs, personal philosophies, and practices aimed at enhancing mental, emotional and physical well-being. All of these have cultural aspects. This chapter will explore spiritual, religious and related practices and examine their relationships with the cultivation of peace.

*

The mainstream view of peace is that it's something which occurs at the macro, elite level, with governments and the United Nations. But what if those organisations are made up of damaged individuals, as we examined in Chapter 7? If they are people with significant inner turmoil, their attempts to create peace may be severely compromised.

There may be little we can do about pro-war politicians apart from voting them out of power when we get a brief say in politics every few years. But we can work on ourselves to find peace within at a micro level, and aim to work outwards to influence our immediate spheres of influence – our families, partners, spouses, friends and workmates. If enough people do this, we may also create political change at the local council level – in the way that debates occur and how people in decision-making roles interact with each other – which can lead to wider change at state and federal government levels and beyond. If we want our present and future politicians to exhibit values and characteristics such as respect, humility, empathy, compassion, emotional intelligence and the ability to listen, a good starting point is to develop and model them in our own lives. There's a song in the peace movement which says:

> There will be peace on Earth
> When there is peace in our hearts.

In other words, having *peace within* is essential for creating peaceful cultures. Without inner peace, our actions in the world are likely to be incompatible with peace. We can have great laws, policies and institutions – peace infrastructure – but these are all compromised if most of us are in internal turmoil.

The same applies to the arts and sciences. As we saw in Chapter 3 on screen violence, there are many films into which incredible technological developments and huge amounts of resources are poured to ensure realistic settings, quality dialogue, credible acting and dramatic cinematography, but if the underlying ethos is puerile or even morally bankrupt, the overall result is shallow, disappointing and unfulfilling cultural violence. It may titillate, distract or entertain briefly, but it does not challenge us to become better people and more peaceful societies.

This can be related to the horror that Einstein expressed when an atomic bomb was first used, at Hiroshima in Japan in 1945. The bomb had developed from his theoretical discoveries and was initially encouraged by him due to a concern that Nazi Germany was developing its own nuclear bomb. He soon changed his mind. For him, the joy and beauty of pure scientific discovery had been converted into the sinister menace of nuclear weapons. Moral development had not kept pace with scientific development: 'The unleashing of the power of the atom has changed everything but our modes of thinking and thus we drift toward unparalleled catastrophes.'[2] He had earlier noted in a speech to students: 'Why does this magnificent applied science which saves work and makes life easier bring us so little happiness? The simple answer runs: Because we have not yet learned to make sensible use of it.'[3]

The quest to abolish war and nuclear weapons, as well as to achieve happiness and fulfilment, can therefore be strongly linked to moral development and inner peace. Inner peace can be referred to as a state of calmness, serenity and equanimity of the mind that surfaces due to minimising distresses or psychological instabilities such as apprehension, greed, hatred and malice.[4]

Finding Inner Peace

There are many ways of finding inner peace, ranging from practices such as tai chi to prayer, and these can be broadly categorised under the term 'personal peacebuilding'. Peacebuilding expert Katerina Standish describes this as 'a form of nonviolent learning and action associated with self-knowledge, wellness, and positive encounter with others and the nonhuman world, [which] makes building peace the work of individuals too'.[5] These individuals may work some of the time to build peace movements and organise mass rallies, but many also spend time doing 'inner work.'

As Robyn Rosenfeldt argues, 'when we focus on what we are passionate about, or what we feel moved by, then we are motivated to make change in that area and we feel empowered when we have success'.[6] Gift economy advocate Charles Eisenstein similarly believes that because 'human degradation and ecological degradation are part of the same fabric [...] neither will change without the other changing. [...] [H]ealing on any level contributes to healing on every level'.[7]

For Standish, '[i]n personal peacebuilding, the "peacebuilder" is the work'.[8] As one activist and *Creating Cultures of Peace* student noted:

> [D]eveloping and maintaining inner peace is crucial. As is 'getting out there' to protest. [I]t is a 'both/and' scenario rather than an 'either/or'. You shouldn't have one without the other. [A] metaphor often applied to people who work with other people all the time (therapists, social workers, teachers, nurses, parents, etc.) [...] imagines each of us as a water jug pouring water into other peoples' cups. If you run dry yourself, you can't keep filling others, so you must take time to keep your own water jug topped up. That is not self-indulgent but what is necessary in order to be able to keep going. I see inner peace as that water. It is not possible to carry on protesting and participating in activism if you run dry – you will burn out and may even become bitter or unhelpful to the cause.

Everyone has different needs and different ways of achieving inner peace, and it's important to find some methods that suit you. These may be found through established religions (discussed below), although many argue that spirituality does not require that one is a member of a church or an adherent of a faith or set of rules.[9] For the latter, secular practices such as jogging or walking in nature may be uplifting or spiritually nourishing and may lead to a deeper connection with the Earth we depend upon. Related to this is the idea of working to make a paradise of this Earth, rather than living for some future heaven or nirvana, succinctly espoused by a character created by the humorous satirist Terry Pratchett:

> [Priests are] always telling folk how much better it's going to be when they're dead. *We* [wizards and witches] tell them it could be pretty good right here if only they'd put their minds to it.[10]

Others rely on yoga, tai chi or meditation, practices which are in between secular and religious, having relationships with Hinduism, Taoism and Buddhism. Still others enjoy the calming effects of listening to music or viewing art, or engaging in their own creative practices, however humble they may be. And, of course, spending time with loved ones is essential for peace of mind. Let's look more closely at some of these practices and traditions.

Empathetic Cooperation

In *Doing Feminist Peace*, Cecilia Confortini[11] refers to a notion developed by Christine Sylvester[12] called 'empathetic cooperation', a method for listening deeply to the concerns, fears and agendas of people one is unaccustomed to heeding, and taking on board the struggles of others.[13] Empathetic cooperation involves a conversational style which doesn't push, direct or break through to any linear progression which gives the comforting illusion that one knows where one is going. Elspeth Liberty is an elderly Tasmanian woman and Peace Studies student who engages actively in such work, which can at times be harrowing:

> One of my practices when I travel is to be open to hear different viewing points. After I travelled to Bosnia and Herzegovina, hearing stories of the rape camps and the siege of Sarajevo, I felt such abhorrence towards the Serbs. I knew I had to go there. I had to be open to whatever conversations presented themselves. I had to try and hear different voices of the country. Some of the voices I heard were brutal. Some of the other voices I had the privilege of listening to were women and men talking of the deep shame they felt to be Serbs. I didn't get to have any conversations with anyone who admitted to committing atrocities, but there is definitely something in the energy of Serbia that makes it feel like it could all easily happen again. Three different people told me of the Serb saying, 'If my neighbour has a cow and I don't have a cow, I will not be happy until my neighbour's cow is dead.' I don't know what I achieve by listening to these stories, but I believe it is extremely important for me to do so. I believe it is my version of being a peace practitioner.[14]

Eastern Traditions

Katerina Standish's concept of personal peacebuilding entails four complementary facets – physiological, interpersonal, immanent/transcendent/biotic and social.[15] From the East have sprung a range of bodily and/or mental practices that can encompass all these facets and help create inner peace. They have some commonalities. Tai chi, for example, is about balance – both physical and in terms of one's emotions and mental alertness. It's related to Taoism and its environmentally linked notion of 'The Way', and it involves the non-dualistic notion of *yin* and *yang*, the dance of two different but complementary elements which each have the other within it. In public parks from Hong Kong to Hornsby, you will see individuals or groups engaging in tai chi to raise or calm their energy levels in a harmonious way.

Meditation is aimed at quieting the constant chatter of our minds (much of it negative), and ideally emptying one's mind of all stresses and attachments – to the material world and to desires. The aim, as with tai chi, is creating mindfulness, perspective and attention to the here-and-now, the eternal present. Many people swear by meditation as a way of reducing worries, achieving tranquillity, working better and enjoying life more. All these have benefits for peacebuilding work, as do findings by Northeastern University College of Science[16] that meditation assists individuals to act virtuously and help people in need.

Yoga arose in India and has spread worldwide – it's a way of bringing together body and mind into an integrated whole. Yoga literally means the yoking together, harnessing or unity of the body and mind,[17] created through movement, stretches, postures, relaxation and mental exercises, with some similarities to the newer discipline of Pilates. As with tai chi, attempting to find balance is important. Tatiyana Bastet shows how yoga and similar practices relate to peacebuilding processes such as nonviolent action:

> The practice of yoga offers various ways of understanding and reflecting on our emotions, allowing us to make more conscious decisions. As with anything, over time and with practice, these methods become second nature. How is this nonviolence? Choosing to be healthy, happy, and continuing to take pleasure in the experiences life has to offer, not at the expense of others, is the practice translated as nonviolence, non-harming, or ahiṃsā.[18]

Self-sacrifice has long been a tenet of Gandhian or orthodox nonviolence, but it has been criticised by feminist authors such as Judy Costello[19] and Starhawk[20] who argue that self-sacrifice is something men can choose, whereas women are often forced into it culturally or socially. Bastet explores both choice and sacrifice in the context of yogic philosophy:

> Personal discord, anxiety, and suffering are all too often viewed as resulting from a lack of choice. These feelings may be exacerbated by the contemporary notion of sacrifice as actively giving up that which brings pleasure and nourishment. How then, do we recognize choice, both passive and active? How does our understanding of sacrifice inform choice? Examining Vedic and pre-Vedic philosophy and practices, including yoga and the concept of ahiṃsā (nonviolence), facilitates

> not only an exploration of choice, but of the understanding of sacrifice, noting that we can choose to sacrifice that which no longer serves us. The sacrificial act is then transformed into a practice of self-reflection, active choice, and self-nourishment, creating an internal cycle of positive peace.[21]

One overtly activist group, 'Yoga for Youth', strives to address both social justice and individual healing by providing opportunities for African American individuals to teach and practice yoga, as well as addressing issues within a wider context, such as the disproportionate number of chronic diseases in African Americans.[22]

Mindfulness

Mindfulness is a tool that allows people to be more aware of their physical and emotional condition. It involves a level of consciousness or awareness that arises through the use of purposeful attention focused on the present moment in a non-judgemental and accepting way. Daily practices in mindfulness can be found in *The Ongo Book: Everyday Nonviolence* by Catherine Cadden and Jesse Wiens,[23] which also has lessons in nonviolent communication for individuals, couples and groups. While mindfulness is cultivated through meditation, yoga, tai chi and related techniques, it can be distinct from these. Particular features of mindfulness can concentrate on physical techniques such as breathing to direct the person to a mindful state; other features draw on cognitive aspects such as exercising awareness and attention.

Mindfulness done well allows one to regain control over destructive feelings and even to capture positive memories that can be enjoyed at a later date. Mindfulness is frequently used in meditation and has many positive benefits, including lowering stress levels and improving our overall health. It is a state of active, open attention to the present. When we are mindful, we carefully observe our thoughts and feelings without judging them as good or bad. Mindfulness can also be a healthy way to identify and manage hidden emotions that may be causing problems in our personal and professional relationships. It means living in the moment and awakening to our current experience, rather than dwelling on the past or anticipating the future. Being mindful can help us to focus on what matters and not dwell on the negative and overlook the positive.

In 2005, a Harvard University study highlighted the fact that individuals who perform mindfulness meditation on a daily basis increase the viscosity of the prefrontal cortex of their brain.[24] This part of the brain is responsible for making decisions, controlling personality expression, planning cognitive behaviour and mediating social behaviour. Mindfulness can also relieve chronic pain and improve aspects of mood, thinking and memory. Recent research by the University of the Sunshine Coast, Australia, shows that it creates changes in brain physiology correlated with improvement in attention. They found that mindfulness training increases the efficiency of brain pathways that process information coming in from the senses, and that it boosts the ability of the brain to direct attention to the information of interest.[25]

Religions and Peace

While atheists such as Richard Dawkins and British historian Tom Holland argue that religion has many problematic elements and is both a source of conflict and a justification for belief without evidence, there have historically been many types of atheists[26] and, increasingly, there is a recognition by atheists that religion has valuable cultural, social and political aspects.[27]

For example, it has created countless extraordinary cultural achievements in multiple fields such as architecture and music, such as the glory of the Sagrada Familia cathedral in Barcelona (Figure 11.1) and the music of

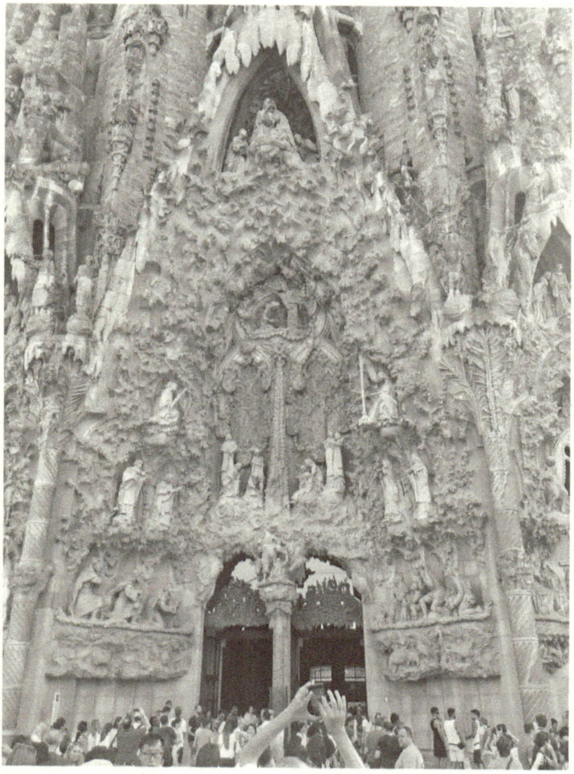

Figure 11.1 Antoni Gaudí's La Sagrada Família Basilica in Barcelona.

Bach and Vivaldi, which deserve to be celebrated and preserved. Alain de Botton's *Religion for Atheists*[28] posits that it is destructive and cruel to mock or humiliate religious belief, as it plays a profound and highly valuable role in the lives of many people. Instead, a constructive approach is imagining how to address the needs that lead individuals to religion, such as 'longings for emotional order, for depth of meaning, for grandeur, beauty, forgiveness and compassion'.[29]

Faith traditions may also bring people peace. Prayer and reflection within a major religion can induce inner peace that translates into action for peace, and many find comfort in the Abrahamic religions – Judaism, Christianity and Islam – which all have pro-peace aspects, such as forgiveness and 'agape': goodwill, benevolence and unselfish love towards others. Religions can play a strong role in building cultures of inner peace internationally by providing 'shelter from the storm' that life can throw at you, and because religions already have established traditions, resources, advisors, organisations, networks and texts, such as the wisdom of the Desiderata.

Engaged Buddhism

Buddhism is often recommended for its ability to create inner and communal peace,[30] as are relevant concepts from Western psychology. Buddhism has an eightfold path towards righteousness, and it also suggests avoiding extremes and taking the middle path, which could be interpreted as eschewing both violence, on the one hand, and inaction or appeasement on the other, for an engaged life of nonviolence. The Zen Buddhist master Thich Nhat Hanh was an initiator of an engaged form of Buddhism dedicated to peace and social justice. The first monastic community founded by him in the West is Plum Village, near Bordeaux in southwest France, which is his largest international practice centre, dedicated to the path to loving one's enemy. Here he realised his dream of 'building a Beloved Community: creating a healthy, nourishing environment where people can learn the art of living in harmony with one another and with the Earth'.[31] Some of his best communication was through poetry (available on the Plum Village website: plumvillage.org), such as 'Please Call Me by My True Names', which reflects a deep insight into how we cannot separate ourselves from the world around us, even those who do major harm.

Judaism and Christianity

There are explicitly peaceful elements of many religions, such as the commandment 'Thou Shalt Not Kill' in Judaism and Christianity, with parallels in Buddhist, Taoist, pagan, Muslim, secular humanist, Socratean philosophical and other traditions.[32] This commandment *does not have caveats or exceptions*; it is a *very simple and clear commandment* which should prevent any adherents to these faiths from joining in warfare.

The commandment not to kill was reinforced by the pacifist exhortation two millennia ago by Jewish man Yesua Ben Miriam (Jesus) to 'turn the other cheek' if someone strikes you, and later hymns such as 'Whatsoever You Do (to the least of my brothers, that you do unto me)', based on the New Testament passage Matthew 25:40. These precepts led early Christians to refuse to take part in war, as have the Anabaptists, Quakers and others from the seventeenth century onwards.[33]

The Mennonite Church continues an activist nonviolence tradition today, with the US chapter voting in 2017 to divest from companies that profit from the Israeli military occupation of Palestinian territories, and expressing strong disapproval of the occupation. Simultaneously, it emphasised a need to build stronger relationships with Jewish communities as well as to combat anti-Semitism.[34] Leading up to this vote, Nonviolence International cofounder Jonathan Kuttab served as a resource for the Mennonites by travelling around the country and talking to delegations about the situation in Palestine and Israel. Another cofounder, Dr Mubarak Awad, stated that 'the Mennonite Church has taken a strong stand for human rights in Palestine' in light of this vote.[35]

Such votes are growing in popularity among religious groups as part of boycott, divestment and sanctions movements intended to place pressure on Israel or to end involvement with fossil fuels and ecological violence. More recently, the Mennonite Church responded to the 2023 Gaza conflict by planning an 'emergency relief response with existing partners, focused on the immediate humanitarian needs in the Gaza Strip. Current programs in Palestine and Israel include education, peacebuilding and food security and livelihood initiatives'; they also support youth vocational training and a trauma healing program for children and youth.[36]

Despite the horrendous and intractable nature of the Israel–Palestine conflict, there are nonviolent campaigns for peace on all sides, involving Muslims, Jewish groups,[i] Christians and people with no religious allegiances, using dialogue, protest, fundraising and cross-cultural programmes of music and education, such as by the Alliance for Middle East Peace, The Parents

i These include Jewish Voice for Peace, Breaking the Silence - former Israeli soldiers – and the Israeli Information Centre for Human Rights in the Occupied Territories.

Circle – Families Forum, and the Seeds of Peace programme discussed in Chapter 8.

On the edges of the larger, more mainstream organisations of Christianity can be found pockets of dedicated peacemaking, often led by women. Dorothy Day, for example, was a strong, outspoken advocate of conscientious objection, a social justice activist, suffragist and cofounder of the Catholic Worker movement,[37] often considered radical but probably more true to the commandments and teachings of Jesus than the larger, more mainstream branches of the church.

Sister Joan Chittister of the Benedictines order of the Catholic Church reinforces the idea that spiritual journeys should not just be directed inwards but need to be rooted in real-world action for peace:

> Benedictine peace is not simply the absence of war. It is a lifestyle that makes war unacceptable and violence unnecessary. It is not a lifestyle dominated by control and a plethora of rules. It is a lifestyle that foregoes violence on every level, for any reason. Most of all, this lifestyle is a simple one. It is basic in its elements, not difficult to achieve, simple to sustain. It nurtures neither ambition nor greed. It is straightforward in its values, without being either esoteric or convoluted. These values are clear ones: community, prayer, stewardship, equality, stability, conversion, peace – all make for communities of love.[38]

Such philosophies have a connection to liberation theology, the engaged social justice movements of Catholicism which emerged in Latin America in the 1960s after the Second Vatican Council. Religious leaders had an important role in the ousting of dictator Ferdinand Marcos in the Philippines in 1986 in the People Power Revolution, also known as the EDSA Revolution or the February Revolution.[39] They also helped end the conflict in Nicaragua in the late 1980s, commencing by performing humanitarian work within both the civilian population and the armed militias. Like their counterparts in the Solomon Islands, they entered war zones unarmed in order to stop the violence.[40] These interventions in Nicaragua created the necessary space for the growth of civilian grassroots movements that evolved into Peace Commissions, which were later joined and further legitimised by international institutions.[41]

In the Solomon Islands conflict involving ethnic militia and non-indigenous settlers, a third party was formed by the 'Melanesian Brotherhood', a religious group with strong traditional values and practices, and trusted by both sides of the conflict. Initially, the group engaged in humanitarian relief, providing sanctuary to the affected communities and delivering medicine and other supplies to villages. However, their intervention later extended to a courageous unarmed presence on battlefields, in order to reduce the violence, negotiate the exchange of prisoners and openly advocate for an end to the conflict.[42]

Occasionally, mainstream church leadership is outspoken in its calls for peace, not just as a vague concept but as practical action. Pope Francis, for example, has drawn attention to those who profit from conflict, claiming that arms merchants are profiteers fuelling war. Calling the arms trade the 'industry of death', he announced that 'it is our duty to confront the problem and to stop the arms trade'.[43] In 2023, he began an unprecedented joint 'pilgrimage of peace', travelling to South Sudan with the Archbishop of Canterbury and a Church of Scotland leader.[44]

An earlier pontiff, Pope Benedict XV, had begged the warring nations in World War I to establish an official truce at Christmas time, asking that 'the guns may fall silent at least upon the night the angels sang'.[45] This attempt was officially rebuffed, but informal, haphazard and unauthorised truces sprang up along parts of the frontlines, as discussed in earlier chapters. Although hatred and suspicion remained in some quarters, fuelled by the cultural violence of government propaganda, xenophobic songs and nationalistic journalism, many truces arose from the singing of Christmas carols, an international language of peace:

> For many, the former hatred was vanished. They now recognized the soldiers from the other side of the trenches as human as themselves. They were not mercenaries, no inhuman monsters eager for war, just humans. The stereotypes they knew from the time before the war and before they met their enemies did not fit after meeting their enemies.[46]

Taking Personal Responsibility

Creating inner peace involves taking personal responsibility, rather than presuming that peace is something we should leave up to governments, non-government organisations and the United Nations. It's a form of prefigurative politics, where we try to live now what we envisage for the future.

Mahatma Gandhi, coming from a Hindu and Jain background which encouraged vegetarianism (taking 'Thou Shalt Not Kill' much further than many from the Abrahamic faiths), was open-minded enough to learn from other traditions such as Christianity and Islam. He was a firm advocate of prefigurative action, keeping the means of social change compatible with the ends (rather than the inconsistency of 'fighting for peace'). His advice was to 'Be the change you want to see in the world.' He has been compared with

St Francis of Assisi, with the nonviolence of both being informed by their deep spirituality.[47] It is less well known that Gandhi admitted learning most of his nonviolent actions from women – in particular, British suffragettes.[48] Although Gandhi has been almost deified in some circles, and was certainly progressive in many regards, Indian writer Bharat Patankar claims that Gandhi 'was patriarchal and supported maintaining the caste system minus untouchability [...] [and that] no low-caste person in India would ever join a green movement that took Gandhi as its exemplar'.[49]

One thing this shows, however, is that we don't have to be perfect before engaging in action. Our search for inner peace needn't exclude engaging constructively in the world around us. We can strive for moral or spiritual perfection while also accepting our imperfections and acting according to our values. When we inevitably make mistakes, we can learn from them. Finding a balance between inner and outer work, between yin and yang, is a lifelong but rewarding quest. As discussed in Chapter 4, Vinya Ariyaratne's chapter 'Building a Culture of Nonviolence and Peace' details the Gandhi-influenced *Sarvodaya* or Self-Development experience in Sri Lanka, involving mass meditation, peace and interfaith dialogues, exchange programmes, training, workshops, language learning and attempts to build friendships and networks.[50]

Islam

Islam has a code of conduct that encourages its adherents to treat everyone, even strangers, with kindness and hospitality. There has long been controversy over claims that Islam is a violent religion, some of which stem from a misunderstanding – a presumption that it is similar to religions like Catholicism with its hierarchical structure led by a pope, whereas Islam has a flatter structure, is less monolithic and has many different centres of power.[51]

To say that all Muslims are violent because some are is as inaccurate as saying that all Christians are violent because of the Crusades or Northern Ireland's 'Troubles'. The larger concern should be any fundamentalists or religious extremists with access to the nuclear weapons button: 'The enemy of peace is not religion, but those who pursue acts of terror and violence against the innocent *in the name of* religion.'[52] There are many Islamic peace groups (e.g. www.islamic-peace.com), and Abu-Nimer[53] details some innovative Islamic (and Buddhist) approaches to conflict resolution.

One *Creating Cultures of Peace* student noted that religion relies on interpretations and that seeking experiences with people of faith can shape our interpretations.

> One of the most beautiful experiences I have ever had involved an afternoon sipping mint tea and gossiping with a group of Muslim women and their children. No men were allowed in this space, and it was wonderful. The beauty was that I was Catholic, and despite our differing beliefs (or not so different really), we were forming friendships that have now lasted for over 30 years. The media has a lot to answer for in creating unfounded fear.

Ecumenicalism and Secular Spirituality

One movement which has grown in recent years is ecumenicalism, where people of different faiths come together to meet, share their stories and beliefs, pray and try to find common ground. Some, such as The Peace Council and Religions for Peace Australia, are explicitly pro-peace. Sometimes, such groups will engage in lobbying, political statements and even nonviolent direct action on issues such as refugees and global warming. For example, the Australian Religious Response to Climate Change (www.arrcc.org.au) is a grassroots network that 'mobilises people of all faiths to take effective action for climate justice [...] the most pressing issue of our time'.

Although some people express concern when they see statistics indicating fewer people in the Western world now go to church or identify as a member of a traditional religion, and that young adults around the world are less religious and therefore lack values,[54] others believe that religion and spirituality are two different things. That is, one can attempt to live a rich life as a good person, to develop one's moral compass in a secular or individually spiritual way, perhaps using what they see as the best of all the religions.[55] Some argue that people are redirecting their faith – not losing it – with religious scholar Linda Woodhead claiming that young people:

> want to find a spiritual, moral and communal life that is personally meaningful for them, and they want to have much more authority in their quest and in their spiritual development.[56]

Non-religious people may express concerns about ongoing issues such as the sexism of many religions, the paedophilia and coverups in Christianity, the exclusionary caste system of Hinduism, Buddhist violence in Myanmar, Islamist jihadists or the fact that religion has so often been a source of conflict and war, such as in the Crusades, witch-burnings or the ill-considered colonial partition of India and Pakistan which led to the slaughter of millions of Muslims and Hindus, a regional wound which has still not healed.[57] As Milad Milani notes, all three monotheistic religions make reference in their religious texts to both violence and peace:

> So the fact that a religious text contains violent verses doesn't make it a violent religion. But it's also a fact that a religious text containing peaceful verses doesn't make that religion peaceful either.[58]

The words attributed to Jesus that 'No-one can come to the Father except through me' (John 14: 1–7), so often used at funerals, assert that Christianity has a monopoly on 'salvation', insist on one 'correct' belief system, and exclude people from all other faiths. Putting enormous pressure on tribal peoples to convert – often at the point of a sword or gun – has also had devastating impacts on many tribal peoples and their cultures. In Australia, Christian missions were

> designed to erase [Aboriginal] peoples' cultural identity. People were separated from their land and their families, and were not allowed to speak their languages, continue their cultural practices or teach them to their children.[59]

These indigenous cultures were often extremely peaceful, such as that of the Native American nation the Hopi, who have a dedication to nonviolent conflict transformation and such ingrained pacifism in their belief systems that leaders such as Thomas Banyacya have been conscientious objectors in the wars in which the United States has been involved.[60] They continue to struggle to sustain their culture and lands against threats from coal interests and the divisive impacts of colonialism.[61]

In the book *ReEnchantment*, David Tacey[62] discusses a new and developing form of down-to-earth spirituality that he has observed emerging in Australia. Exploring issues of social ecology and the intersections of religion and geography, he examines some of the influences on this uniquely Australian spirituality which include both the land and Aboriginal spirituality. Tacey suggests that it may eventually lead us towards a harmonious marriage between rational, secular humanism and the spiritual realms.

This ecologically-linked spirituality that Tacey sees occurring even in urban areas is subtle and understated yet often present. It is a spirituality more embodied than the Judeo-Christianity many have moved away from, with its Cartesian mind–body dualism that prioritises the spiritual over the corporeal, the human over the environmental and the academic over the manual.

Nature-Based Spirituality and Deep Ecology

This form of spirituality has cousins in the nature-based spirituality practised by neo-pagans, and the deep ecology advocated by Arne Næss,[63]

Joanna Macy,[64] John Seed and Ruth Rosenhek,[65] and practised by many environmentalists and alternative lifestylers, who claim that inner peace comes from a close, intimate connection with the land and sea, the air we breathe, the water we drink and the food we eat. They aim to reduce their separateness from nature and redress the imbalance of *koyaniskaatsi* (which is Hopi for 'life-out-of-balance') of a dualistic society where reductionist science rules (provided it doesn't produce inconvenient truths), technology and growth are the answers to most questions, and the city dominates the country, as sociologist Ferdinand Tönnies wrote in his influential work on *Gemeinschaft/ Gesellschaft*.[66]

An enduring example of a community that puts its eco-friendly beliefs into practice is Scotland's Findhorn Ecovillage (www.ecovillagefindhorn.com), which has become a buzzword for alternate farming, community living and planetary awareness. Initially derided for its eclectic spirituality, such as belief in nature spirits, the 61-home village has survived for 60 years, gained international fame and become a learning centre, attracting people from all over the world. Its ecological ethos, once regarded as 'wacky', now has mainstream acceptance, partly due to recognition that Findhorn has the lowest ecological footprint of any community measured to date in the industrialised world.[67]

Another example is northern New South Wales's Bodhi Farm, founded in 1977 on principles of 'voluntary simplicity' and five Buddhist precepts: do no harm, do not steal, do not lie, do not misuse sex and do not consume alcohol or drugs. Often dismissed as drop-out hippies, dirty and uneducated, many were in fact university-educated and widely travelled, bringing philosophies of community from India and what was then Portuguese Timor.[68] Their affordable housing, usually hand-built over time using recycled materials and set in a beautifully regenerated forest, is a beacon of hope in the current housing affordability crisis.

Other traditions include the Chinese tradition of Taoism, which focuses on seeking harmony within and with nature. It has similarities to Earth-based spirituality, which goes under names such as Wicca, Goddess worship or neo-paganism. A Californian woman named Starhawk is one of Wicca's most famous practitioners and advocates, educating through novels like *The Fifth Sacred Thing*,[69] which is also a landmark tale of nonviolent resistance to an invasion.

Cognitive Dissonance

Cognitive dissonance is the mental discomfort or psychological stress experienced by a person who simultaneously holds two or more contradictory or inconsistent thoughts, beliefs, ideas or attitudes, especially as relating to behavioural decisions and attitude change. This is something we can encounter if we have a devout pacifist religious background but are conscripted or forced because of poverty into the army and told to kill people. It can occur if we're concerned about global warming but work in the fossil fuel industry or have to fly or drive everywhere for work, or if we hate war but have an account in a bank linked to the arms industry.

In such cases, it's difficult to reconcile these inconsistencies and find any inner peace. Something must change to eliminate this *dissonance.* So, inner peace is not just about our beliefs but how we live them. To remove the dissonance between our inner selves and outer lives in the world, we may need to take action in the areas we've covered in this book – in how we communicate and interact with others, in the language we use, the films we watch, the media sources we support, the way we parent, the education we support and so on.

We might also need to re-evaluate our work–life balance to ensure that we spend more time socialising with friends and relaxing with family. Relating back to the last chapter, finding inner peace might require a conscious effort to listen to more music, view more art, force ourselves to undertake some creative activities and go beyond the notion that only people born with talent can do art. Art is an integral and inextricable part of many indigenous cultures.

One *Creating Cultures of Peace* student observed:

> I was really struck by the idea of the lack of inner peace that dissonance between one's values and work (or the language/education/influences etc. around them) can cause. [...] Just a few months ago I decided to step away from my teaching career for essentially this reason. There was an increasing divide between my work and the place I was living to do it and my own values and interests (essentially I was feeling more and more that I didn't agree with and didn't want to be a part of our current education system anymore) and it was causing me great distress and inner turmoil. Since I left and changed jobs, I have been able to spend much more time working on art and engaging with volunteer activities etc. that simply were not possible when I was teaching, and I have truly noticed a huge difference in my inner peace and happiness and even the way I treat others as a result. I had insomnia when I was teaching and now I can sleep well. I was physically sick all the time, always getting colds/flus etc. and now I am healthy.

The praxis of 'permaculture' (discussed in Chapter 5), designed to minimise ecological and structural violence in how we eat and live, arose from co-founder Bill Mollison realising the cognitive dissonance of how he was living in the 1950s. Having grown up in a small village in Tasmania, where natural abundance and beauty were taken for granted, he noticed that large parts of the system in which he hunted and fished were disappearing or dwindling. He began to protest but found this ineffectual. He withdrew from society in order to ponder the situation deeply, later saying that 'I wanted to come back only with something very positive, something that would allow us all to exist without the wholescale collapse of biological systems'.[70] The result was permaculture, developed jointly with David Holmgren and others, utilising wisdom from ancient and modern cultures. It has now spread globally.

Actions for Inner Peace

Let us conclude this discussion with some examples of simple, grounded acts that can lead to and spread inner peace. *Zen* by Japanese monk and garden designer Shunmyo Masuno[71] has some simple, practical advice about finding peace within. This includes savouring the morning air – 'nourish the mind and body by breathing in the beautiful morning air'.[72] Practice gratitude for your food by pausing after every bite, go barefoot to connect to nature and improve physical health, seek out the sunset to practice gratitude for the day and try to take care of something, such as a plant or a miniature garden, because nurturing helps 'develop a mind that cares for things'.[73]

One emerging holistic health practice is 'forest therapy', a practice of mindfully engaging in multisensory, immersive experiences in forests and other natural environments to achieve well-being outcomes. Initially formalised in the 1980s as a health-based activity in Japan, forest therapy encompasses forest bathing (*shinrin yoku*), nature therapy and forest walks. As with yoga and meditation, it involves quieting the mind and directing embodied awareness to the present moment, but it does this not indoors but 'surrounded by a rich array of living, changing, multisensory natural phenomena'.[74] This helps people build connections with the natural world and can lead to short- and sometimes long-term improvements in mental and physical health.

Lindy Schneider espouses the benefits of simply walking:

> Walking is essential to awareness. Walking in nature is the way we come to understand our deeper world, to garner a sense of the quality of our lives and to connect deeply with the underlying nature of life in all its glory. When we walk regularly we embrace a practice that leads to clarity. What cannot be solved by the ruminations of the mind can be handed with grace to the seasons. Walking stills our racing thoughts and allows them to return to the vast oceans of our interiors, creating a space for new ideas to crescendo from the depths of our subconscious.[75]

This practice can also deepen relationships, according to Schneider:

> When I walk with my friend Linda something vast opens up between us, an energy that does not feel present in other ways we share time. Our creative spirits seem to expand and mingle among the trees and ferns, and we feed from nature and each other with a vigour that can only be described as joyful and intense. Our friendship is deepened with each walk we take, our silences more profound, our support of one another's creative pursuits, and beauty as women, a direct expression of our encounters together. A walk with Linda is a creative tonic: our ideas blossom and we step away at the end with new visions and projects.[76]

Clinical psychologist Melanie O'Shea advocates creating and maintaining a gratitude list, a daily routine of recording and reflecting on things that you are grateful for.[77] This amplifies the strength of that gratitude and the emotions which are attached to it, essentially refurbishing the brain to concentrate more on all aspects which are positive and creating a resistance to negative ones. Elspeth Liberty, mentioned above, and a friend share every morning one thing that they are grateful for and maintain that it's a great way to start the day with a positive 'glass half full' mindset.

Acts of kindness, generosity and giving can also be beneficial, according to *The Kindness Revolution* by Hugh Mackay, who claims that '[w]e were born to cooperate not compete'.[78] Mackay notes that the world is filled with constant, unremarked acts of kindness, and argues that there is 'an identifiable "cooperative centre" in the brain'.[79] (This is an ideal theme for positive news stories in peace journalism.) Some obvious examples include vegan restaurants in Melbourne and Newtown, Sydney, where diners are asked merely to give a donation. Contrary to 'economic rationalism' theories, these restaurants continue to thrive. The concept has spread to top-end restaurants such as Adelaide's Africola and Soi.38, whose dine-by-donation dinners use food rescued through OzHarvest. Their concept, 'Share', aims to feed the less fortunate and to reduce food waste and its contributions to landfill and methane emissions.[80]

Dadirri

Dadirri is a word, concept and spiritual practice from the Ngan'gikurunggurr and Ngen'giwumirri languages of the Aboriginal peoples of the Daly River region (Northern Territory, Australia) which means inner deep listening and quiet, still awareness. Traditional owner Miriam-Rose Ungunmerr explains that

> Dadirri recognises the deep spring that is inside us. We call on it and it calls to us. […] My people are not threatened by silence. They are completely at home in it. They have lived for thousands of years with Nature's quietness. […] To be still brings peace – and it brings understanding.[81]

A simple dadirri exercise is this:

> Reserve a space regularly for about 5 minutes, in the morning or evening. Go outside if you can. Simply sit and look at and listen to the earth and environment that surrounds you. Focus on something specific, such as a bird, a blade of grass, a clump of soil, cracked earth, a flower, bush or leaf, a cloud in the sky or a body of water, whatever you can see. You can also let something find you, be it a leaf, the sound of a bird, the feel of the breeze, the light on a tree trunk. There's no need to try, just wait a while. Be still and silent and listen.[82]

Conclusion

The more we learn, the more it seems there is to learn. At the same time, it's possible to attain a modicum of inner peace. We may never be entirely satisfied with our spiritual strivings, but we can develop some contentment that we have developed beneficial practices which help both us and the world around us.

An ancient story is told about a sage being asked by a seeker what he did before enlightenment. He responded: 'I chopped wood, baked bread, meditated and walked in the forest'. When asked what he did now that he was enlightened, he responded: 'I chop wood, bake bread, meditate and walk in the forest'. In this perspective, enlightenment is an ongoing process involving 'dharma yoga' – viewing everyday work as a yogic practice. That is, no matter how wise you become and how much inner peace you attain, the chores (such as doing the dishes) still have to be done. It's a down-to-earth philosophy rather than one based in the clouds.

Following Eswaran, Tatiyana Bastet notes that

> ahiṃsā [nonviolence] stems from an internal practice that, like the ripple effect, is seen outwardly […] If life is lived fully from a place and practice of self-knowledge and self-reflection, with a focus on ever increasing vitality, the result of that, though not always a smooth ride – because what's the fun in that – must certainly be that of one lived in play, joy, and curiosity for the next experience to come.[83]

Some of the most inspirational nonviolent campaigns – and developments in nonviolence – have sprung from playful, joyful, humorous, celebratory activism rather than fearful or angry protests. Examples include the OTPOR-led deposing of Serbian dictator Slobodan Milosevic[84] and the anti-logging and anti-coal seam gas campaigns of northern New South Wales in Australia.[85] These successes occurred because of dedicated, courageous activists, discipline, clever leadership and effective strategy, but it was also because of inner work performed by the actors in social movements. Rather than merely reacting unthinkingly and striking out, those strategies emanated from calm, patient, determined interiors. They consciously involved positivity and humour and were solutions-oriented rather than simplistic opposition, such as Nancy Reagan's advocacy to 'just say no' in the ineffectual 'war on drugs'.

Major social change requires cultural change and nonviolent action, supported by high-level political and economic reform. It can happen unexpectedly fast, such as with the rapid dismantling of the Iron Curtain from 1989, which took the world by surprise. Sometimes the quieter but no less important changes go unnoticed:

> Faced with litanies of bad news, it is easy to become disheartened about the future of human society. But there are [...] reasons to think that change for the better is possible. [...] [E]normous change has taken place in the recent past. [...] In many countries women can now vote, obtain abortions and become heads of government. Outspoken bigotry is increasingly viewed as unacceptable. Malnutrition has become less common, at least on some measures. Support for strong action on climate change is growing. Social media exists. Whether or not one approves of all these changes, they have happened, and fast.[86]

Wrap-up and Future Directions

To wrap up, I hope you have found this book informative and thought-provoking, and that you can forgive its many flaws and omissions. I have argued that many of our societies are drenched in cultural violence, and that this is a root cause of the more visible direct violence which is regularly splashed across the media.

There are also many counter-currents of cultural peacebuilding and exemplary islands of peace which deserve far more attention. Reducing direct and structural violence requires an understanding of the many facets of cultural violence, and support for those counter-currents and peace islands. Fighting fire with fire has set the planet ablaze. Dousing the fires of violence with the waters of love, inner peace and imaginative nonviolent action makes much more sense.

We have covered a wide range of topics, including language, communication, narratives and discourses; screen violence and peace; peaceful communities, nations and regions; peace history, journalism, parenting and education; gender issues; artistic activism; and religion and spirituality.

There are many other topics which could have been covered, and which future research could explore, such as bullying; the pornography industry; conspiracy theories (including anti-science ones); over-reliance on science and technology as solutions; and cultural and gender issues within police and peacekeeping forces. How cultural peacebuilding and artistic activism can better complement economic and political peacebuilding and peace infrastructures, and the intersections between grassroots and top-down actions, are also worth exploring.

The rapidly evolving information and communication technology field warrants more research, including deep fakes; artificial intelligence; misogynist, racist or violent online content; vitriolic social media content, language and narratives hiding behind anonymity; free speech versus responsible limits; the time-wasting and exhaustion created by email and information overload; deliberately engineered phone addiction; invasive data collection by unaccountable corporations and states; corporate control and shaping of our consumption patterns; the 'dark web' and crime; and the relations between these topics. There are opportunities to delve deeply into all these issues of direct, structural and cultural violence, and to research and support artistic activism and cultural peacebuilding which undermines them, envisages better futures and creates positive, peaceful solutions and alternatives.

*

There are some great leaders in the struggle to develop peaceful cultures globally, such as the city of Hiroshima, with its peace museum and park, its Peace Institute, its art gallery dedicated to 'Love and Peace' and its central role in creating the Mayors for Peace organisation. This is understandable, given Hiroshima's history as the site of the most horrific mass violence imaginable. The city values peace because it has suffered the worst consequences of war.

Elsewhere, however, peace is often taken for granted. Peace practitioners, teachers, researchers, activists, advocates and academics are often underfunded and rarely included in high-level media or public discourse. Yet peace is essential for civilisation, trade, education and culture. Without it, a society may survive, but it cannot thrive.

Although deeply affected by conflict and very conscious of the need for peace, a war-torn society may be too traumatised, too devastated, too much in pain to think clearly about how to achieve peace. This is why the responsibility falls to wealthier, more peaceful countries to take on the role of peacebuilder, to recognise the violence in their own cultures, to reform them and to spread that peace outwards to the world.

It's in these fortunate places that much of the world's power and influence resides. Those of us who are privileged enough to be able to read books and reflect on them without missiles whistling over our heads, military forces taking our homes or suicide bombers threatening our safety often do not realise how much power we have to make positive changes through our cultures, through the way we communicate, the movies we watch, the way we raise and educate our children, the media sources we rely on, our museums, art and music, gendered interactions, environmental mores and spiritual practices.

Yet we do have power, particularly when we work together. According to chaos theory, the right action at the right time can make a huge difference (think butterflies causing hurricanes), and small changes, when magnified across many people, can lead to fundamental transformation of our cultures and societies. Every drop of mindful, compassionate action makes a ripple of change towards a global culture of peace and adds to the streams of love, compassion, equality, justice and sustainability, and the 'infinite ocean of peace' that peace educator Prem Rawat says resides within us all.

Notes

1 Goldhahn, Joakim and Taçon, Paul 2021 'How aboriginal rock art can live on even when gone', *University of Western Australia*, 13 April, www.uwa.edu.au/news/article/2021/april/how-aboriginal-rock-art-can-live-on-even-when-gone

2 Cited in Krieger, David 2019 'New modes of Thinking', *Waging Peace,* 17 June, www.wagingpeace.org/new-modes-of-thinking/

3 Samuel, Lawrence R. 2019 'Einstein on happiness', *Psychology Today*, 10 January, www.psychologytoday.com/au/blog/psychology-yesterday/201901/einstein-happiness

4 Gogava, I., Poghosyan, L. and Aslanovet, B. 2018, *Strengthening Culture of Peace,* Peace Education, https://peaceducation.net/wp-content/uploads/2018/07/Manual-for-Educators_Eng.pdf

5 Standish, Katerina 2022 'Personal peacebuilding and COVID-19' in Katerina Standish et al. (eds.), *The Palgrave Handbook of Positive Peace,* Springer, Singapore, p. 42.

6 Rosenfeldt, Robyn 2020 'Climate activism: Find your calling', *Pip: Australian Permaculture,* March–June, p. 64.

7 Cited in Rosenfedt 2020, p. 64.

8 Standish 2022, p. 41.

9 Tacey, David 2000 *ReEnchantment: The New Australian Spirituality*, HarperCollins, Sydney.

10 Pratchett, Terry 1987 *Mort*, Gollancz, London, p. 74.

11 Confortini, Cecilia 2011 'Doing feminist peace', *International Feminist Journal of Politics*, vol. 13, no. 3, pp. 349–370.

12 Sylvester, Christine 1994 *Feminist Theory and International Relations in a Postmodern Era*, Cambridge University Press, New York, pp. 317–326.

13 Ibid., p. 317.
14 Liberty, Elspeth 2022 personal communication (email), 25 May.
15 Standish 2022, p. 42.
16 Northeastern University College of Science 2013 *Can Meditation Make You a More Compassionate Person?* https://cos.northeastern.edu/news/release-can-meditation-make-you-a-more-compassionate-person/
17 Bastet, Tatiyana 2022 'The nature of reflective choice and nonviolence as a personal practice of yoga', in Katerina Standish et al. (eds.), *The Palgrave Handbook of Positive Peace,* Springer, Singapore, p. 29.
18 Bastet 2022, p. 28.
19 Costello, Judy 1982 'Beyond Gandhi: An American feminist's approach to nonviolence', in Pam McAllister (ed.), *Reweaving the Web of Life,* New Society Publishers, Philadelphia, p. 178.
20 Starhawk (Miriam Samos) 2006 'Reclaiming nonviolence from Gandhian puritanism', *Peacework,* vol. 33, no. 368, pp. 14–15, 25.
21 Bastet 2022, p. 27.
22 Davis, B. 2007 'Inner peace', *Colorlines,* Oakland, United States, p. 49.
23 Cadden, Catherine and Wiens, Jesse 2017 *The Ongo Book: Everyday Nonviolence*, Baba Tree International, Jeffersonville.
24 Gaia 2016 *10 Science-backed Reasons to Make Inner Peace a Priority,* www.gaia.com/article/10-reasons-make-inner-peace-priority
25 Budson, Andrew E. 2021 'Can mindfulness change your brain?' *Harvard Health Publishing,* 13 May, www.health.harvard.edu/blog/can-mindfulness-change-your-brain-202105132455
26 Gray 2015 'A point of view: Does atheism have to be anti-religious?' *BBC News,* 30 August, www.bbc.com/news/magazine-34054057
27 Armstrong, John 2012 'Religion for atheists: The struggle for the heart and soul of non-believers', *Conversation,* 28 February, https://theconversation.com/religion-for-atheists-the-struggle-for-the-heart-and-soul-of-non-believers-5542
28 De Botton, Alain 2012 *Religion for Atheists: A non-believer's guide to the uses of religion,* Hamish Hamilton, UK.
29 Armstrong 2012.
30 Brenes, Abelardo 2009 'Personal transformations needed for cultures of peace', in Joseph de Rivera (ed.), *Handbook on Building Cultures of Peace,* Peace Psychology Book Series, Springer, New York.
31 Plum Village n.d. https://plumvillage.org/about/plum-village
32 Woito, Robert 1997 'Nonviolence, principled', in Roger S. Powers and William B. Vogele (eds.), *Protest, Power and Change: An Encyclopaedia of Nonviolent Action from ACT-UP to Women's Suffrage,* Garland Publishing Inc, New York, London, p. 358.
33 Yolton, L. William 1997 'Conscientious objection', ibid., pp. 125–126.
34 Houser, Gordon 2017 'Delegates pass resolution on Israel–Palestine overwhelmingly', *Anabaptist World,* 6 July, https://anabaptistworld.org/delegates-pass-resolution-israel-palestine-overwhelmingly/
35 'Nonviolence International' 2021 NGO Monitor, 20 April, www.ngo-monitor.org/ngos/nonviolence_international_/
36 'MCC plans relief, advocates for just peace in Palestine and Israel' 2023 *MCC* (Mennonite Central Committee), 13 October, https://mcc.org/our-stories/mcc-plans-relief-advocates-just-peace-palestine-and-israel

37 Cep, Casey 2020 'Dorothy Day's radical faith', *New Yorker*, 6 April, www.newyorker.com/magazine/2020/04/13/dorothy-days-radical-faith
38 Chittister, Joan 2011 'Benedictine spirituality: Peace in the monastery of the heart', *HuffPost*, 18 June, www.huffpost.com/entry/benedictine-monastery-of-the-heart_b_849190
39 Astorga, Ma. Christina A. 2006 'Culture, religion, and moral vision: A theological discourse on the Filipino people power revolution of 1986', *Theological Studies*, vol. 67, no. 3, pp. 567–601.
40 Mouly, C. 2013 'The Nicaraguan peace commissions: A sustainable bottom-up peace infrastructure', *International Peacekeeping*, vol. 20, no. 1, p. 51.
41 Ibid., p. 52.
42 Wake, J. 2004 'Lessons learned from the peacebuilding practices in Asia Pacific', in A. Heijmans, N. Simmonds and H. Veen (eds.), *Searching for Peace in Asia Pacific: An Overview of Conflict Prevention and Peacebuilding Activities*, Lynne Rienner Publishers, Boulder, CO, p. 109.
43 Gaetan, Victor 2016 '"Industry of Death": Pope Francis on arms dealers and causes of World War III', *National Catholic Register*, 9 February, www.ncregister.com/news/industry-of-death-pope-francis-on-arms-dealers-and-causes-of-world-war-iii
44 Pullella, Philip and Shirbon, Estelle 2023 'Pope arrives in volatile South Sudan for "pilgrimage of peace"', *EuroNews*, 4 February, www.euronews.com/2023/02/04/pope-africa
45 Philpot, Terry 2014 'World War I's Pope Benedict XV and the pursuit of peace', *National Catholic Reporter*, 19 July, www.ncronline.org/news/justice/world-war-pope-benedict-xv-and-pursuit-peace
46 Löwer, Thomas n.d. 'Demystifying the Christmas Truce', *The Great War*, https://greatwar.nl/frames/default-christmastruce.html
47 Ramachandra 1978 'Blessed are the peacemakers', *Messenger of St Anthony*, April, pp. 19–22.
48 Brock-Utne, Birgit 1994 'Listen to women, for a change', in R. Elias and J. Turpin (eds.), *Rethinking Peace*, Lynne Rienner Publishers, Boulder and London, p. 206.
49 Gaard, Greta 1998 *Ecological Politics: Ecofeminists and the Greens*, Temple University Press, Philadelphia, p. 200.
50 Ariyaratne, Vinya 2006 'Building a culture of nonviolence and peace: The Sarvodaya experience in Sri Lanka', in Toh Swee-Hin and Virginia F. Cawagas (eds.), *Cultivating Wisdom, Harvesting Peace*, Multi-Faith Centre, Griffith University, Brisbane, pp. 87–95.
51 Chamas, Zena and Shelton, Tracey 2021 'Australian Muslim communities are a lot more diverse than you may have thought', *ABC News*, 23 August, www.abc.net.au/news/2021-07-20/muslim-minorities-sunni-shia-multicultural-islam-cham-sufi-/100164492
52 Milani, Milad 2014 'The truth about whether Islam is a religion of violence or peace', *Conversation*, 6 October, https://theconversation.com/the-truth-about-whether-islam-is-a-religion-of-violence-or-peace-32437
53 Abu-Nimer, M. 2001 'Conflict resolution, culture, and religion: Toward a training model of interreligious peacebuilding', *Journal of Peace Research*, vol. 38, no. 6, pp. 685–704.
54 Pew Research Center 2018 'Young adults around the world are less religious by several measures', 13 June, www.pewresearch.org/religion/2018/06/13/young-adults-around-the-world-are-less-religious-by-several-measures/

55 Tacey 2000.
56 Cited in Funnell, Antony 2021 'As some in the Western world reject traditional religion, they're redirecting their faith – not losing it', *ABC News,* 24 October, www.abc.net.au/news/2021-10-24/religion-humans-are-hardwired-for-religious-spiritual-belief/100556060
57 Banerjee, Neel, Taranto, Claudia and Kelsey-Sugg, Anna 2023 'The partition of India in 1947 came suddenly, creating chaos, bloodshed and mass migration', *ABC News,* 21 February, www.abc.net.au/news/2023-02-21/partition-of-india-and-pakistan-led-to-chaos-and-bloodshed/101980234
58 Milani 2014.
59 AIATSIS (Australian Institute of Aboriginal and Torres Strait Islander Studies) n.d. 'Missions, stations and reserves', https://aiatsis.gov.au/explore/missions-stations-and-reserves
60 National Library of Medicine n.d. 'Native voices 1941: Hopis argue for conscientious objector status', www.nlm.nih.gov/nativevoices/timeline/466.html
61 Kaye, Eugene 2010 'Hopi fight for survival and peace in the next Millennium', *Cultural Survival,* 2 April, www.culturalsurvival.org/publications/cultural-survival-quarterly/hopi-fight-survival-and-peace-next-millennium
62 Tacey 2000.
63 Næss, Arne 1973 'The shallow and the deep, long-range ecology movement: A summary', *Inquiry: An Interdisciplinary Journal of Philosophy,* vol. 16, no.s 1–4, pp. 95–100.
64 Macy, Joanna (edited by Stephanie Kaza) 2020 *A Wild Love for the World: Joanna Macy and the* work *of* our time, Shambhala Publications, Boulder.
65 Seed, John and Rosenhek, Ruth 2012 'Climate change, despair and empowerment', *Social Alternatives,* vol. 31, no. 1, p. 36.
66 Tönnies, Ferdinand 1964 (ed) *Community & Society,* The Michigan State University Press, East Lansing.
67 Tinsley, S. and George, H. 2006 *Ecological Footprint of the Findhorn Foundation and Community,* Sustainable Development Research Centre, UHI Millennium Institute.
68 Faulkner, Heather and Stickells, Lee 2019 'Bodhi Farm and other countercultural communities live like the 1970s never ended', *ABC News,* 15 December, www.abc.net.au/news/2019-12-15/what-can-we-learn-from-countercultural-communities-bodhi-farm/11409046
69 Starhawk 1993 *The Fifth Sacred Thing,* Bantam Books, New York.
70 Rosenfeldt 2020, p. 64.
71 Masuno, Shunmyo 2019 *Zen,* Michael Joseph, London.
72 Ibid., p. 22.
73 Ibid., p. 168.
74 Gobster, P. H., Kruger, L. E., Schultz, C. L. and Henderson, J. R. 2023 'Key characteristics of forest therapy trails: A guided, integrative approach', *Forests,* vol. 14, no. 186, p. 1.
75 Schneider, Lindy 2018 'Still steps', *Remember the Wild,* 22 September, www.rememberthewild.org.au/still-steps/
76 Ibid.
77 O'Shea, M. 2013 *The Totality of Now: 30 techniques to achieve inner peace and live in the now,* https://books.google.ca/books?id=50vUxyDStiAC&pg=PA77&dq=inner+peace+techniques
78 Mackay, Hugh 2021 *The Kindness Revolution,* Allen and Unwin, Sydney, p. 43.

79 Ibid., p. 44.
80 Galletly, Jessica 2020 'Dine-by-donation' dinners in Adelaide aim to reduce food waste and feed the less fortunate', *Advertiser,* 30 August.
81 Cited in Korf, Jens 2022 'Deep listening (Dadirri)', *Creative Spirits,* 22 February, www.creativespirits.info/aboriginalculture/education/deep-listening-dadirri
82 Korf 2022.
83 Bastet 2022, p. 39.
84 Popovic, Srdja and Miller, Matthew 2015 *Blueprint for Revolution,* Spigel & Grau Trade, New York.
85 Ricketts, Aidan 2021 *Complexity Theory and Social Movement Praxis: Emergence, Adaptability and Unpredictability*, PhD thesis, University of New England.
86 Marshall, Michael 2023 'Rethinking civilisation', *New Scientist,* July, p. 38.

APPENDIX

Examples of Violent Language

Bullets	*Guns*	*Gun-related*
dodge a bullet	*young gun*	*staring down the barrel*
bite the bullet	*jump the gun*	*we're targets (e.g. in a work place restructure)*
the silver bullet	*a hired gun*	*targets (economic or work)*
bullet points	*gun it/he gunned the engine*	*off like a shot*
bullet train	*gunning for someone*	*shoot through*
he thinks he's bulletproof	*stick to your guns*	*shoot it over to you (email)*
Soldiers	*bring out the big guns*	*What are the triggers?*
to soldier on	*to go in with all guns blazing*	*to shoot someone (or an argument)*
		down in flames
toast soldiers	*a gun shearer*	*shooting the messenger*
he's a trooper	*to be outgunned*	*keep your powder dry*
my comrade-in-arms	*the scatter-gun approach*	*guns for hire*
our foot soldiers	*a shotgun wedding*	*returning fire*
just a foot-soldier	*the smoking gun*	*have a shot*
Bombs	**Bomb-related**	*call the shots*
dropped a bombshell	*blow them out of the water*	*give it your best shot*
it bombed (e.g. movie)	*it blew up in our face*	*shot in the dark*
to bomb someone (jump near them in water)	*bang for your buck*	*shot in the arm*
a blonde bombshell	**Violence-related**	*that's the shot*
mind-bombs (used in Greenpeace documentary)	*break the back (of some work)*	*come out with all their guns blazing*
getting bombed (drunk)	*take a stab at something*	*troubleshooting*
bath bombs, bliss bombs	*a stab in the dark*	*gave him both barrels*
bomber jackets	*a multi-pronged approach*	*shoot from the hip*
yarn bombing	*stone the crows*	*shot full of holes*
Wars	*a murder of crows*	*shoot yourself in the foot*
been in the wars	*a policy with teeth*	**Sport-related**

(*Continued*)

(Continued)

Bullets	*Guns*	*Gun-related*
It's war now!	*the Gunbarrel Highway*	*roll with the punches (used by a Rugby League coach after a player was suspended for violent assault)*
(kids) having 'war wounds'	*set the world on fire*	*punch above one's weight*
War-related	*on razor's edge*	*an opportunity to punch into*
It's a minefield (legal)	*hit me (in cards)*	*pack a punch*
it's a battlefield	*hits those learning outcomes*	*lacking punch*
loose cannon	*HMU – hit me up (send me a message)*	*punch on*
on the frontline	*hit someone up (for money)*	*we smashed them*
hold the fort	*to beat yourself up about something*	*we smashed a record*
leading the charge	*a political ambush*	*we got slaughtered*
(in argument) defending our positions	*strike me pink*	*fighting fit*
massacred a joke	*it's a knockout*	*a tilt at another premiership*
(in election) hitting the battlegrounds	*hit the nail on the head*	*torpedo kick*
round up the troops	*a big hitter*	*torpedo pass*
speaking to the assembled troops	*you've nailed it*	*A bomb (ball kicked up high)*
a call to arms	*knock 'em dead*	*carving it up (surfing)*
blitzed it (exam or game)	*hard-hitting exposé*	*you're killing it*
keep your head down	*let the cat out of the bag*	*shoot the breeze*
up in arms	*use the carrot and stick*	*the game was on a knife's edge*
a double-edged sword	*break the back of some work*	*hit a purple patch*
here comes the cavalry	*death of a thousand cuts*	
strike a blow	*give someone the boot*	
enough to feed an army	*under siege*	
an army of helpers	*explode a myth*	
hold the fort	*bombarded with emails*	
soldier on	*under the gun*	
bootcamps	*hard-hitting*	
going over the top [i.e. out of the trenches]	*punchy*	
battle stations	*a real coup*	
fighting the good fight	*the spearhead (of a movement)*	
cop a lot of flak	*deadlines*	
stay below the parapet	*a kick-arse film*	

Some ungrouped examples include the following:

- *tackle the final topics*
- *a stone's throw away*
- *a battle against cancer*

- *take no prisoners*
- *crack the whip*
- *fire away*
- *punch numbers into a phone*
- *how many hits (on a website)*
- the environmentally violent terms *earth-shattering* and *ground-breaking.*

Other examples from activists include the following:

- *On the peace front*
- *another song in your armoury*
- *punching home the message*
- *the weapons of boycotts, blockades, non-cooperation, lobbying and publicising wrongdoing.*

INDEX

Page locators in **bold** indicates tables

www.ingramcontent.com/pod-product-compliance
Lightning Source LLC
LaVergne TN
LVHW091343280826
846697LV00027B/88
* 9 7 8 1 8 0 1 3 6 0 5 0 0 *